Elite Migrants
South Asian Doctors in the UK

To my parents, in particular my late, much missed father, Nur Mohammed, my children and grandchildren

In this excellent work of scholarship, Farooq provides us with a rich and insightful account of the experiences of a remarkably important migrant group - South Asian doctors who came to Britain to work in the NHS. This rich and multifaceted work provides a vital and engaging account of this remarkable group. Essential reading for anyone interested in the role of migrant workers in the NHS, and in the experiences and challenges faced by migrants settling to Britain during the 1960s and 1970s.

- **Robert Ford**, *Professor of Political Science, University of Manchester, UK*

Dr Farooq's research into the lives and contributions of South Asian doctors working in NHS GP practices in the North of England is insightful as well as timely. Her work examines the complex intersections between class, race and migration. The analysis are supplemented with some wonderful quotes by the doctors on how they responded to their migration journeys, and adapted to their local communities and the changing demands of working within the NHS. The research provides a unique insight into the experiences of different generations of South Asian GPs who contributed so much to our local communities.

- **Tarani Chandola**, *Professor of Medical Sociology, University of Manchester, UK*

Often seen as a uniquely British institution, the NHS is really an international institution where international medical graduates, international nurses and migrant labour have contributed to it its values, its identity and its purpose. Dr Yasmin Farooq, together with her contemporary Julian Simpson who both worked with me to document this history will ensure that future historians and sociologists will acknowledge and recognise the hidden contribution of these architects and pioneers to British Society and the International NHS.

- **Aneez Esmail**, *Professor of General Practice, University of Manchester, UK*

Migration of healthcare professionals is a global phenomenon and I believe this is a very timely book as most countries are struggling with migration issues. The author describes the impact of migration of South Asian doctors on the UK society and discusses in detail the role of social remittances and how these doctors used their own social capital which they culturally diffused within their new settings thus becoming remittance transmitters which greatly enhanced entrepreneurship. This book is the first of its kind that weaves together issues of identity, migration and integration of elite migrants and will be of interest to social scientists and policy makers on an international level.

- **Barış Alpaslan**, *Associate Professor of Macroeconomics, Social Sciences University of Ankara, Turkey*

Elite Migrants

South Asian Doctors in the UK

Dr Yasmin Ghazala Farooq

TRANSNATIONAL PRESS LONDON
2020

Migration Series: 24

Elite Migrants: South Asian Doctors in the UK

By Dr Yasmin Ghazala Farooq

First Published in 2020 by TRANSNATIONAL PRESS LONDON in the United Kingdom, 12 Ridgeway Gardens, London, N6 5XR, UK.
www.tplondon.com

Paperback
ISBN: 978-1-912997-63-3
Hardcover
ISBN: 978-1-912997-70-1

Cover Design: Nihal Yazgan
Cover Photo provided by Dr Aneez Esmail

www.tplondon.com

CONTENT

ABOUT AUTHOR

Dr Yasmin Ghazala FAROOQ is a social researcher. She originates from Azad Kashmir, Pakistan. She has worked in the health and social care settings for over three decades as a social work practitioner and a lecturer and has undertaken various research projects. She completed her funded PhD at the University of Manchester in 2014 where she subsequently worked as a lecturer in Social Statistics until 2019. Her research interests include migration, identity, ethnicity, race and health inequalities. She is particularly interested in exploring the integration experiences of elite migrants which has remained an under-researched area until very recently. She has presented her work in numerous international migration conferences. She has co-written a research blog titled *Migrant doctors keep the NHS going* published at the Manchester Policy Blogs. She is also the author of two book chapters in which she documents the various aspects of experiences of overseas-trained South Asian doctors in the UK which contribute towards the growing field of migration studies.

FOREWORD

The NHS has, since its inception depended on a vast army of international medical graduates in meeting its medical workforce needs. The majority of these doctors qualified in the Indian subcontinent and have made a huge contribution to the NHS - working in the most unpopular specialties and in the most deprived areas of the UK. Frequently written out of its history, their own stories and experiences have rarely been documented. As a group of highly skilled migrants, they have a different experience to that of many migrants, experiencing racism from professional organisations and from the NHS itself. Often forgotten, frequently ostracised but always wanted when their skills and experience were required to supplement the specialised labour shortages that have been a hallmark of the NHS. Dr Yasmin Farooq has written a rich and detailed account of the experiences of this group of doctors, linking their narratives with contemporary debates around migration, community cohesion and racism.

In addition, she provides a detailed account of the entrepreneurial initiatives and processes that these doctors used through general practice to provide healthcare services to the most marginalised communities in the UK. The unique perspective which she brings to these narratives is enhanced because many of the interviews were carried out in Urdu/Hindi and Punjabi and then translated - revealing insights that would never have been possible had they been conducted in English.

Although it has been in existence for over 70 years, the NHS has still to acknowledge the debt that it owes to these doctors. Often seen as a uniquely British institution, the NHS is really an international institution where international medical graduates, international nurses and migrant labour have contributed to it its values, its identity and its purpose. Dr Yasmin Farooq, together with her contemporary Julian Simpson who both worked with me to document this history will ensure that future historians and sociologists will acknowledge and recognise the hidden contribution of these architects and pioneers to British Society and the International NHS.

Aneez Esmail

Professor of General Practice, University of Manchester, UK

PREFACE AND ACKNOWLEDGEMENTS

This book presents my research work that I undertook for over a decade in the area of identity and migration. Being a migrant myself, it is a subject that is very close to my heart. It is based on an investigation I undertook with overseas-trained South Asian doctors. The idea for this study sprang from a conversation between some academics in the social sciences, namely Dr Kingsley Purdam, Professor Rob Ford and Professor Aneez Esmail, following the delivery of his annual public lecture at the University of Manchester by the lattermost.

His lecture, titled *Asian doctors in the NHS: service and betrayal,* was also published in The British Journal of General Practice (Esmail, 2007). This lecture provided a historical background regarding the migration of doctors from the Indian sub-continent in the context of post-colonial links, looking at how medical education in India has been influenced and controlled by Britain and suited to western medical practice. Esmail described the inequalities experienced by overseas-trained South Asian doctors while working in the lower status "Cinderella" services of the NHS, for example, working as junior doctors or registrars, and posed the question as to why their position in the NHS has not been considered in the same context as "indentured labour". Moreover, he asserted that overseas-trained South Asian doctors are more likely to work in specialties that are less attractive among white doctors, for example, geriatrics and psychiatry. His lecture played a pivotal role in instigating the research agenda of this study. Professor Ford and Dr Kingsley Purdam were working in the social sciences discipline and were keen to marry the contemporary debates of identity, community cohesion and migration with Professor Esmail's interest in the migration experiences of overseas-trained South Asian doctors in the UK. In particular, they were interested in collecting the narratives of highly skilled migrants. This collaborative work took place in 2008, which was subsequent to community cohesion becoming a major policy concern following the race riots in 2001. The team was later joined by Professor Tarani Chandola, whose expertise in medical sociology served as an asset in this project. I became the person who inherited this research proposal, which I was able to pursue during my doctoral study.

A researcher is always implicated in the research process, in one way or another and it is always helpful for the reader to have a sense of where the author is coming from, what influenced them socially, politically and culturally. Most academic work starts from the invented premise that the scholar looked at the evidence and found a gap, which, may very well align with an aspect of their identity. It is therefore important to talk about my identity and how it has been impacted upon by my experiences as well as discussion of a transparent research process. I will describe in length, the methodological considerations I undertook, that helped me overcome any biases that I may have had.

I migrated as a young adult from Pakistan (Kashmir) to join my father, who had answered Britain's call to address the labour shortage in the 1960s and worked in the steel industry. I was well aware of identity issues prior to my migration to the UK, as my family had migrated from the Indian side of the Kashmir to the Pakistani side after the 1947 partition of India. I remember the stories that my father used to tell us of his experiences in the UK. He was full of admiration for the British values and often praised the British for even some colonial projects, such as the railway system in India etc. He had also directly witnessed an era when some bed and breakfast places displayed sign in the windows stating, 'no blacks, no Irish, no dogs', but he had a tendency to focus on positive experiences.

Having worked in both social and health care settings in the UK as well as being an academic for over three decades, I believed that I had a good insight into the issues that I set out to explore. I believed that my lived experiences of what it is like to be an Asian woman, born and brought up in the country of origin now living and working in Britain would facilitate access to my subjects and enhance the quality of the research findings.

The writing of this book is very much owed to the inspiration I received from my late father, who was very passionate about education. He was a very learned man and a role model for me in many respects. He was proficient in Urdu and Persian languages and would often recite Shaikh Saadi's poetry. Growing up with him, I witnessed his feelings of frustration at being downgraded during his working life in the steel industry.

Whilst he enjoyed his supervisory role in the industry, the job did not fully reflect his abilities and his life came to revolve around community development work with the Asian community that he undertook in his own time. He was a pioneer in setting up a local luncheon club for the Asian older people for whom no culturally appropriate service existed previously. Since the majority of Asian people were not literate in both English and Asian languages, he often completed all sorts of paperwork for them. I believe he achieved social recognition through his community work which his day job lacked. I was greatly influenced by his hard work and his vision for a better future. He believed in investing in human capital and one thing that he emphasised throughout his life was education for his children as he did not want them to go through the same struggles he himself had experienced. He believed that education adds value to one's human capital, especially western education, as his educational qualifications (proficiency in Urdu and Farsi) were not recognised in the UK. As this concept was instilled in our brains very early on, it is no surprise to me that I became a lifelong learner. Whilst I also shared his thirst and passion for education, there have been times, however, when I became less convinced by the Human Capital Theory, as I often experienced being 'othered'. By way of explanation, my experiences in all walks of life have made me aware of the limitations of the Human Capital Theory, which only acknowledges individuals' skills, educational qualifications, and abilities, but does not take into account other intersecting characteristics, such as race and gender.

One such vivid memory that has stayed with me is when I became a member of the Social Security Tribunal in the early 1990s. It was quite an achievement for me finally to become part of some decision-making body and I felt quite privileged to have earned that position. It was quite common in those days either to have no black institutional representation, or occasionally I would see a tokenistic black/Asian male in a position of power. On my first day, I reported to the receptionist on my arrival by showing a letter I had received. She took a cursory look and asked me to take a seat in the waiting area. After waiting for half an hour I wondered what had happened as the tribunal should have started a while ago. As I was thinking what to do, someone came out to announce that the tribunal had been delayed as the third presiding member had not arrived yet. It dawned on me at that point that I may have not been counted as a tribunal member by the receptionist, but rather, an assumption had been made that I was a client. I went back to the reception desk and I asked if they were waiting for me. It turned out to be the case and everyone was apologetic later, but it took away some element of pride from me that day. It felt like I was trespassing and had no right to be in that space. This type of experience inspired me to explore issues of identity and sowed the seeds for me to undertake research in this area.

Little did I know that I would be reading some 30 years later The Guardian newspaper reporting similar experiences of a black barrister, who was stopped and mistaken for a defendant three times in one day[1].

As I have always a taken a keen interest in the intersectionality of race, class and gender issues, as part of my MA degree in 1996, I undertook research into the experiences of South Asian women in the area of domestic

---

[1] https://www.theguardian.com/law/2020/sep/24/investigation-launched-after-black-barrister-mistaken-for-defendant-three-times-in-a-day

abuse and how their identities were impacted upon as a result. I became acutely aware of the impact of cultural and structural constraints on the identity of individuals. I was surprised to learn that my study was the first of its kind and that no previous empirical evidence existed relating to the experiences of Asian women in this area. I was awarded an equal opportunities prize by Sheffield Hallam University for the quality of my work. I was also informed that my research was instrumental in securing a lottery grant for a local domestic violence forum.

The opportunity of undertaking this research study and analysing its findings has been very exciting. The writing of this book, which is a product of my research over a decade, has been quite a journey. Following the completion of my research study, I have been able to disseminate findings not only to national conferences, but also, to a much wider audience. I have been invited to numerous international conferences to present papers and have written book chapters and research blogs. This process has offered external validity and credibility to my research findings, which is the very essence of effective social research. Through the publication of this book, I wish my work to be shared with the wider world, anticipating that it will make a significant contribution to the literature of elite experiences of identity, migration, community cohesion and healthcare.

This book would not have been possible without the support of my family, in particular my children, my academic and non-academic friends and the doctors in the study who were keen to share their narratives with the wider world. First and foremost, I would like to say how indebted I feel to Almighty God for His continuous guidance and goodness in allowing me to reach many milestones during the writing of this book. Undertaking this research study and compiling the evidence in the form of this book has been quite a journey in recent years. I feel greatly indebted to my late father for inspiring me to be creative and join the literary world. His interest in Persian and Indian/Pakistani poetry that he passed down to me helped me tremendously to engage with the doctors in the study.

I would like to acknowledge the doctors who gave up their precious time to tell their stories. I very much hope that I have been able to do justice in retelling their stories as they are. I enjoyed the poetic expressions that they used to articulate their thoughts and feelings. Many years after my fieldwork, I still hear echoes of a poetic account of an interviewee who was trying to describe his hybrid identity:

Hum Log Sumandar Ke Bichrey Huey do Sahil hein

Is Paar Bhi Tanhai Us Paar Bhi Tanhai

[Translation: we people are like the two separated seashores that

> feel apart from each other]
>
> The people from there [India] say you live in England now and become Valaytey [Westernised] and the people from here say we are Hindustani or Pakistani... that feeling is there. Yes, that is there, love for the home country (gp5s).

I am grateful for their time, enthusiasm and knowledge, which contributed immensely to the quality of this research. I also had the opportunity to visit interesting locations and attended a number of interesting networking events.

It has been a great privilege for me to also have had an incredible network of institutional support, which included: Dr Kingsley Purdam, Professor Rob Ford, Professor Aneez Esmail and Professor Tarani Chandola. I am grateful to all of them for the passion and dedication that each one showed, as well as for their patience, suggestions and constructive feedback over the course of the many months of this study. I am also grateful to Professor Ford for taking the time and effort to read my draft copies and make detailed suggestions.

I would like to thank my fellow researchers, who have been invaluable for support and the development of ideas, in particular Dr Julian Simpson, who was also undertaking research with overseas-trained South Asian doctors at the time and investigating their role in the development of general practice. He has since authored a book titled, *Migrant architects of the NHS: South Asian doctors and the reinvention of British general practice (1940s-1980s) (Social Histories of Medicine).*

I am truly and greatly indebted to my family, who provided practical and emotional support throughout this study, in particular to my daughter, Zara, for transcribing, proofreading, commenting on my work and being an incredible teacher. Her input as a GP has also been invaluable. Many thanks must go to my daughter-in-law, Liza Molinari, who joined my family household during the course of this study and often provided me with lifts to and from the train station along with meals on late wintry evenings. She keenly read my chapters and was amazed to find that the migration trajectories of her own grandparents of Italian origin were, in many ways, not so dissimilar. During the writing of this book there was subtraction from and addition to my family. Sadly, my father, who instilled in me the value of education, lost his battle with Parkinson's disease. I can only imagine how pleased he would have been to see my work in print and also for me to have raised three daughters, who all became GPs.

I would also like to acknowledge the intellectual debt I owe to my nephew Dr Wasim Ahmed, a lecturer in Digital Business at Newcastle University

Business School, for taking his time to read the manuscript thoroughly and for his valuable feedback.

I would like to extend my gratitude to the University of Manchester for securing the scholarship funded by ESRC, which enabled me to carry out this study and the case partner, the British Association of Physicians of Indian Origin (BAPIO), for co-sponsoring. In particular, I would like to thank Dr Ramesh Mehta, Professor Rajan Madhok, Dr Tariq Chauhan, Dr Javed Iqbal and Councillor Dr Zahid Chauhan OBE in facilitating access for me.

I would also like to thank Professor Wendy Olsen, head of the department of Social Statistics at the University of Manchester, Dr Baris Alpaslan, an Associate Professor of Economics and an Associate Dean at the Social Sciences University of Ankara in Turkey and Dr Amina Bargawi, Director of Community Health Nursing Services, Primary Health Care, Ministry of National Guard, Health Affairs, Jeddah, Saudi Arabia for their invaluable input to my research. I am grateful to all of you and many other well-wishers who cannot be individually named for remaining constant throughout this drawn out process of writing.

INTRODUCTION

Contemporary social policy debates on community cohesion in Britain appear to have very prescribed identities for migrants, which often centre on the concepts of 'Britishness', having 'common values' and one national language 'English' for their successful integration. That is, the role of established migrant communities and new immigrants to the UK has invariably been scrutinised in the context of how well the migrants have integrated into British society. Much of the existing literature in this area relates to the experiences of low or unskilled labour migrants. The experiences of elite migrants, however, have often been overlooked in such debates, which, nevertheless, is an important area of research. The growing body of community cohesion literature lacks specific empirical data regarding what accounts for the particularities of migration of highly-skilled migrants in the UK, and how they settle in their respective communities, post-migration. This book is aimed at documenting the identity and integration experiences of overseas-trained South Asian doctors, an elite group of migrants who form a large group within the UK medical workforce. Why study the integration experiences of overseas-trained South Asian doctors one might ask? These doctors constitute a large proportion of highly-skilled migrants to the UK and yet, they have remained an under-researched group until very recently. Smith (1980), for example, reported that in the late 1970s, 40% of hospital doctors and 20% of GPs in the UK were born overseas. They are the second single largest group of doctors working in the NHS after doctors qualified in the UK (Hann et al., 2008). Doyal et al. (1980, 1) commented on the invisibility of migrant workers in the NHS, despite the fact that they make a significant contribution to the NHS, pointing out that the extent and the details of their role in the NHS have gone almost entirely unrecorded.

Research studies in recent years have acknowledged the high level of workforce participation that is required by migrant workers, which is considered vital to continue to alleviate medical labour shortages in the NHS. *Against the Odds: Black and Minority Ethnic Clinicians and Manchester: 1948 to 2009 (2010)* and *Migrant architects of the NHS* by Simpson, *(2018)* are among those few studies that have highlighted the impact of the migration of these high skilled people and the significance of their contribution to the NHS from the point of its conception in 1948. Simpson highlighted the contribution of overseas-trained South Asian general practitioners in the development of general practice and the impact these doctors had beyond the 'surgery boundaries' in their local communities. Evidence from Simpson's study suggests that overseas-trained South Asian doctors are more than just healers, for as social actors they play a vital role in wider community engagement, which is an important element of the community cohesion agenda.

However, little is still known about the nature of the social aspects of their lives and the roles that they play in their local communities. It is within this context that I seek to redress this imbalance, by investigating the integration experiences of this distinct group within UK society. I have chosen general practitioners (GPs) as the subject of my research study given that in the UK they are based in primary care settings. They are the first point of contact for most patients.[1] As health care professionals, the GPs have a wide remit for the provision of health and social care to their patients and they are, due to their unique position, often at the 'heart of networks within and between communities' (Farmer et al., 2003, 673). They often have intimate relationships with their local communities and this makes them an interesting group to study as they are likely to have a unique insight into the lives of their patients (Wise, 2010).

The terms 'overseas-trained South Asian doctors' and 'migrant South Asian doctors' here refer to those doctors who obtained their basic medical degrees in India and Pakistan. These terms are often used interchangeably in this book. An understanding of these doctors' experiences can shed light on many of the abovementioned hotly debated topics relating to community cohesion.

This chapter provides an overview of the Community Cohesion framework within which this study is located as well as the methodology I employed. It also describes the contents of each subsequent chapter.

The Community Cohesion Framework

The Community Cohesion framework replaced the old multicultural policy in 2001 and became a policy concern. Following the race riots in 2001, the first published report to investigate their causes reported how communities both white and Asian were polarised and segregated, and that people within these communities lived 'parallel lives', with physical segregation of housing estates, educational arrangements, community and voluntary bodies, employment, places of worship, language, social and cultural networks, thus experiencing a lack of meaningful interaction and community cohesion. Since then, the question of migrant identities has

[1] Royal College of General Practitioners

become more pertinent than ever, because in the government's community cohesion agenda identities are regarded as an important element (Khan, 2007). As a result, emphasis is placed on Britishness.

It has been argued that our identities are socially produced and that they determine our relationships with the external world. Identity is defined as a significant factor in the community cohesion agenda, whereby it relates to how people understand their relationship to the world, how that relationship is constructed across time and space, as well as how people understand their possibilities for the future.

Norton (1997, 410) describes identity as follows:

> *...how people understand their relationship to the world, how that relationship is constructed across time and space, and how people understand their possibilities for the future.*

Gilchrist et al. (2010) explain the significance of one's identity in the community, contending that it is important to recognise how people 'define, resist or adapt' their identities so as to enhance our own understanding of their engagement with their fellow citizens and with government. Welzel et al. (2005) contend that an individual's level of involvement in the community is determined by his or her personal attributes as well as being conditioned by the level of opportunities to which they are exposed. This implies that contextual factors also need to be considered alongside socio-economic background when analysing the differences between individuals and how well they integrate into the communities as migrants; those with different social statuses may have different identity and integration experiences in different contexts. It is vitally important to develop an understanding of the dynamics that impact on cohesion in order to ensure effective policy interventions (Jayaweera and Choudhary, 2008).

According to the Institute of Community Cohesion, the term 'community cohesion' is not new in the writing of political theorists', and can be broadly applied to 'describe a state of harmony or tolerance between people from different backgrounds living within a community.'[2] However, the concept of community cohesion has evolved over the last few years.

Following the urban disorder that occurred in Bradford, Oldham and Burnley in 2001, much of which was attributed to racial tension, several government reports were published investigating the status of community relations in the cities that experienced the disturbances (Clarke, 2001,

[2] The Institute of Community Cohesion was established in 2006 to provide a new approach to race, diversity and multiculturalism following the urban riots in Lancashire. http://www.cohesioninstitute.org.uk/Resources/Toolkits/Health/TheNatureOfCommunityCohesion

Ouseley, 2001, Ritchie, 2001, Denham, 2001). All these reports identified the 'segregation' of different racial groups as a significant contributory factor towards the disturbances. The concept of community cohesion re-emerged when the government reports concluded that a lack of it was a fundamental cause of these riots (Jayaweera and Choudhary, 2008). This absolute separateness, based on religion, education, housing and employment, leading to a lack of contact and knowledge about each other's group, was envisaged to have contributed to the growth of fear and conflict (Cantle, 2001). The diversity issues that had previously been promoted under the remit of multicultural policy were now considered in a negative way. Following such an analysis, community cohesion became an important goal of British public policy. Initiatives aimed at promoting it required a built-in process for ensuring that their impact could be measured (Jayaweera and Choudhary, 2008). The Home Office biennial Citizenship Survey of England and Wales was an example of such a measure. Here, the emphasis was placed on acquiring a national identity, this being perceived as 'potential super glue' for those communities considered to be too diverse and divided (Wetherell et al., 2007).

The Commission on Integration and Cohesion (CIC) undertook development work that involved adopting a clear definition of community cohesion before it could be incorporated into the policy framework. Various national indicators were initially used against which each area was measured for its cohesiveness. In 2008, the commission provided the following definition of community cohesion and integration:

> *Community Cohesion is what must happen in all communities to enable different groups of people to get on well together. A key contributor to cohesion is integration which is what must happen to enable new and existing residents to adjust to one another (DCLG, 2008a, 10).*

In order to tackle the problem of perceived 'parallel lives', as identified in the analysis of the 2001 disturbances, the community cohesion policies introduced were of a multifaceted nature, drawing upon a diverse range of implicit rather than explicit ideas (Lowndes and Thorp, 2011). Regarding which, the Community Cohesion Pathfinder Programme, a key element of the government's initiative on community cohesion, focused on the social capital approach and increasing the level of intercultural communication. It was anticipated that such an action would bring about increased cohesion (Ratcliffe et al., 2008).

Since the development of community cohesion policy, a common sociological theory used to distinguish forms of community interaction is that of 'bonding' and 'bridging' social capital. Bonding social capital refers to social ties within various community groups, whereas bridging pertains to social ties across social groups. One of the criticisms of the old multicultural policy has been that it was pre-occupied with bonding social capital and not enough emphasis was placed on bridging (Khan, 2007). Hence, since the implementation of Community Cohesion policy, importance has been accorded to bridging social capital that connects across groups rather than bonding social capital.

The policy focus of the Community Cohesion Framework has also been shaped around ideas of common vision and sense of belonging in order to move towards the integration and cohesion of 'different' communities into a (British) whole (Worley, 2005). However, despite the growing interest in the value of cross-cultural interactions and in the ethos of the Community Cohesion Framework literature, there appears to be a gap in the knowledge as to how elite migrants manage such processes and their own identity. I will firstly discuss the criticism that the Community Cohesion Framework has received.

Apart from the methodological flaws, there are a number of other areas which have attracted criticism. However, I will only discuss specific areas that directly relate to this study, this is because a detailed overview or critique of community cohesion policy in the UK is beyond the scope of this book. My focus is on two central themes that have attracted a lot of academic scholarship in relation to the Community Cohesion Framework. One relates to the fact that there is a lack of emphasis on the impact of racism within the policy framework that prevents structural integration of migrants whereas the other theme relates to socio-cultural integration and what Parekh (2007) refers to as 'exhorting people to become or feel British'. I will now discuss each of these themes in depth.

Critique of Community Cohesion Discourse

Intercultural Communication initiatives aimed at increasing the knowledge of 'the other' have been criticised for their failure to acknowledge the role of racism in achieving community cohesion. Ratcliffe (2011) points out that while the suitability of such initiatives is not disputed, it is the ideology implied in such approaches that has been the subject of much of the academic debate. Since cohesion policies are targeted mainly at the local level, problems are therefore perceived to be stemming from ethnic, cultural and religious difference rather than material and power-based inequality (Ratcliffe, 2011). The author adds that such an approach assumes that historically entrenched/endemic racism, and prejudice, can be educated away by simply employing cross-cultural interaction in the same way that multiculturalism posited that such differences could be 'negotiated'.

In an article *'It's not about race. It's about the community': New Labour and 'community cohesion'* Worley (2005), sums up the criticism relating to the community cohesion policy framework and pointing out that the concept of 'community' which is central to the community cohesion agenda has implications for processes in relation to lived experiences of race and gender and that such usage allows for language to be become de-racialised. The author also adds that the new framework also draws on earlier discourses of assimilation through notions of 'integration'. Drawing on their own research, Yuval-Davis et al. (1989) additionally contend that the survival of 'communities' owes much to both gendered and racialised processes.

The social capital approach has been further criticised for the emphasis it places on bridging social capital following on from the criticism of the old multicultural policy which, it has been argued was pre-occupied with bonding social capital (Khan, 2007, 47). Khan argues that the formation of bonding social capital can be an important way of providing disadvantaged communities with the necessary resources that eventually enables them to participate in the wider society with more confidence.

Central to the above criticism is the argument that racial prejudice continues to play a significant role in ethnic inequalities. A key research question in this study is concerned with the nature of the structural and socio-cultural integration experiences of overseas-trained South Asian doctors who are an elite group of migrants as well as members of disadvantaged communities. It was anticipated that the findings of this research will be able to contribute to what type of social capital the elites in this study utilise and what strategies they employ to combat racial prejudice which has been historically described as 'entrenched and endemic' racism. Through their work, the doctors engage in cross-cultural interactions, and knowledge about their experiences can shed light on whether or not prejudice can be can be educated away and, if the difference can be 'negotiated' as implied in the Community Cohesion Framework. In the following section, I will discuss the criticism that relates to identity debates in such discourses.

In relation to identity debates, the pre-occupation of the community cohesion agenda with unitary national identity has been heavily criticised in the academic literature. Brah (1985, 9) draws on the earlier influential work of Berger and Luckmann (1971) who argued that identity is formed by social processes which are involved not only in the formation but also in the maintenance of identities, and that identities are produced in a dialectal relationship with society. They argue that identities are produced by an interplay between an indivisual and their consciousness and social strucutres that react upon a given social structure, thus preserving, adapting or even reshaping them.

Ethnicity is socially construced with an ethnic group referring to communities who feel a common sense of identity, often based on shared language, religion and cultural traditions (Coker, 2001). Brah (1985) argues that ethnic identity is a specific facet of an individual's or a group's global identity, and that it becomes meaningful to refer to ethnic identity only when two or more ethnic groups are brought into contact within a common social context with other ethnic groups. However, it is the social structure of society that determines the social context. To elaborate upon this this further, Brah (1985, 9) also reminds us of colonial history and its impact on individuals:

> *Thus discussions of 'ethnic' and cultural' identity in contemporary Britain must be grounded in an analysis of the complex social and historical processes which account for the subordination of black groups in British society. It needs to be borne in mind that the social relations between white and black groups are predicated against a backdrop of colonialism and imperialism.*

The above highlights two important points which are interlinked, one refers to the historical subordination of black groups in British society, and the other relates to the impact of imperialism on individuals' identities.

The key research question that I will explore in this book is how structural and socio-cultural integration has been experienced by highly skilled migrant South Asian doctors in the UK. I will discuss how their own experiences relate to Britishness, sense of belonging, integration and social capital, which are key concepts of the community cohesion framework. I will examine whether their personal attributes, such as being highly skilled healthcare professionals and the level of opportunities to which they have been exposed have shaped their worldview differently from that of their low/unskilled counterparts.

It is argued that identity is formed by social processes, which are involved not only in the formation, but also, in the maintenance of identities, and that these are produced in a dialectal relationship with society. It is further argued that identities are produced by interplay between an individual and their consciousness and social structures that react to a given social structure, thus preserving, adapting or even reshaping them. Evidence suggests that all migrant workers are exposed to some form of prejudice by individuals and institutions. Various scholars have drawn attention to the structural inequalities embedded in the NHS that overseas-trained South Asian doctors encounter. I will examine the doctors' own accounts and analyse what their perceptions are regarding racism in the NHS. I will examine whether they have different identity experiences and whether they have been subjected to the same level of racism as their counterparts, or whether their class identity buffers them in any way as well as whether their experiences vary in different

UK geographical locales.

Methodological Considerations

As well as the lack of knowledge on the identity experiences of elite migrants, a general lack of an appropriate methodology in this area of research has also been highlighted (Iredale, 2001). The methodology applied previously to measure the level of integration was mainly of a quantitative nature, the Home Office biennial Citizenship Survey of England and Wales being an example of one such approach. The survey investigated issues relating to family networks, views of the local area, fear of crime, local services and political institutions, volunteering and charity, civil renewal, racial and religious prejudice, discrimination and views about rights and responsibilities. The Place Survey was another such example, where ward level data was obtained in the context of national indicators and individuals were asked about the extent to which they agreed or disagreed that their local area was a place where people from different backgrounds got on well together and how they felt about their immediate neighbourhood.

The aim of my research was to gain insights into the structural and socio-cultural integration experiences of overseas-trained South Asian doctors in the UK. The time period considered is from the 1960s onwards, as this encapsulates the era of their most significant migration to the UK. It allows for uncovering their professional and social experiences over a longer timeframe, that is, from early migration to settlement. I employed a qualitative approach, with my findings being based on 27 in depth interviews with overseas-trained South Asian GPs in three different geographical locales in England with varying ethnic populations.

Since the primary research aim was to investigate how these GPs construe their experiences and the meaning that they ascribe to these, which is of a subjective nature, I decided that the study was more suited to qualitative research and analysis. Interviewing is considered to be one of the most powerful tools for gaining insights into the world of others (Legard et al., 2003). I applied a case study approach to explore processes specific to local areas. The focus here was to compare experiences of GPs in three contrasting geographical contexts at a smaller scale but in greater depth. The interviews undertaken were semi-structured and the themes explored were derived from the theoretical concepts identified previously, including community cohesion indicators and social capital. The data collection covered demographic information of the participants, migration and settlement experiences, narratives on employment in the NHS, links with other professionals and organisations, transnational role and reflections on their personal and professional journeys in UK.

Semi-structured interviews have a degree of structure, however, the use of open ended questions allow interviewees' flexibility to tell their stories spontaneously in their own words (Bowling, 2009) with richness and detail (Oppenheim, 2000) and to pursue topics of particular interest to them (Bryman, 2009). Within this approach, Seidman (1991, 69) advocates in-depth interviewing as this method is 'primarily designed to facilitate informants to reconstruct their experience and to explore their meaning'. This appears eminently suited to eliciting overseas-trained South Asian doctors' understanding of their own experiences and the meaning they make of their experiences. Semi-structured interviewing presents a space for investigating in great detail the perceptions of participants in relation to their lived professional and personal experiences, whilst Wengraf (2001,6) emphasises the meaning of 'depth' stating that:

> *To go into something 'in-depth is to get a sense of how the apparently straight-forward is actually more complicated, of how the 'surface appearances' may be quite misleading about 'depth realities'.*

Other positive aspects of such an interview technique, include the choice participants have for expressing themselves in their preferred language and in addition, any confusion arising from the use of particular words can be instantly dealt with using standardised explanations (Oppenheim, 2000). Participants can also help identify themes that may not previously have been considered by researchers, thus providing more depth to concepts in the study (Putnam, 2000).

Kvale (2008) regards the interviewer as the 'primary research instrument' in qualitative research and the 'interrelationship' between interviewer and interviewee as significant in relation to obtaining knowledge. Kvale reminds us about the demands that this places on researchers regarding the quality of their research, and their ability to be empathetic and creative in their approach.

In any social research, the decisions about how to study the social world, through the assumptions of ontology or epistemology, are two important aspects that are integral to deciding on the appropriate set of techniques. Ontological assumptions are concerned with social reality and what there is to know about the world (Ritchie and Lewis, 2003), whereas epistemological ones are concerned with how knowledge is produced or reproduced (Moss, 2002). The ontology and epistemology of my research study was very much influenced by the literature review I undertook, which pertained to what is the perceived social reality and what research methods have already been applied for its discovery along with consideration of their shortcomings. These previous studies helped me to pin down my ontological stance. The epistemological position taken for my research is that of a social constructivist, which implies that our knowledge of the world and how we understand it is derived from how people construct it between them (Burr, 2003) and that our experiences as well as perceptions are '*mediated historically, culturally and linguistically*' (Willig, 1995,13). In other words, social constructionists believe that there are more 'knowledges' rather than there being 'one knowledge'. Social reality is also assumed to be an ongoing dynamic process that people produce daily according to their own knowledge and its interpretation.

My research aim was to discover the perceived reality of the individual doctors, who were likely to have their own particular construction of social reality, and which would be co-constructed collaboratively between myself as a researcher and the researched. This process of co-construction is further explained in what is referred as reflexivity. Reflexivity requires the process of data collection and its analysis to be made explicit, there being two types: epistemological and personal reflexivity.

Epistemological reflexivity requires the researcher to analyse the research questions. For example, the researcher needs to ask himself/herself whether the way the research question was set aided or limited what could be '*found*', and should make it explicit how their design of the study contributed towards the construction of the data and the research findings. That is, whether the research study could have been investigated in a different way than to the proposed one and what impact this may have had on the understanding of the phenomenon under investigation. To summarise, epistemological reflexivity assists a researcher to reflect on the assumptions she or he has made during the course of the research study, which consequently helps her or him understand the implications and limitations of the study findings (Willig, 1995, Bryman, 2009).

Personal reflexivity relates to researchers' own impact on the research process and their contribution in the research process. Willig (1995, 10) describes it as follows:

> *Personal reflexivity involves reflecting upon the ways in which our own values, experiences, interests, beliefs, political commitments, wider aims in life and social identities have shaped the research.*

Bolognani (2007) refers to literature which places emphasis on "interview matching" in the context of ethnic or linguistic similarity. I believe that the experiences of being a migrant, Asian, a woman, having had several professional roles in the UK, and of being "othered" while living in Britain, served me well in enriching the quality of my research (Oguntokun, 1998). Moreover, my attributes enabled the participants to disclose information that may be regarded as being of a highly sensitive nature (Song and Parker, 1995). Moss (2002) takes the above a step further and questions the type of epistemology applied in research, such as Marxist, anti-racist or feminist epistemology. She argues how feminist scholars have had to fight, to ensure not only that "knowledge" is inclusive of "women's voices", but also, how the data might be affected by the gender of the researchers and the researched. The principles of anti-racist research are explained by Dei and Johal (2005, 257) as follows:

> *Anti-racist research does not just deal with 'social facts', it is also about how people interpret those facts, how the researcher interprets those interpretations, contextualizes them, and assists the subject in developing theoretical understandings of their lived experiences.*

The epistemology of my research study was very much influenced by the abovementioned elements and the application of a qualitative approach was considered to provide a comprehensive picture.

A cornerstone of the process in interpretive research is the researcher's own reflexivity (Paulus et al., 2008) as a researcher is always implicated in the research process of all qualitative methodologies in one way or another (Willig, 1995). My own background is in social work and having worked in the field for three decades, so I perceived that this experience would ensure my interviewing skills were of a high standard. I migrated from Kashmir (Pakistan) to the UK after having completed my secondary and further education in Pakistan, where the education medium was Urdu. The combination of different fields of knowledge that I have gained over the years, my own migration experience as well as being the daughter of a migrant (who had come to the UK to work in the steel industry due to the post-war labour shortage), as well as and being the parent of three daughters, who are doctors, helped me enormously in understanding the complexity of these issues. Hence, I believe I was well placed for this particular project. I have had a lot of personal and professional experience of interacting with this group of people whose contribution I personally value. As a migrant and female, I have had my own struggles in relation to structural inequalities, including racism. I am aware that my own interests and experiences were helpful in the research process, however, through a transparent reflexive process, I needed critically to examine the evidence that was grounded in the accounts of the interviewees, while recognising my own biases.

I believe that my research is organic in various ways and that I played a central role in constructing the social reality of the research subjects. I designed the research strategy, developed the topic guide, and conducted the face to face interviews, incorporating my expertise regarding the cultural and linguistic aspects. I am of the view that my own characteristics and networks helped tremendously in negotiating access to the respondents, in particular, because they helped me to convey *an implicit message about credibility and openness* (Ritichie et al (2003, 65).

I allowed the interviewees to articulate their feelings/responses in the languages that they felt most comfortable with. From my own experience, I was well aware that discussions around sensitive issues can be more usefully articulated by individuals in their first language as it is a fact that, in emotional situations, we, as humans, always have a tendency to regress to that language. This assertion of mine was proven correct during the interviews, where interviewees often articulated their feelings by means of referring to and reciting Urdu/Hindi poetry, which I was able to fully comprehend, because of my own secondary education in Pakistan. The pre-occupation of the doctors from the Indian subcontinent with using poetry as an expressive mode was related to the fact that they all had been exposed to a similar educational style, prior to partition in 1947 and possibly after this period. Communicating to the masses through the medium of poetic expression is a norm, and also a language of the elite.

The above knowledge and skills enabled me to build a rapport with this elite group of people and elicit the information required with relative ease.

Kvale (2008) discusses the significance of the first minutes of an interview and states that they are crucial in relation to its quality as a whole, as the participants will want to have some knowledge of the interviewer before opening up and allowing their inner world to be exposed. In order to ease them gently into the research topic, I began by explaining the aims and objectives of the research and shared my own history as a migrant in this country (Rubin and Rubin, 2011). This was done with a view to breaking down the barriers between us, thereby creating a safe environment and a "climate of mutual disclosure" in which the participants were able to share their deepest thoughts, feelings and emotions. The exposure of my inner feelings and experiences 'legitimised' the interviewee's account by the articulation of our "reciprocal revelations" and enabled the doctors to continue by sharing their own story (Holstein and Gubrium, 2010). I believe that for the discovery of "truth" that I was after in this research, self-disclosures were important at appropriate times, for example, the interviewee seemed to open up more when I shared my own experiences of racism. I also felt that my communication was further facilitated by sharing personal information about being a parent of a doctor, who was born and educated in the UK; the interviewees appeared to be more 'approving' of me.

In spite of there being similarities, I believe there was still constant fluctuation of my status in terms of being an insider and outsider. The interviewees regarded me as an insider in relation to religious, cultural and linguistic background, whereas at other times I was informed that I was not a medic and that I would not understand the issues. Welch et al. (2002, 611) discuss challenges that are compounded in elite interviewing by "differences in professional values, seniority, gender, culture and language skills", all of which I encountered. I was very aware of power dynamics in that there were issues related to the interviewees being of an older generation. Issues pertaining to their membership of a professional status, cultural difference, gender, class, and religion all had to be navigated in a sensitive manner to manage the power dynamics of the interviews.

As I was interested in the meaning that the doctors ascribed to their experiences throughout the interview, I always asked them for clarification, rather than relying on "taken-for-granted assumptions" (Rubin and Rubin, 2011). This was achieved by gentle probing into the remarks the interviewees made from time to time, where I repeated their words and asked them to elaborate upon what they had said. The interviewees were asked similar questions, however, additional questions were put based on their responses.

Reliability relates to the consistency of a measure of a concept, whereas validity pertains to whether a devised indicator really measures the concept in question. An IQ test is an example where the validity of the measurement for the concept of intelligence can be questioned (Bryman, 2009). Whilst reliability and validity can be analytically distinguished, these concepts are also inter-related in that validity supposes reliability, in other words, a measure is not valid, if it is not reliable (Bryman, 2009).

In qualitative research, the assessment of quality is about the suitability of the design, including the accuracy and adequacy of the measurement tools used to measure the intended social phenomenon (Creswell, 2007, 206).The author contends that validity concerns alignment between research design and data gathering and how they allow for a conclusions to be drawn in a confident manner. In other words, it pertains to how well data interpretation can take place based on the specific procedure utilised. Strategies suggested by Creswell for validity in social research also include external evaluation through debriefing sessions in which questions can be asked about the credibility of the research process. I achieved this by presenting the preliminary findings to internal research seminars as well as delivering external poster and paper presentations.

Interviewing elite subjects, such as the participants in this study, can be a challenging task (Harvey, 2001) and characteristics such as ethnicity, gender, religion, culture of both the researcher and researched can hinder the research process. Interviewers need to build a rapport and present themselves in a manner that is acceptable to such subjects. This is important not only to obtain high quality responses, but also, because these participants can act as gatekeepers and restrict additional contact, if they do not approve of the interviewee (Harvey, 2011). I was aware that lack of a rapport between myself and the interviewee, and the problem of interviewer bias could have hindered the research process.

Central to this study was the question of how the contextual factors in different localities impact on the identities of overseas-trained South Asian doctors. A case study based approach was chosen in order to capture comparisons of GP experiences in three contrasting geographical contexts. The case study approach allowed for the consideration of different patterns of settlement, the overcoming of structural barriers and how the doctors in the study negotiated their own agency in different geographical contexts. The characteristics of the three case study areas are illustrated in the following table.

Table 1. Characteristics of Geographical Locales

	Characteristics of Place	**Place**
1	A major urban area with high ethnic density	Manchester
2	A large urban area with average ethnic density	Sheffield
3	A semi-rural area with low ethnic density	Barnsley

The choice of Barnsley, Sheffield and Manchester was motivated by the similarities and the differences in their locations. All three areas have a high density of overseas-trained South Asian doctors, however, the ethnic density and physical environment of the cities are different. The varied contextual factors allowed for an analysis of the key factors that can impact on social interactions, place attachment and identities.

In the qualitative data investigation, it was important to address the characteristics of the potential interviewees, sampling method, sample size and techniques used. The decision to select the characteristics of this research sample was guided by the criteria requirements of the research questions (Ritchie, 2003) and included overseas-trained South Asian GPs of both sexes, aged over 50 years, who had practiced in any one of the case study areas. It was decided to focus on doctors of over 50 years of age as they were more likely to have been in the UK and general practice for at least the last two decades. It was anticipated that using this timeframe was likely to capture earlier and more varied experiences of migration, as well as a longer term perspective on community cohesion. The use of the term 'South Asian' only included overseas-trained doctors of Indian and Pakistani origin, with Bangladeshi and Sri Lankan doctors being omitted due to fieldwork access issues. The interviewees were aged 50-76 years and had migrated from either of these two countries. The majority of the GPs were concentrated in the age band 60-75.

Table 2 shows the ethnic, gender and religious breakdown of the GPs interviewed in each of the case study areas. As can be seen, there were no overseas-trained doctors from Bangladeshi or Sri Lankan origin, which relates to fieldwork access issues in the case study areas. Given that community cohesion debates are increasingly concerned with religious identities in the UK, it was considered important to refer to religion in the analysis.

Table 2. Ethnic, Gender and Religious Breakdown of GPs in the Case Study Areas

Ethnic Origin	**Sheffield**		**Barnsley**		**Manchester**		**Religion**	
	Male	Female	Male	Female	Male	Female	Hindu	Muslim
Indian	7	1	2	1	6	1	14	4
Pakistani	3	0	4	1	1	0	0	9
Total	11		8		8		14	13

The qualitative research strategy involved undertaking a sample in a strategic manner rather than sampling on a random basis. A purposive and stratified sample was taken and the approaches applied in this research study are criterion and snowballing. This meant that the participants were purposively selected to ensure that they reflected diversity in the context of demography and geographical location, i.e. rural/urban as required. A quota sample was envisaged to ensure that an equal number of participants were selected from each case study area.

The interviewees were identified by the snowballing method that focused on professional networks and searching GP practices in the case study areas. This is a technique for finding research subjects that entails making initial contact with one or two research subjects, who give the name of another subject, who in turn, gives the name of another and so on (Atkinson and Flint, 2001, Bryman, 2009). The snowballing strategy was used with the anticipation that it was essential to have someone's trust to initiate contact as these are an elite group of individuals, and likely to be hard-to-reach by other means by nature of their employment status and their ethnicity (Atkinson and Flint, 2001). This method involved utilising their social networks to provide further potential contacts. In sum, the interviewees in my study shared the characteristics listed above and snowballing was considered an effective strategy. To overcome possible 'selection bias' associated with snowballing strategy, attempts were made to generate a large sample to include 'isolates' (Atkinson and Flint, 2001) and other complimentary strategies were used alongside snowballing to recruit interviewees. In this respect, information regarding the research project was sent out to GP practices managed by those with South Asian names as well as to BAPIO, the CASE partner organisation and other user organisations.

The interviewees in my research study can be described as relatively homogenous in many respects, such as their age when they entered into general practice, practice conditions and gender. In the light of the above considerations and available resources, the sample was restricted to a total of 27 in-depth interviews with GPs and based on a quota from each of the three contrasting geographical contexts, the profiles of which have been discussed above. A quota sample consisting of 8 participants was purposively selected in each of the case study areas, however, the sample size in Sheffield increased to 11.

I developed guidance notes for the in-depth interviews through informal discussions with GPs from the targeted research population. I contacted the interviewees by telephone and the interviews were arranged either at their home or at their practices. Written consent was taken for quotations to be used in the publications and the interviews were digitally recorded. The topic guide used during the interviews involved incorporating techniques advocated by Lazarsfeld (1972) in that questions should be fitted to the experience of the researched and that they should be fixed in *meaning* rather than *wording*. The art of asking the right questions triggered interviewees' memory accordingly and they felt at ease in remembering sequences of events. Consultations also took place with the user organisation, the British Association of Physicians of Indian Origin (BAPIO). Following the approval of the ethical procedures, pre-piloting was undertaken followed by a pilot study to test and evaluate the question guide regarding the wording, clarity of the proposed questions, ease of understanding, time needed to complete the interviews, the order of the questions and to ensure that the questions were focused on the core goals of the research. An interesting and important aspect was uncovered during this stage: the significance of first language. The interviewees were somewhat hesitant, at first, to express themselves in their first language, then they spontaneously switched into it and were articulating in poetry and prose in the South Asian languages. The interviewees' responses echoed what Burr (2003) argues, that is, that language is about more than simply expressing ourselves. Burr (2003, 4) adds:

> *It is through the daily interactions between people in the course of social life that our versions of knowledge become fabricated. Therefore social interaction of all kinds and particularly language is of great interest to social constructionists.*

Burr refers to the work of Whorf (1941), who believed that it is a person's language that determines the way she or he perceives the world. Burr adds that:

> *.....this means that the way a person thinks, the very categories and concepts that*

provide a framework of meaning for them are provided by the language that they use.

As the interviewees appeared relaxed and responded positively, this confirmed that the content and art of questioning were working effectively. Some other minor changes were made regarding the wording and the sequence of the questions. For instance, the interviewees were given the choice to express themselves in the language that they felt most at ease with.

This book is organised into six chapters. The introductory chapter has set out the context of this research study. Chapter one describes the context of migration and the driving forces behind that of the doctors in the study. The role of religion is also explored, which impacted on the decisions to migrate among other social, cultural and political reasons, this having previously been neglected. In chapters 2 to 4, I discuss the migratory processes leading up to settlement followed by discussion of how the overseas-trained South Asian doctors settled into their respective communities, and how identities were experienced in different contexts.

Chapter 2 delves into experiences upon arrival in the UK, whereas chapter 3 probes how the focal doctors negotiated their entry into general practice utilising an entrepreneurial process. In chapter 4, I describe their experiences of social interaction, and how they were able to fit into their respective communities. It explores how identities were experienced in each of the case study areas and how the local environment impacted on their feeling of belonging to Britain. In chapter 5, I provide exploration and analysis of the doctors' own perceptions and experiences of racism and coping strategies that they utilised. In the final chapter, I present the overall findings of the study and consider how elite migrants' experiences add a new dimension to our existing understanding of community cohesion in the UK.

The review of the community cohesion literature has highlighted a number of deficiencies, for example, it has uncovered the need for an appropriate methodology suited to investigating the experiences of this cohesion, such as in depth interviews. It has also shown that little is known about the nature and extent of the social roles played by highly-skilled overseas-trained South Asian migrant doctors. This study is the first of its kind to investigate the integration experiences of highly skilled overseas-trained South Asian doctors in relation to community cohesion concerns, that is, no previous studies have been undertaken in this regard.

CHAPTER 1

THE CONTEXT OF MIGRATION

In this chapter, I examine the empirical evidence that relates to the context of migration of overseas-trained south Asian doctors, the driving forces behind their migration and how these experiences relate to the existing theories of migration. Firstly, I will provide a brief overview of the historical perspectives on the migration of overseas-trained south Asian doctors in the UK.

Following the creation of the NHS in the UK, which resulted in the expansion of the health workforce in 1948, a significant number of doctors came to the UK from the British ex-colonies. This was a result of an active recruitment attempt by the UK government to alleviate the critical labour shortage in terms of medical manpower, something which became a theme in subsequent recruitment policies (Doyal et al., 1980). However, Doyal et al. (1980) cited that the 'most basic historical and statistical material' had not been recorded despite the fact that the migrant workers had made a significant contribution towards the maintenance of the NHS operation and its ability to provide cost effective healthcare. The earliest study of medical migration into and out of Great Britain was published in 1968 by the Ministry of Health[1]. According to this study, the overseas-doctors represented one-fifth of all doctors in the UK in 1966 with 60% of all 14,500 foreign-born doctors coming from developing countries, the largest number (44%) of all foreign-born doctors being from the Indian sub-continent (Gish, 1971).

In subsequent years the data collection regarding overseas doctors took place in the context of discussions to ensure that the NHS workforce had the right number of doctors at the right place and the right time. Different studies provide different accounts as to exactly how many such doctors came to the UK. Smith's (1980) study refers to the DHSS statistics stating that more than one third (40%) and one fifth (20%) of the medical workforce were doctors

[1] It has subsequently been known as the 'Department of Health and Social Security' and 'Department of Health'.

and GPs respectively, who had trained overseas. According to Doyal et al. (1980) 14% of GPs were overseas-qualified. Robinson and Carey (2000) found that in 1995, 32% of all NHS staff born outside the EU while in 1980, 14% of NHS doctors in 1980 came form Asian subcontinent. Jones and Snow (2010, 35) describe this period as follows:

> *Within twelve years of the creation of the NHS, Manchester was growing increasingly reliant on overseas junior staff for the day-to-day running of its hospitals, while doctors from India and Pakistan were shoring up the city's GP and dental practices.*

Doyal et al. (1980) argue that the presence of overseas doctors in the UK has stimulated 'discussion' and 'controversy'. Ironically, the earliest of the studies do not seem to discuss the type of jobs these doctors occupied, their career prospects or the relevancy of their post-graduate training to their needs (Anwar and Ali, 1987). Rather, these debates appear pre-occupied with two inter-related themes. Firstly, the recruitment of overseas doctors was explained in the context of the 'Brain Drain', that is the loss of doctors to richer countries, which paid limited attention to the implications of sending expensively trained migrant doctors outside their poor countries of whereas the second debate was concerned with professional competence of overseas doctors (Doyal et al., 1981).

The remaining literature regarding the migration of overseas-trained South Asian doctors generally relates to the contribution of overseas-trained doctors working in the NHS, their experience of racism and the implications of the gap created by their departure such as retirement. In order to understand how overseas-trained South Asian doctors came to put down roots in UK society, an important first step is to explore the context of their migration, and the theoretical framework that informs such migration, before looking at an overall settlement pattern.

Various migration theories have been put forward to explain this sociological phenomenon. I believe that the newly emerging Migration Systems Theory, which incorporates all dimensions of the migration experience, including the historical colonial link, has much to offer in analysing the complex sets of factors involved in overseas-trained South Asian doctors' migration into the UK (Castles and Miller, 2003). The approach adopted under this theory is based on a basic principle that assumes a migratory movement as being a consequence of the interaction of macro-micro-structures, which are linked by a number of other intermediary agents, known as meso-structures. The macro-structures are concerned with institutional factors, government policies etc., whereas micro-structures relate to the motivation of individuals/groups and their social networks. The meso-structures consist of intermediaries (such as recruitment agents) that link the macro- and micro-structures.

The process of migration is discussed in the context of macro-micro-meso structures, which cover the reasons for and mechanics of migration, for example, how it was facilitated as well as how social networks were developed and utilised. The discussion also addresses the economic, social, political and cultural practices involved in the migration process.

Macro-Structures

The macro-structures relate to institutional factors and include the laws, relationships and practices between sending and receiving countries that occur in order to control migration settlement. They can act as lubricators in the migration process (Castles and Miller, 2003). A common route described for coming to the UK was by way of an application to the GMC for a recognised clinical attachment under the supervision of a UK consultant, which was offered for an initial period of four weeks. One interviewee explains the process:

> *I suppose if I want to apply for clinical attachment... my professor talks to your professor here and he says 'okay you send your boy here I will give him a clinical attachment'. It used to be a recognised training for 4 weeks, just to give exposure to the local system and they used to pay just nominal salary, some eighty pounds or something for the whole month period (gpm7).*

However, four of the Pakistani origin and three of the Indian origin doctors had come to the UK prior to 1965 under the voucher scheme[2] that was in operation at the time to overcome the labour shortage in Britain. The 1948 Nationality Act allowed Commonwealth citizens who were also British subjects a guaranteed right of entry to the UK. This 'open door' immigration policy remained in place until 1962, when it was replaced with a quota system, which restricted admission to those holding employment vouchers. Historically, doctors came to the UK to gain a post-graduate qualification, and while immigration control was in existence for unskilled/low/semiskilled migrants from the Indian subcontinent countries, doctors were not subject to strict immigration controls until 1994 (Robinson and Carey, 2000). Gish (1971) comments that the immigration acts of the 1960s and early 1970s were

[2] The Commonwealth Immigration Act 1962 introduced employment vouchers, where anyone in possession had the right to enter and settle in Britain. There were three categories: A, B and C. The 'A' voucher was granted to those who had a specific job to come to and where the initiative had to come from the employer. The 'B' category voucher was issued to those who possessed recognised skills and qualifications that were in short supply, such as medical; these were skills that were likely to be useful in the UK. The professionals included in this category were teachers, nurses, doctors, dentists, etc. All other unskilled applicants were included in the category 'C' (Doyal et al.,1981). Those who obtained vouchers could enter the UK provided they were going to work in areas with a labour shortage (Panayi, 2010).

intentionally designed, such that the recruitment of new Commonwealth doctors was exempt from any restrictions. The majority of other non-professional potential migrants from these countries were excluded.

Six Indian origin doctors stated that they had undertaken a post-graduation qualification, which exempted them from the clinical attachment requirement and had been given full registration status prior to coming to the UK. Their accounts show that they obtained jobs with relative ease in less prestigious specialties:

> *I was lucky also that, er, as I landed in London on Saturday morning… er, BMJ [British Medical Journal] we saw and there was a job[advertised] next door to my friend's hospital, yes and he rang the hospital and they said 'okay come... ask him to come with his, er, documents and we'll interview him and give him'... it was a locum job... stopgap job, they gave me a 10 weeks, er, locum job, because somebody who took the job he became ill or he might have left the job and they couldn't fill that job up for 10 weeks. Yes, they wanted somebody to join. A lot of people started, like, doing short term jobs, in certain specialties it was easier, such as casualty, orthopaedics... but not in paediatrics, for example… (gpm7).*

The above account highlights the significance of the role of social networks, which is discussed later. The interviewees talked about how they had to meet the criteria, which included qualifying from specified medical colleges, obtaining house jobs in specific specialties and being resident doctors in such specialties. These requirements were laid down by the GMC and the frequency with which clinical attachments were offered suggests that such screening undertaken was in fact an indirect recruitment process for doctors to work in the NHS, rather than the intention of providing a learning opportunity for them. It is not known whether this type of indirect recruitment related to the circumvention of migration restrictions, or simply occurred because it was the most convenient mechanism for recruiting from South Asia. The interviewees stated that most of the time these clinical attachments were in disciplines and areas where there was shortage of doctors, with the four week attachment often extending to a short term contract, with their being offered jobs in the same hospitals when a vacancy arose. These findings support Raghuram and Kofman's (2002) observation of the altering of state regulations, both of immigration and those governing the medical labour force, to meet the specificities of internal labour-market shortages.

Micro-Structures and the Driving Forces of Migration to the UK

The micro-structures relate to the motivation of individuals/groups and their social networks. Micro approaches also pertain to the processes underlying the decision to migrate and the influences that come to bear on the individual's decision to do so as well as the choice of destination (Stillwell and Congdon, 1991). The interviewees highlighted various reasons for their migration, some of which were disclosed in response to direct questioning, others came to light during the more general discussions. This section is divided into subsections that reveal the nuances and complex sets of factors involved in the motivation to migrate.

Gaining of Post-Graduate Qualifications and UK Medical Training

Almost all the doctors stated that their primary purpose for migration was to obtain a post-graduate medical qualification in support of their career aspirations. Three out of four of the female doctors stated that their main purpose was to support their spouses in the pursuit of higher education; however, they had also hoped to undertake some specific diplomas during their stay in the UK. One male doctor migrated to join his wife-to-be; however, he also stated that his motivation was to undertake a postgraduate qualification. The interviewees emphasised that coming to the UK for post-graduation education was a well-established practice in that era and that this was also a closer match in terms of the structure/qualifications of the South Asian medical system.

Several interviewees of both Indian and Pakistani origin talked about the perceived superiority of UK qualifications to those of their countries of origin and the value that it added to one's human capital. There was some anticipation about the ensuing exposure to the high standards of education and training provided in Britain, which was likely to enhance their status upon returning from migration. Below is a typical response in this regard:

> *I came to do an MSc and I wanted to specialise in medicine. I wanted to get experience in a UK hospital, because this experience means a lot in Pakistan. Everyone respects and is willing to offer you a job, if you have experience from a British institution (gpb5).*

The majority of the doctors had specifically wanted to acquire fellowships from a British Royal College, which they believed was highly valued in their countries of origin. This is the qualification that is required to become a consultant, whereas others had wanted to obtain diplomas in specific specialties. These findings support those of earlier studies that overseas-trained doctors are more likely to have a career intention of progressing to the consultant grade in comparison to UK-trained doctors (Oikelome and Healy, 2007, Anwar and Ali, 1987, Smith, 1980, Esmail, 2007, Rashid, 1990).

In the following, one doctor explains that he wanted to specialise in ENT

(Ear Nose and Throat) and the resources were insufficient in the country of origin. It appears that long after the British left India, the medical profession continued to impose its influence:

> *There was post grad in India and I had taken part one for the fellowship, but there were not good prospects for my specialty, I was specialising in ENT. A British degree is always preferred, well at that time anyway (gp6b).*

Another interviewee stated that he wanted to specialise in gynaecology; however, he was discouraged by his professors as this specialty was not a norm for male doctors at the time in India. Whilst the interviewee below describes the migration decision being made on the spur of the moment, the account also reveals other factors and conditions influencing such a decision. The medical colleges were regularly visited by British medical personnel who acted as an inspiration for the overseas-trained South Asian doctors. It has been stated that the standards for medical education in India were set and regulated by the GMC to ensure compatibility for those Indian doctors who wished to work in Britain (Esmail, 2007). The purpose of these visits from British professors may have been to ensure that the Indian medical colleges were adhering to British standards:

> *What happened was that one of my friends said to me, 'I am thinking of going (to Britain), will you come', I said 'OK' (laughs). So we came.....UK qualification is preferred especially in medicine. Our medical system was set up in the same way and everyone more or less came here to upgrade their education at some stage. Now, I hear that doctors go to Australia from India and Pakistan. In India, only the UK fellowship was recognised, membership or FRCP, MRCP, which you could do in Britain. All of our professors had been educated from here and they had fellowship; membership from England. We also had British professors visiting our colleges on a regular basis (gp6b).*

Decisions to migrate to particular countries were influenced according to the doctors' motivation at the time. Migration to the UK was associated with academic opportunities:

> *When I finished my house job, there had been invitations from the USA and Britain for us. Some of my colleagues went to the USA, but I chose Britain as I wanted to do FRCP. There was another choice, an invitation from Saudi Arabia as well. You go to other countries for economic reasons, but you come to Britain to do your post-graduation (gp2s).*

The relevance of the medical education and training the physicians receive on the Indian sub-continent has been questioned for its relevance to the health needs of the majority of people, as it has been modelled on the British medical education (Mejia, 1978); (Esmail, 2007). The benefit to the less developed donor country of postgraduate training undertaken in a technologically advanced country that has a highly specialised and capital intensive medicine has been also questioned. (Mejia, 1978) argues that a returning migrant physician is relatively unsuited to perform the tasks that are most needed in developing countries. Esmail (2007) provides a different explanation, referring to the colonial context, where coming to Britain to study was considered a badge of honour and upon return the migrant would command considerable distinction in Indian society. This practice, the author argues, has continued since 1800 to the present day.

Professional Experience and Income

The ability to work with renowned professors and within prestigious hospitals in the UK, as well as to gain practical experience and clinical excellence were things that cropped up in numerous accounts, being described as a tradition for those doctors migrating here. The interviewees emphasised that broadening their horizons by learning new ways of practising medicine and eventually taking these skills back home, was their primary objective. Whilst the interviewees did not refer to themselves as economic migrants, the following doctor explains how his friend inspired him to come to the UK when he talked about his success in the country:

> *This was 1965, before the war, [between India and Pakistan] so I received the voucher, my friend H had already come. He wrote to me and said that he had already got provisional registration and that he worked in a hospital A & E department [Accident and Emergency]. He also said, I earn between 100-150 rupees (£10-£15) a month, whereas he earnt that much in a week. He said I should come to UK (gp2s).*

The above illustrates how migration can become a self-perpetuating general system if it impacts positively on the migrant. Satisfaction with the move is communicated back to friends and relatives of the migrant in the sending countries, which can lead to a process of chain-migration (White and Woods, 1980). Many interviewees mentioned that they had been influenced by others' success stories. Being financially supported during post qualification training was also mentioned by a few others as an incentive for migrating to the UK, which also suggests an economic context as a pull factor for migration. Doyal et al. (1980) argue that upon completing vocational training in India and Pakistan, many new graduates were being targeted by countries with medical staff shortages, with Britain being one of these. The UK qualification was described as acting as a subsequent guarantee for better job prospects in the country of origin, providing a wider choice of branches within medicine than the Indian system.

By and large, the well-established concept of the 'Brain Drain' is associated with the one way movement of highly-skilled professionals, such as doctors from developing countries, to developed ones (Pang et al., 2002). The doctors' accounts show that intended outcome was 'Brain Gain', where knowledge was to be taken back to the home country:

> *...Oh, that you wanted perhaps to broaden your horizon, improve your qualifications, and see how medicine is practised in one of the best. I still say today that the National Health Service, it still is the envy of the world and that you want to see how health, universal healthcare is provided in the most reputable hospitals in the world and then, you wanted to learn from this aspect and once, if that could be somehow implemented back home (gpm8).*

The following account sums up the push factors for this interview's migration, which included poor working conditions, lack of training opportunities and medical training not being geared to meeting the needs of physicians and patients. It would appear from his account that he sees the UK system as superior:

> *There was no improvement in the system, no changes, there is corruption, in hospitals, in all fields including the NHS, everywhere, there are no facilities, there is no educational training programmes. We have got an NHS service in Kashmir, but it could be better, if there were other facilities and educational programmes, e.g. when I came here I had to go for GP training for three years. The system here is so well developed. Over there we were trained for something that we didn't have, the equipment, the training, the whole system (gp8s).*

The above accounts provide evidence of the specific colonial contribution in this area through institutional linkages, and the prestige associated with the profession, by downgrading the Indian medical system. The interviewee refers to feeling 'left high and dry' by the western model of medical education, with its lack of relevance to the needs and systems of countries on the Indian subcontinent (Esmail, 2007, 828). Others were of the opinion that Britain is a just society:

> *They [teachers] said that the system is a lot fairer here and that one does not need to be acquainted with some high-powered minister or his relatives to get a job (gp6s).*

The perception of fairness relates to the individual positive experiences that migrants relay back, constantly comparing them with their experiences in the country of origin, without analysing the wider context in which they take place. For example, the same interviewee later stated that he was 'headhunted' by a British professor, who imported him to work in a British hospital as he was the best in his specialty. He lacked the support networks crucial for migration and had no means to migrate otherwise. Hence, his perception of the British being fair, possibly developed from his conditioning in English medium schooling, was subsequently reinforced by his actual experiences. Ironically, his later experiences in the UK when he was not able to penetrate the 'glass ceiling' that he and many other doctors in the study described as preventing them from progressing to consultants' roles, do not appear to have negatively impacted on his views concerning Britain. His failure to look at the bigger picture, in particular, regarding how structural inequalities impacted on the career progression of overseas-trained South Asian doctors, may have been related to the values embodied by the NHS. There was evidence of this, where the negative experiences were silenced or underplayed and I return later to consider as to why this may have been the case.

Ambiguity about the relevance of the UK postgraduate qualification in the country of origin also surfaced in a few interviewees' accounts:

> *Another thing, you are exposed to is the different way of practising. Developed countries have got different ways of doing the things, especially the UK, and if you have first-hand experience and you can translate that thing back into your country when you go back, and you can improve your services also. But it may suit to that country or not I don't know, because our way of teachings are different, our way of... our cultures are different, we go with the religious views, we go with caste culture. There are so many things, you know, people go out of the country to get experience that is the main reason people go out (gpm7).*

The interviewees' accounts clearly show their passion for learning, acquiring knowledge and for the medical profession. The colonial historical context previously discussed may explain the urge of the doctors in the study to invest in their human capital by acquiring a western education, for this would promise them social status in a prestigious profession, such as medicine (Husband, 1982).

Fascination with Britain: A Colonial Legacy

Explanations given by the interviewees, such as 'bettering' themselves and accessing post-graduate training opportunities, provided just minor visibility to a more intricate scheme (Robinson and Carey, 2000). The individual stories uncovered subtle factors that appear to have played a key role in migration decisions, such as fascination with Britain as a place. As previously stated, the interviewees' exposure to English medium-stage schools shows how they had been conditioned to think of Britain in a positive way:

> *We had heard a lot about Britain in schools. We had an image of Britain as nice and clean; like a paradise on earth, country. My wife and I had only just qualified*

and got married; we wanted to see the country that our parents and their parents used to talk about (gp3b).

I went to an English school and read all about Britain from a young age, poetry, prose, Shakespeare, Wordsworth and I was always curious what this beautiful country looked like. You see, so I always wanted to come and see for myself what it looked like (gp4b).

A few of the interviewees came from an army background, where direct or indirect contact with the British had been inspirational for generations. (Husband, 1982). The author refers to the experiences of African Caribbean people, who also felt a 'legitimate bond' with Britain, seeking membership here. Indeed, long after the British had left India, it was still being remembered as the 'Mother Country'.

The interviewees' accounts related to the legacy of colonial relations, which was personal, and emotional, as well as institutional (Robinson and Carey, 2000, 100). Robinson and Carey refer to their empirical study of Indian doctors in which colonial links figured strongly in the doctors' accounts. The authors contend that decisions to migrate to 'better themselves' are based on economic as well as other non-economical 'taken for granted than instrumental' factors, such as the kind of novels one reads as a child. The majority of the interviewees in this study described how they had a pre-conceived image of the UK as a 'paradise'. Their accounts provide evidence of how an English medium-stage education, the school curriculum and the role of missionaries led to the mythologisation of England and impacted on their social lives as ex-colonised people. This impact is likely to be particularly strong for those towards the top of the status hierarchy, which most of these doctors were:

I used to read a lot in my school days, I went to a school which was run by nuns. I knew all about Shakespeare.... I had an image of England as some kind of paradise... where everyone was so nice and friendly, everything clean and orderly (gp1b).

The Role of the Family in the Migration Decision

The majority of the doctors described their social background as elite middle class in that they came from well-educated families. The doctors variously described the professions of their parents as teachers, psychologists, government officers, army officers and influential people in the community, with the exception of a couple of doctors from more modest backgrounds whose families belonged to farming communities. These doctors stated that their parents had worked very hard and ensured the best education for their children so that they could get onto the social mobility ladder. Three of the Pakistani origin doctors said they came from families where their fathers and grandfathers had served in the army; the British army. Only three out of the 27 doctors interviewed had prior familial links within the UK. The role of the family has been stated as being central to migratory movement from the Indian sub-continent countries (Castles and Miller, 2003). Lahiri (2000, 39) also contends that obtaining a British qualification was rarely an individual choice, and that parental aspirations lay behind this enterprise, for they perceived it as a window of opportunity for their children and an English hall-mark as a ticket to success.

Mixed evidence was found in this study concerning the role played by families in the migration decision. Two thirds of the interviewees confirmed that family had played a significant part in their planning to move. They talked about how their parents and even grandparents had held aspirations for them to go to England for higher education in medicine to enhance their social status and fulfil what they described as 'family honour':

> *My family, not just my parents, but grandparents, uncles and aunts, had always said that they wanted one of their family members as a doctor, because it raised your social standing in the community and if you were UK qualified, this was even better for the family honour (gp1s).*

The interviewees' accounts show that the families with a religious background were no different and they all had similar aspirations for their sons:

> *My father, although was a religious man, and had a strong Indian Muslim identity, he very much wanted one of us to do medicine and go to the UK to do higher education [explaining a potential conflict]. You would be regarded as a highly respectable person in Indian society, if you had raised and educated a son who managed to get a UK qualification in medicine. I was the one who fulfilled my father's ambition, but unfortunately, by the time this happened, he had passed away (gp7s).*

Views regarding migration emanating from among South Asian religions vary. While Muslims believe their religion supports travelling abroad for education (Sayeed, 2006), Hindu Brahmans vigorously oppose foreign travel (Lahiri, 2000, 39).

Robinson and Carey's (2000) study also highlights the significance of the notion of family honour (*Izzet*) in its findings and the authors argue that the linkage between spatial, social mobility and Izzet is central to understanding migration from the Asian subcontinent. Sayeed (2006), in an autobiographical account, states that he fulfilled a heartfelt wish that his grandmother made four decades prior to him becoming a doctor, thus being sixteen years before his birth.

Contrary to the much discussed role of family being central to the migratory process, migration might also be described as a solo act. As many as one third of the interviewees emphasised that migration had been solely their own decision. The account of the following interviewee provides contrasting evidence regarding family support for migration:

My plan was to go back to India eventually. You see my father hated me to come to Britain. In fact, he did not even want me to study medicine, because he was fearful that I would lose my Indian identity. He never liked the British. He wanted his all sons to be farmers, but we had seen the other side you see, none of us wanted to do that. He used to say 'the British will corrupt your minds'(laughs). It was funny, he was pulling us to his Indian heritage and we wanted to see and work with those prestigious doctors and professors that we read about in books. I think that the British did us good in many respects and medicine is one example, they set up a good medical system in India (gp6s).

The above account shows how the doctors had to deal with conflicting motives, on the one hand, a desire for status and professional advancement (either by themselves only or their family) and on the other, a desire to maintain their cultural identity and links to their homeland. It also shows how colonisation impacted upon two members within the same family differently; one who believed in the anti-westernisation movement, and the other being directly influenced through medical education based on the western model. However, the laughter of the interviewee did indicate that he appreciated his father's views as well. Lahiri (2000, 42) argues that it would be too simple to state that there was increasing rejection of the west in Indian society, as rejection and admiration of the west seem to co-exist. Others refer to this phenomenon as a direct result of colonialism, which has left scars on the colonised (Chew and Rutherford, 1993).

Teachers as Role Models

According to Samers (2010), the inspiration for migration may be located in the social networks that communicate the value of a particular destination among migrants. Almost all the doctors talked about how they were influenced by their teachers, professors and/or consultants, who were part of the medical establishment and who either originated from Britain or had been trained in UK hospitals and who had shared stories of their positive experiences. Within the Indian sub-continent cultures, the learner-teacher relationship is such that teachers are accorded a lot of respect for their wisdom, knowledge and expertise; they are looked upon as role models. The fact that the teachers made personal recommendations was meaningful for the students, as illustrated in the following accounts:

I came to the UK to, to advance my medical training, because people from the UK, who trained in the UK, who were... came back to India, my consultant and professors, not all of them, a number of them.. they all, they all, were quite happy with the training they had so and so forth and when I was training to be...(gp2m).

He adds that career discussions were a regular occurrence:

...after my qualification as a junior doctor we had talks like this... generally, what we will do and where we will go for training and they particularly said, if you want to train abroad, the UK is the place to go, because it's the training, it's pretty good and it's... as far as medicine and surgery is concerned it's a... very methodological and it's done properly and it's a good experience (gp2m).

The teachers, thus, played a significant role in reinforcing the superiority of a British education and professional experiences in the UK as well as in providing information about migration opportunities, thus aiding preparation for the migratory process. The interviewees' accounts show that their teachers had wholeheartedly embraced the British medical model imposed upon India during colonisation. The role played by the teachers is an important example of the colonial institutional legacy, and its effects upon the shaping of attitudes. The historical context of Indian Medical Services (IMS), as described by Esmail (2007), provides an explanation for the influential role of the teachers as described by the interviewees.

Political/Social/Cultural Reasons

The cultural, social and political complexities of migration also surfaced in the interviewees' accounts when discussing reasons for coming to Britain. Structural inequalities based on caste and class were cited most in this regard by interviewees of both Indian and Pakistani origin:

...you are only successful, if you can 'approach' the right (influential) people (gp5s).

The interviewees themselves acknowledged that there was no simple single reason for their migration. However, among other things, lack of political freedom was cited as a motivating factor:

Main reason was very complex it's not easy and straightforward...I think essentially it was a political reason, I was very much involved in student politics in college days, things became very difficult, it's a very very difficult time. So, when you are involved in politics you are targeted, it was essentially political. It was dangerous for me to remain there (gpm4).

Migrants sometimes return home when the primary goal has been achieved (Castles and Miller, 2003). A few of the interviewees who had returned after gaining post graduate qualification stated that their remigration was due to political disturbances in their country of origin.

An Indian origin female stated how her husband could not obtain a post-graduate qualification in India due to political issues at the time:

> *So, when he applied for a post-graduate position, because he wanted to do Orthopedics, MSA in Orthopedics, three times he was turned down, because he couldn't write in Tamil. That was the main reason, so then we found there was no reason, no point in sticking to this place.' I'm going to apply and go abroad' [Refers to husband], that's how it came about. He was born and brought up in Bombay, at that time; they had all these unnecessary unwanted rules and regulations (gp1b).*

The instability of Indian and Pakistani politics in the migration and post-migration period was identified in one third of the interviewees' accounts, with Britain being valued as a potential 'haven'. This type of behaviour was also witnessed in the colonial period, where some villagers were said to hold the British in great esteem as their rule had brought some 'stability' following the insecurity created by resistance and conflict among the ruling Indian classes (Husband, 1982).

Apart from the influence of a western education, motivations for moving to the UK were also described in a cultural context. Culture can be defined in terms of language religion, and values (Castles and Miller, 2003). The findings of this study lend support to the assertion of Hagan and Ebaugh (2003), that the role of religion and spirituality in the stages of the migratory process has been neglected by scholars of both immigration and the sociology of religion, despite its prominence in immigrants' lives. Majority of the interviewees described how they were influenced by revolutionary literary writings and Urdu poetry of their era. The following Pakistani origin interviewee explained this by reciting the following poetic verse, which he said had been inspirational for him in his decision to migrate; it also indicates how his faith shaped his way of thinking:

> *When I was young, I used to read this Urdu poetry which I found very inspirational: Mohabat mujhe un jwanu se hey,*
>
> *Sitarun pa jo dalten hey Kamand.*
>
> *[Explains the meaning] The poet says, 'I love those kinds of people who have the ability to capture stars by throwing a noose at them. What is meaningful here is that one must not make poverty or other problems an excuse, My own interpretation of this is that you try, God will then help (gp2s).*

For gp2s, reaching out to the stars equated to coming to the UK, which was considered a huge achievement in his era, and he proved that, with a show of determination he was able to do what may have been undoable for many. An Indian origin doctor articulated similar views by reciting a different poetic verse that he had found inspirational with regard to migration:

> *You see I was very much influenced by this poetry verse in my youth,*
> *Tufan ki zindgi pe sadqe hazar janein*
> *muj ko gawara nahien sahil ki moat marna*
>
> *What exactly it means is that I like storms, because they bring challenges and I like to live a life which is challenging. Challenge inspires you to do something, you are in the middle of a storm and you work hard to reach the seashore, but after you reach the seashore, there is no more struggle left. Tufan [storm] is another name for doing something extra-ordinary and I would rather give a thousand lives to a life that is spent in doing something to fight with injustices. I preferred to migrate than to sit helplessly and do nothing, but I also hoped to return one day (gpm8).*

A third of the doctors in the study referred to the strong cultural influences and values that they had been brought up with, which included the belief in *takdir* (destiny); that it is *He who makes the plans and you are destined to it by your creator* (Sayeed, 2006). One interviewee of the Hindu faith commented that his future was destined this way:

> *It's got to do with destiny; it's not what you decide you would do (gp2b).*

Similarly, another interviewee explained that his Muslim faith had provided guidance for him:

> *We (as Muslims) believe that any migratory movement is a blessing for you (harkat mein barkat hai). We come from a risk-taking culture, its ingrained in us, we took a huge journey, crossed many seas, just a few pounds in our pockets, because we had faith in us, in our ability and hard work (gp7b).*

The migrants' creative use of religion in the above quotes is clearly evident, not only in their decision-making processes, but also with regard to its provision as a spiritual resource. Their accounts show that the psychological effects of religious values resulted in their commitment towards enduring the hardship of migration (Hagan and Ebaugh, 2003). The findings show that causes of migration can be found in the cultural, political and social marginalisation of specific groups of people (Samers, 2010). They add to our knowledge as to how the doctors used creative ways forward, where aspects of culture, language, religion and values, became integrated in the organisation of the migratory process.

Professional and Elite Social Networks

In this section, I will discuss the informal social networks that the migrants developed in order to manage migration and settlement. In migration studies, chain migration has received a lot of attention; it implies that social ties that are based on kinship and community membership facilitate a process by which migration leads to more migration. This terminology has been replaced with 'migrant networks', which are defined as 'interpersonal ties' connecting key actors, such as migrants, former migrants and non-migrants, in both origin and destination countries, by means of kinship, friendship and shared community origin (de Haas, 2010).

Researchers of migration studies associate the bulk of migration of South Asian origin people with networks that are based on kinship; however, the focus of such research has been on peasant/low/unskilled migrants. The networks utilised by migrants vary considerably and a qualitative variation has been shown to exist in the types that different occupational classes utilise. Regarding which, unskilled migrants' networks are likely to be based on kinship, whereas 'high occupation groups' tend to rely on their colleagues and institutions (Shah and Menon, 1999). The findings of this study bring to light the heterogeneous nature of networking utilised by the doctors in the study pre- and post-migration. Very few of the interviewees had prior familial links to the UK. Two key institutional links were described by all the interviewees as providing information concerning migration, one being the medical colleges themselves, where teachers inspired students to travel to UK universities for exposure to professional experiences and technological advancements, as discussed in the previous section concerning the motivation to migrate. The second instrumental institutional link, described as the first port of call for these migrants, was the GMC, which provided key information as to what they had to do prior to and post-migration. This is very different to the networks typically discussed in chain migration, which are informal and community based. A couple of interviewees discussed utilising networks, which can be classed as non-traditional links that had evolved. One described how he had networked with a UK origin doctor, with whom he had become a pen friend during his studies in Pakistan:

> *When we were at college, we were encouraged to have contact with other medical students in Europe, our teachers used to say you must have links with Europe, then you will know what they are studying. I had a pen friend D in Somerset in the UK; I used to write to her regularly. She was very helpful, she could not come to meet me at the airport, but told me about flights, hotels airport etc. I was a little nervous, new country; I did not know the country at all. She also explained what I should do, like contact GMC and look for jobs in BMJ (gp2s).*

The above interviewee remarks how he was apprehensive about coming to a new country, which was also mentioned by several others. Some interviewees had the belief that only those who have strong networks can migrate:

> *Most doctors who are able to come to the UK are from upper middle classes, with well-established links. I had no contacts or important links with anyone, because I come from a farming community and was the first one to become a doctor. If I had not been headhunted by an English professor who had gone to our hospital where I was working, I probably wouldn't have been able to make it (gp6s).*

However, this belief is not borne out by the experiences of doctors from more privileged backgrounds. Only a few of the interviewees (4/27) described how in the initial period of migration they had networked with friends and colleagues, who were either from the same medical college or had occupied similar social/professional positions, and had been inspirational and facilitated the migration process. Emphasis was placed on long standing relationships between families and the social positions of these links, as the following response illustrates:

> *I had, yes, I had a friend who was here for a few years before I came, a family friend, she's a consultant in Obs & Gynae [Obstetrics & Gynecolog]), err and he [husband] was working in a hospital. Yes, they were helpful, because when I arrived here, they, they came and met me and then put me up with them for a few days until I moved on to Southampton and so on (gpm2).*

The doctor in the following describes how friends had facilitated his social mobility by providing employment links and introducing him to key contacts:

> *I had some doctor friends, they said, 'what we can do is to introduce you to our consultants and then it is up to you how you perform'. They did introduce me to the consultants, let me stay with them for a week so that I could acclimatise and get used to things. I got an attachment in Kettering in Northamptonshire (gp1b).*

The most frequent response however, was where interviewees reported that they did not know anyone when they came to the UK, which may suggest social networks are less important for skilled professionals, a finding that was also revealed by (Shah and Menon, 1999). A few talked about having some transient non-medical links upon arrival in the country that became useful in their finding their way round and providing accommodation for the first few days in a new country:

> *There were no infrastructures available in the 60s really to help you; I was very independent any way. There was no network at all that I could access, but we just coped with the situation, when you are faced with the situation, you don't just back out, you face it (gp5b).*

The interviewees placed emphasis on being independent, which was a theme present in the majority of the interviews, implying that they did not wish to ask others for information or other forms of support. Some reported proudly how they had not taken up their family's wishes and feelings about migrating to the UK, because they preferred to be independent. Their confidence could have been down to their entrepreneurial thinking and the professional training they had received.

The doctors were less likely to seek support from friends, especially from friends/colleagues originating from the same city and country. They preferred to be independent and stated that in years to come they did not want reminding that they had been successful, because of someone's favours. Additionally, they did not want news travelling back to their home towns about their struggles. In part, this may also be a reaction against a system where personal contacts seemed too important a factor in success. Reacting against this system, it perhaps became important for these doctors to succeed through merit; not social contacts. The following quotes illustrate how doctors gave preference to institutional links:

> *Yeah, we had a few friends as well, yeah, but they were not known straight away, but you make your own place and then actually you meet people, you find out people, we did not know anybody before coming. I would not have relied on friends in any case, because I did not want them to tell me after 10 years that I was only able to navigate my way round, because of their help. I preferred institutional help in the first instance (gp3s).*
>
> *I had been in touch with GMC before coming here and they offered me a clinical attachment for four weeks; so I came. I did not seek help from friends, because it's better to receive help from institutions, you don't have to pay back favours for ever to them. They [friends] also remind you from time to time, I was the one who brought you here, remember etc. (gp4s).*

While some doctors acknowledged the significance of support from their networks in the initial period of settling in, they also talked about the implications of such social relationships that arose from a shared ethnic community:

> *Our community is very tight knit and news of any failure travels fast and even before you know, it reaches your hometown and gossip starts. Also, we were going for the same jobs and you did not want to lower your own chances of securing a position by helping your comrade. That's not to say that I have not helped anyone or that no one has helped me, but I think networking is based on certain criteria and what that means is that you don't just help anyone from your city or place, you have to be cautious. I have helped friends who were my friends from college comradeship or who have been family friends for a long time and who I trust (gp7b).*

The above quote highlights the significance of the trust required for networking and the complexity involved when a community is close-nit, with individuals competing with each other, along with the unconscious rules of individuals' social backgrounds determining the strength of these networks. The majority of interviewees with both Indian and Pakistani origin described networking across beneficial, as one put it:

> *I [Pakistani origin] found Indian doctors very supportive in work related issues; they gave me detailed information about what to expect in interviews, selection processes, which consultants to avoid, but my own [Pakistani] were trying to avoid me, so that I couldn't reach out to them. They did not tell me a single thing. I have heard them often bitching about others from their own cities and saying things like, look at so and so, he is trying to act bigger than his boots. His mother was only a primary school teacher or that his father was only a coolie. That's why I did not associate with doctors from my own city and country. I would rather seek help from an Indian doctor, because there is no such threat in that relationship. They won't let your hometown know if you failed an exam or did not get a job in your specialty etc. My Indian friend told me the same; he said the person who helped him most was a Pakistani doctor (gp4s).*

The above quote shows how conscious the interviewee appeared to be about social status, not wishing to take any risk that may damage his reputation. The above also suggests another motive for doctors choosing to migrate, which was to get away from the class/caste judgments still so prevalent in the homeland, and their desire to acquire social status through their profession, rather than 'hereditary privilege' as previously discussed. Most doctors were determined to use their own agency in navigating the system and not contacting their friends or colleagues for support:

> *I knew Dr X from before coming here. I met him when he had just got the job in the same hospital as me here in the UK. When we met, he took me to one corner and said, no one here must know that we know each other, because they will assume that you helped me to get here. He thought that this will give people a bad impression of him and that he had it easy and they would doubt his own capability (gp6s).*

The above account shows that networking was considered in a negative way. This may have been related to the interviewee's perception that he should be selected on merit, rather than through networks. Many interviewees said that they left the country of origin, because the system was flawed and unless you could 'approach' the right personnel, the chances of success were slim. They rejected networks, because a meritocratic system was important to them; however, their views appeared to be based on rather an idealised meritocracy and an assumption that the elites in Britain could achieve their position on the basis of ability and achievement.

It is often assumed that established migrants help out new one in terms of settlement. However, the interviewees' accounts show the complexity involved in networking and whilst having a desire to escape ascribed status was one motive for migration, a wish to generate status in the homeland was another. There was also a general consensus that friends/colleagues expected each other to find their own feet:

> *I think it's because they think that it did not come by easy to us, so why should we help someone else, they should also be thrown about like we were (gp3s).*

The following doctor stated how his friends avoided contact with him in the work setting as they did not want to be stereotyped by others:

> *They [friends] did not want to be known as Mirpuris [Kashmiri region in Pakistan], because others make fun of you, that you are from a backward area (gp4s).*

The above and other quotes show that while there was some level of mutual support among the interviewees, there were also prejudiced perceptions of each other. Apart from cultural reasons, this form of behaviour may be reflective of the racism experienced by overseas-trained South Asian doctors, who in turn, projected such feelings on to others, who they thought were of lower status than themselves (Husband, 1982). Linblad (1993, 125) also echoes the above regarding her experiences in the UK and associates such behaviour with how racism impacts on individuals:

> *Having been looked down by the British made me enjoy looking down on others myself.*

All four female doctors in the study had had their husbands (doctors) either accompany them or arrived earlier. They can therefore be regarded as chain migrants, who had networked into existing networks. As explained previously, the female interviewees entered into already networked communities. There were also examples of family migration, where husband and wife both entered the UK at the same time, which differs from the usual pattern of young, male migration. It also shows that temporary highly-skilled permit holders were allowed family migration and exempted from immigration restriction when other immigrants from South Asian countries were not exempted (Kofman, 2004).

Meso-Structures

Intermediate 'meso- structures' play an important role in facilitating migration. Individuals, groups and institutions take on the role of mediators between migrants and institutions, which has led to the emergence of a migration industry. These mediators can be recruitment organisations, lawyers, agents and other intermediaries (Castles and Miller, 2003).

Evidence from the interviewees' accounts suggests that the migration industry was also in operation in their era, and there were local recruiters who were in an advantageous position to facilitate migration. The interviewees mentioned vouchers being distributed and work permit schemes also being in operation. As explained earlier, the voucher scheme in operation in the early 1960s encouraged migrants to accept invitations to migrate. The following account shows that there was an exchange of favours, rather than the brokers charging high fees, which may have been reflective of the higher social status of the doctors and their ability to access influential networks:

> *One of the managers from the local job centre had an appendicitis operation which I performed. After the operation, he came up to me and said doctor sahib, we have those vouchers for the UK, if you are interested. By this time, I was already working after my qualifying. He said, come to me and I will give you the voucher. There were three of us, a professor of ophthalmology, a colleague who was a house surgeon, and another boy who I forgot to mention, we all went (gp5m).*

The interviewees' accounts showed that there was a large network of people working in the migration industry and working with various governmental officials in both the receiving and sending countries. The account of the following interviewee, who came to the UK in 1964, shows a pattern of 'aggressive recruitment' activities mediated through extensive networks and the use of the voucher scheme:

> *I was offered a voucher by the labour ministry at the time. I had no passport, no intention to come. I was well off, father was a businessman. My uncle was also very influential in the city. One of the travel agents my uncle knew, he was an international traveller, he said 'you must go there even for six months; they will treat you like a hot cake'. He said. 'They (UK) will receive you overenthusiastically', because they desperately needed us doctors, and there was a shortage of labour force, but there was a shortage of doctors too. Anyway, I started thinking about what this man had said; I think he had sown the seeds. But I had no passport and it used to take two years to get one unless you used bribes, which neither I nor my father liked to do. The agent said, I will deal with all of that, you just get ready, within two weeks (gp2s).*

The period referred in the above account closely ties in with the period referred to by Gish (1971), who argues that the immigration Acts of the 1960s and 1970s were intentionally designed to favour Commonwealth doctors over their less skilled counterparts, and that 40% of all vouchers issued between 1966-1968 to New Commonwealth and Pakistani origin professionals were allocated to doctors. The above account suggests that this practice was being implemented even earlier than the period referred to by Gish.

Migration, in general, is perceived as a process in which migrants are active actors, who employ their own agency in making the decision to migrate. This was not the case for the following interviewee, who talked about being plucked out from the country of origin for his skills and experiences:

> *I got an offer to come to Edinburgh through a WHO scholarship, because one of the professors from Edinburgh went to look for the brightest medical students. So, he made an offer to me and asked if I would like to come to UK and I said, ok. So, I grabbed the opportunity. He came..., he made observations of my work for a few weeks. My professor was very good as well, after observations I was offered the scholarship and invited to work in Edinburgh in 1966. Although it was a scholarship, they changed my job to house officer and then senior house officer after a while (gp6s).*

The above account reflects the labour shortages and informality of the systems that operated at the time, with no explicit criteria for recruitment or consideration of equal opportunities. The interviewees' accounts also confirm that migratory movement becomes a self-sustaining social process once it has started (Castles and Miller, 2003). For example, the migrants might find partners in the new country, which three of the interviewees did. Migrants who find living and working conditions better than their own country of origin may remigrate. In two of the cases, this was so, as illustrated by the following account, where the interviewee describes how he was summoned back after returning to India, thus adhering to the original plan of settling back:

> *It was a rural area and there were only five to six other Asian doctors in the whole of the area (UK). I said to myself 'let's go back now', so I went back to India. I had only worked for about two months in a hospital when one day I received a phone call from the consultant in Kettering hospital inviting me back to work for him. He said, 'please come back; we need you and we have a job for you'. I discussed with my wife this job proposal. I said to her that, 'there is ongoing politics in India, in order to survive here, you have to know so many important officials for little things to be done, if you don't know anyone, you stand at the bottom of the queue. On the other hand, these people from UK are inviting me to come and work for them, what more do I want?' She said, ok, you go first and then I will come. So she joined me later after eight months (gp1m).*

The above also highlights how family, especially spouses, were closely involved in the migration decision, as discussed previously. It also demonstrates the importance of social networks in the UK in encouraging remigration and how access to information/job offers could tempt doctors back again.

This chapter has discussed the empirical evidence in regarding to how the migration experiences of overseas-trained South Asian doctors relates to existing theories of migration. The findings show the nuances and complexities of the migratory process and the intertwining of macro-, meso- and micro-structures, making it difficult to highlight one single cause for migration. The GPs' accounts have revealed the significance of the micro-level role of religion and spirituality in the dynamic process of international migration, which has not been explored previously. The role of the family in the migration decision was only significant for a quarter of the doctors in this study. The macro-structures facilitating migratory movement included provision of structural support in the form of exemption from strict immigration controls. The availability of opportunities in Britain, such as vouchers, work permits and clinical attachments, acted as catalysts and mechanisms for promoting the migratory processes. These methods of enabling doctors to migrate appear to be a combination of an active and subtle recruitment drive on the part of the NHS.

While the primary purpose of migration was stated as being the obtaining of a postgraduate qualification, the interviewees' accounts testify that beneath the surface lie much more complex and deep-seated issues that appear to relate to the legacy of colonialism and its impact on people. At first glance, the typology of these highly-skilled migrants may appear to fit with what Iredale (2001) describes as 'Government induced' or 'industry led', as there is evidence of active recruitment by the government and the NHS. However, the subtle reasons behind this, such as a fascination with Britain, its culture, its perceived superiority in medical training and education facilities, including advanced equipment as well as how British degrees and experiences are held in high esteem in the countries of origin, all being associated with improving a migrant's status, can be seen to figure strongly in the migrants' accounts. They provide evidence for the dependency and opportunities created by the colonial legacy on the personal, emotional and institutional levels. In light of the findings of this research so far, I argue that the migration of overseas-trained doctors is a social phenomenon that has been colonially induced through the educational and social processes that were part of the colonial rule at the time, and that continue to play a role in conditioning individuals, communities and nations' ways of thinking.

In relation to social networks, the key networks described are institutional rather than based on kinship. The findings show that, so far, Migration

Network Theory has not incorporated the cultural issues that rendered some networks as obstructive/ facilitative for the doctors in the study. I now turn to the post migration experiences of the interviewees. In the following chapter, I will explore the immediate experiences of the migrants following their arrival in the UK, along with discussion of how the medical system was navigated by the interviewees.

CHAPTER 2

NAVIGATING THE UK MEDICAL SYSTEM UPON ARRIVAL

I will now turn to the post migration experiences of the doctors in the study. In this chapter, I will explore their immediate experiences upon arrival in the UK, followed by their narratives on how they navigated the medical system. I will also explore their perceptions of what factors led to their entry into general practice and how they negotiated entry into this discipline.

Unlike their unskilled counterparts, the majority of doctors' accounts show that special entry privileges were granted to them. The doctors' pre-conceived positive attitudes about Britain were reinforced from the point of entry by such experiences:

> *When I arrived in the country, an Englishman came and met me at the airport. He had been sent by the hospital to pick me up. He took care of my suitcase immediately. I was so impressed. I wrote a letter to my wife the same day and I remember to this day that I wrote to her that I was in heaven on earth (gp8s).*

The interviewees' accounts show that their experiences sharply contrast with those of lay South Asian migrants. For example, in 1979, an Indian woman was subjected to a 'virginity test' on her arrival at the Heathrow airport. It was alleged that this was undertaken to ascertain that she was the 'bona fide virgin or fiancée' of the man who had sponsored her.[1] Similarly, Asian children were being x-rayed upon arrival in the UK to determine their ages and whether they were dependent children of the sponsor (Husband, 1982).

A most common experience among interviewees upon arrival to the UK was that of working several temporary locum jobs, ranging between 3-6 months before securing one year's contract. Some jobs lasted only a few weeks. Specialties considered less prestigious were cited as their most

[1] Virginity tests for immigrants 'reflected Dark Age prejudices' of 1970s Britain. 8 May 2011, The Guardian. http://www.guardian.co.uk/uk/2011/may/08/virginity-tests-immigrants-prejudices-britain

common forms of work:

> *With some specialties it was very easy, like orthopaedics, psychiatry. There was a divide for all, even geriatric medicine, because local people were not interested in doing those types of jobs, but these are jobs which we filled up, Geriatrics, psychiatry, casualty, orthopaedics and then to get a general surgery, general medicine, paediatrics, it used to be very hard (gpm7).*

Since being in employment was crucial as it provided accommodation and extension of a visa as well as a salary, the interviewees stated they were left with no alternative other than to accept any job that became available:

> *First, initially for 6 months, I did 10 weeks locum, then I went in to do another locum for 2 weeks. See what used to happen, with a job you used to get a room, if it is a resident on-call, yes, resident on-call, then you always used to have a roof over your head, if you have got a poor job, you don't have a roof (gp7m).*

For many, lack of family support was an added dimension:

> *I had no relations. We had no family member here whom I could rely on and therefore you had to get any job, whatever comes your way (gp1s).*

As many interviewees talked about being approached by consultants for temporary jobs via their friends, this would suggest that their vulnerability was exploited by NHS employers, who needed persons to take on a post.

Following The Merrison Report (1975), which highlighted the competence issues of overseas doctors, the interviewees who came to the UK after 1975 had to undertake a Temporary Registration Assessment Board (TRAB) test. This was a new system introduced by the GMC for the purpose of evaluating the professional and linguistic ability of a physician who was trained outside the UK, which covered knowledge of both English and medicine (Douglas, 2000). The test only applied to those doctors who had not qualified from a medical college which had reciprocal arrangements with the UK. In one case, where a respondent's wife had been given full registration prior to entry into the country, she was asked to take the PLAB[2] exam before she could be granted full registration upon her entry into the country, as the test had since been introduced.

The following interviewee talked about the informality of the recruitment process, with a consultant offering a job without any formal application. Interestingly, the doctors previously talked about obtaining jobs on merit rather than from knowing someone, however, they stated with pride that they

---

[2] TRAB was later renamed the Professional and Linguistic Assessment Board (PLAB)

had been selected, as the following account states:

> *...then I got a locum job in Gloucester, that consultant there, he liked me, he said OK there's a regular job coming, in September you can have that (gp2b).*

Several of the interviewees recalled being headhunted for their expertise which would suggest that overseas-trained South Asian doctors were vulnerable and being exploited:

> *We worked hard, and previously, many times in peripheral and district general hospitals, they always used to prefer experienced people, because we had done most of the jobs in India, technically we are alright, our hands are OK (gpm7)*

Another interviewee's account suggests vulnerability, unequal power relations and exploitation:

> *It is because, when you are thrown into the deep end we don't have any cosy life, we don't have protection, and we are in a different environment and you can't go and stay anywhere and, you have to get... beggar has got no choice, you have to take a job, whatever job comes your way (gpm1).*

The metaphor of the beggar was used by a couple of other interviewees, which is ironic, in that the majority of the doctors in the study did come from very privileged backgrounds. Such professional downgrading is likely to be reflective of the particular culture of the NHS operating at the time, and its potential impact on people.

In general, the interviewees' accounts lend support to the findings of earlier studies such as that of Doyal et al.(1980, 54) who stated that overseas-trained doctors provided cheap labour:

> *...the traditional justification for the above situation offered is that it constitutes a form of British 'aid' to the third world, training health workers who then go back to their own countries. However, a closer examination reveals that in reality these workers provide a crucial source of cheap labour and their utilisation has always been an important component both in keeping down the costs and in rationalising the labour process in health care.*

Negotiating Entry into General Practice

In the previous section, I explored the migration processes, how the doctors in the study navigated their way into the UK system and the barriers that they encountered to integrating fully into the institution of NHS. I was interested in exploring their perceptions of their mobility in the NHS in terms of working conditions and career development as well as their contributions to this area of work. This section builds on their subsequent experiences. I will now discuss the push and pull factors regarding entry into general practice.

Migrants often occupy low level positions in the labour market on the point of entry, as a result of a combination of factors, such as arriving from a poor country to a rich country, unfamiliarity with local ways of working, lack of proficiency in English and/or, few or no local networks. This segmented structure of the labour market is owed to the migratory process; however, an important question is the extent to which migrants have a fair chance of upward social mobility (Castles and Miller, 2003). It appears from the accounts of the doctors that this upward social mobility was blocked for them.

The doctors described the push factors for entry into General Practice as: harsh working conditions, mostly having to work as junior doctors despite having several years of experience under their belt in the country of origin, frequently moving to temporary jobs in high demand areas, and being pigeon-holed into the least desired specialties. Most of them stated that they were stagnating in jobs that did not relate to their career progression and there was no career path planned. However, a few stated that they had progressed to the post of a registrar, although they knew that they were going to be held back at some stage, as they had seen it happening so frequently with their friends/colleagues. Many were unable to pass part of the postgraduate qualification exams, partly because their clinical experiences did not relate to the desired qualification. Return home was not an option, after having been engulfed in the migratory process, and for many, the only viable option was that of general practice, as explained below by one of the interviewees:

> *At that time, the only compulsion was that if you want to stay on here, career progression in the hospital..was... looked blocked, so then the second alternative was to go and do general practice (gpm4).*

Another doctor commented on the harsh working conditions and being pigeon-holed into specialties that are the least desired in medicine:

> *...in those days, job was thanklessly hard, very busy, you see, nowadays they are doing quite a good job. I mean, they're not on call no more than 8 hours at a time, whereas when we came we were on call alternate days, Very very hectic, on call, very very busy job. So, there is no question of only this many hours the doctor should work, nothing like that. I mean, have to do this job and then, I mean, that's it, you keep your mouth shut, you carry on working, at that time, because this country didn't have enough, you see. It was majority from India, Pakistan and Bangladesh, mainly in geriatrics, psychiatric, casualty, because it's all hard working posts, unsociable hours, you see. A surgical post, a medical post, obs & gynae posts will*

be taken up by the local... white, but Asians, will fill up these psychiatric, geriatrics also in anaesthesia...Asian. So, it was very very difficult, you see. Orthopaedics is another branch mainly Asians (gp1b).

In nearly all cases, the doctors showed hesitation in the use of terminology such as white, black, instead frequently used terms such as *locals* to describe white or English and *our own* to refer to patients or others from same race/culture Reasons as to why hesitation of describing people in racial terms exists are discussed elsewhere in this book. Reference to *our own,* however, may be related to their acknowledgement of my identity as a researcher.

The above account refers to *keeping mouth shut*, which would suggest that this was a survival strategy in an environment where there was a culture of fear among overseas-trained South Asian doctors.

The doctors in the study were a group of professionals, who were motivated to return to relatively privileged lives on the Indian subcontinent once they had gained a qualification here. Hence, an understanding of why that did not materialise for many is quite important. Almost all the interviewees stated that as the length of stay increased, family formation took place and the birth of children required stability in life. The UK system offered new kinds of opportunities than initially envisaged, such as the new niches carved out in the general practice industry. Personal and professional relationships built over the years were mentioned by all those interviewed, while such networks were weakening in the countries of origin. Whilst poor working conditions in the UK were described, comparisons were drawn with the conditions in the countries of origin and preferences were stated over the practice style in the UK, which offered them autonomous positions and social status. The UK was also preferred as it offered enhanced education and career opportunities for their children, the majority of whom also went into medicine as a career. In one case, a child's specific disability needs being better met within the context of the UK was also mentioned. Attachments with places/people/communities that they worked with were also cited as common reasons to stay on, whereas lack of improvement in social/economic/political situations in the country of origin cropped up in many accounts as an ongoing push factor. The interviewees' experiences in this respect were quite similar to other less privileged groups of migrants, who also often intend to return, however, due to growing ties with the new country, their return becomes a myth. The role of institutional racism in the NHS was acknowledged by several of the doctors in the study:

The bad thing here, is that, if you were competing with a local doctor, no matter how good you were, the English or the Scottish will always get the job. There is discrimination, and the thing is you could not even complain about it as it would be noted and then, it will follow you wherever you go for the job and then, you will have difficulty (gp3b).

The above quote suggests that the interviewees were well aware of widespread discrimination and victimisation, but felt unable to complain as a result of the existence of power inequalities and the likely implications for them, if they were to speak up against powerful people. This can be evidenced in the account below:

One of my friends decided to take it all the way to GMC to defend his case and won. There, they asked him the question that, 'it appears in the court that this is a case of racism, do you want to pursue it further? He said, 'look I am living in a sea, I don't want to be enemy with crocodiles' (laughs). He said, 'I have got a few more years to go; I want to live peacefully with the crocodiles' (gp9s).

Some interviewees were more explicit than others in naming their experiences:

There was definitely racism shown towards us, on the basis of who we were and because of our overseas qualifications. One of my friends was of mixed parentage, his mother was Welsh and father Pakistani. His father went back to Pakistan, he and his brother were brought up in Pakistan; he graduated in Pakistan but came here to do his post graduation. He had difficulty getting jobs. Once, he was told that if he changed his name to an English name, he was likely to get jobs as he was very light skinned and could pass as a white person. He changed his name, got his qualification and went back, because he said he could not bear the racism shown (gp9s).

The following interviewee's account shows the differential experiences he was subjected to:

I was talking about glass ceiling earlier on, that was quite explicit you know, you were not being given the training that you needed, whereas they were providing training to their local people that was very obvious, because they (NHS) were preparing them (local) for a certain direction (gpm8).

The above accounts affirm Collins's (2001) findings in a study undertaken to address the implementation of *Tackling Racial Harassment in the NHS, A Plan for Action (1998)*, in which he concluded that the fear of victimisation was a significant factor in the non-reporting of numerous racial harassment cases (Collins, 2001). The nurses from black and minority ethnic (BME) background working in the UK have also been reported as being over-represented in auxiliary roles providing a cheap source of labour in the NHS (Baxter, 1988). Jones and Snow (2010) also reported how BME nurses in their study identified difficulties in promotion and career development.

Many of the doctors described having no identity and feeling frustrated as it contradicted with their motivation to come to the UK which was to gain a higher professional status. They had become more settled in the UK and a number had started to build their family lives after their spouses had joined them. The needs of raising young families and the demands of the NHS produced conflicts in personal lives as described below:

> *I worked there in Accident and Emergency department, for 6 months. So then, my dream was that I have to do post graduate training in something, so actually I joined the school of tropical medicine in Liverpool after that and I did diploma in tropical medicine in Liverpool. After that, circumstances, family circumstances changed, my wife joined me and we had our first son born. I took up a job, first in A&E, then I worked a little while in geriatric medicine also, in a different hospital, in Liverpool and Manchester, I did my diploma from Liverpool, then came back and did geriatric medicine for a while. I think.. I came in '78 and until '81.. 3 years I did from one hospital to the other. In one place, the maximum length I stayed was 1 year, but the others were 3 months… in some hospitals 3 months. Yes, you had to apply, not only that, the hard part was you have 2 children as well. It's busy and you don't have a house either, that is dependent on your job, if you have a job the hospital would give you accommodation. Yes, if you don't have a home, where will you go? You'll become homeless. It was very frustrating, very frustrating disappointing also, ermm... you had no identity, then I took up general practice (gpm4).*

The above account shows how the overseas trained South Asian doctors were being used as a 'pair of hands' (Sayeed, 2006) on a needs led basis without any consideration for their training or future careers. Similar concerns have also been echoed in anecdotal evidence by the overseas trained doctors in the medical press (Unwin, 2001). A number of studies, such as those of McKeigue et al. (1990) and Anwar and Ali (1987), also refer to the disproportionate difficulties experienced by ethnic minority doctors. A small-scale study conducted by Esmail and Everington in 1999, found that English applicants were twice as likely to be shortlisted as applicants with foreign sounding names, thus confirming that there was racial discrimination against doctors from ethnic minorities.

The above interviewee's account, which was a typical response in this area, shows that overseas trained South Asian doctors had other pressures to deal with, such as family reunion/ formation and/or work-life balance. In such circumstances, where there was constant job insecurity and the need to travel around, general practice was likely to be a more attractive option. Careers advice being given by white consultants was also strongly pointing them in the GP direction. In nearly all cases, the interviewees talked about being advised by their consultants to go into it:

> *...he (consultant) said 'why you don't do general practice? You would settle better and your family will be settled as well'. He was Irish, very nice man. I asked him, how do I go about it. He goes, 'alright'. He arranged it with someone that I will do general practice for one year with them (gp3b).*
> *Well, when I was doing Gynae/Obs, my consultant.. he (consultants) was very very good and I wanted to do do.. be a consultant, but.. I realised when talking to him that I will never get a consultant post in my life.. at that time it was very difficult. He told me that, if I wanted to live here, it will be good for me, if you go into general practice, so I did.. I came into general practice (gp1s).*

This experience was common among other interviewees. Their consultants were directing them to go into the discipline of general practice, rather than continuing to pursue the consultant route. The interviewees held the consultants in high esteem and generally viewed their advice in a positive way, except in the following account, which sheds some doubt on the advice being authentic:

> *No idea why they were doing it, but I think probably they didn't want Asian or outsiders to go in consultancy... I think he advised me, he was a very good friendly consultant and... yes, he was white. He asked me, 'what do you want to do?' I told him, 'I want to, I am interested, I want to be a gynaecologist'. Then, he gave me the impression that I don't think you will get a consultant post, you might be just an SHO or registrar and that's it, nothing else. I think he knew, yeah, but he liked me very much, so he advised me right and I'm happy he advised me in that way (gp1b).*

The above quote raises a number of issues. Firstly, Gish's (1971, 52) assertion that "... the National Health Service simply could not function without overseas doctors " suggests that it would have been in the consultants' own best interests at the time to have sufficient competent junior doctors at hand to run the hospital service effectively. This heavy reliance would have necessitated the forming of a good working relationship. This is not to deny that some genuine working relationships would not have been built among individuals; however, overwhelming evidence exists suggesting that class (Navarro, 1978) and race (Collins, 2001) are factors that have been used to oppress doctors from the lower classes and ethnic minority backgrounds by consultants who are predominantly drawn from the white upper middle classes.

The interviewee concludes in his account that, *'I'm happy he advised me that way'*. The interviewees' accounts are based on their own retrospective analysis of experiences, which may have been shaped by the relative success that they have since had in their current position as GPs. Cultural beliefs are also likely to have influenced to their reflections, whereby interviewees referred to cultural codes, which required them not to say unpleasant things about others who had been supportive, in whatever capacity, small or great, in the past (detailed discussion on experiences of racism and cultural beliefs is provided elsewhere). In the following, the interviewee points out the overseas trained South Asian doctors felt a void in their lives in not having extended family around in the UK, who could be called upon instantly for advice. The nature of work would have brought them closer to the consultants, with whom they inevitably developed closer relationships and so, they trusted their wisdom:

> *I think we missed out on older brothers and fathers and developed close relationships with consultants, whose advice we took seriously. He (consultant) always gave me good advice and I took up his advice (gp9s).*

The following account describes the nature of a close relationship between one interviewee and the consultant, which the former only perceives as being a positive one:

> *He (consultants) would sometimes come and ask what I was doing that afternoon. I said nothing and he would say, 'let's go somewhere for tea/coffee'. They knew me and I knew them, they trusted me because they knew I knew what to do. I was in-charge of 120-150 beds on my own; there was no other consultant around when Dr A was on holiday. He used to come back from his holiday and he used to say, 'Now you must go on holiday'. He was a great person. He was very caring and when he said, 'Go home to your family', you had to listen to him (gp7s).*

The above account describes the working conditions, consultants' heavy reliance on junior doctors, the majority of whom were overseas trained doctors and the social dimension of the personalising of the relationship between individuals of a different professional status and class. In a study of Turkish Greek factory workers, Ladbury (1984) observed that such relationships, in which an employer rewarded an employee with personal favours, were associated with constraints that they placed on the employee, such as an expectation of working until 9pm every day in a busy week. It would appear that the interviewee did not perceive such offers in an exploitative manner, even though, as shown below, he goes on to say it was seen as normal by his seniors for him to finish late in the evening:

> *At that time, there used to be a lot of smoke, because of factories and what not, so people had a lot of chest problems, TB was common, bronchitis etc. Dr A accepted me, because I had a lot of experience in that area of medicine in India and I was also a hard worker. We were so busy that at 7-8pm at night, we would be still doing the clinic (gp7s).*

The above accounts overall present a positive picture of working relationships with senior members of medical staff; however, they also provide compelling evidence that overseas trained South Asian doctors were being channelled into particular jobs. Unwin (2001) reported the findings of a research study exploring the question *Is the selection process for becoming a consultant racist?*, for which various factors were examined, such as *the training requirement, culture of fear, career advice, hospital appointments, differences in short listing, comparisons of careers of white and ethnic minority doctors and membership of the royal colleges*. The author concluded that the evidence suggested that overseas trained doctors were discriminated against by the medical establishment.

Samers (2010, 126) also draws our attention to the limitation of Human Capital Theory, which whilst acknowledging individuals' skills, educational qualifications, and abilities does not take account of other intersecting characteristics, such as race and gender.

Navarro (1978) provided a detailed historical perspective of deep-seated class inequalities in medicine in Great Britain, a thorough understanding of which would cast some doubt on the alleged objectivity of the consultants who held the power. The author pointed out how the division of labour and specialisation in medicine produced via education and research, could be attributed to the licensing and regulation with the help of state intervention, which strengthens and legitimises a hierarchical order that already exists in our societies based on distribution of power relations along class, sex and race. Furthermore, the distribution of responsibilities of teams is such that the upper middle class physicians sit at the top, whilst the attendants and auxiliaries, who are pre-dominantly women, are at the bottom of hierarchy. This hierarchical arrangement primarily relates to class background and/or sex role, with technological knowledge being subordinate. Navarro described how class difference contributes to inequality in service provision. For example, the hospitals, being regarded as workshops for the consultants, have priority over general practice and receive far more generous funding than general practitioner services. This is further evidenced by the fact that the teaching hospitals, referred to as the 'cream', have priority over non-teaching ones. An example of this inequality is provided for the period 1963-1969, where the non-teaching hospitals, despite the fact that they had a heavier load of patients that were sicker than the teaching hospitals, received less capital expenditure than the teaching ones (Navarro, 1978).

Navorro contended that one possible explanation for this inequity is that the non-teaching hospitals had more working class and elderly patients than the teaching ones and that the latter had more middle class and younger patients than the former. Similarly, the regional differences in the distribution of services reflect the social class of the individuals in the respective communities, such that the higher the percentage of working class residents, the lower the availability of consultants and general practitioners. Another example of inequity provided by Navorro is the secret system of awards given to consultants which once awarded, means that they receive financial rewards for life. Navorro (1978-43) states,

> *The class-conscious Royal Colleges made quite sure that there would not be equality within the system of rewards to different branches of medicine.*

According to Navorro, Lord Moran, a close health advisor to Bevan[3], and the representative of Royal Colleges, had responded to a suggestion of equalising the income levels between the consultants and general practitioners by stating that it was absurd to treat the people who get to the top of the ladder the same as the people who fall off it. Navorro concluded that, whilst professional dominance will be challenged, it is highly unlikely that the current pattern of class control, which is different from professional control, will be changed, as it would be considered 'unnatural' in a capitalist society. In the light of Navorro and Unwin's assertion regarding the significance of race and class issues in maintaining consultants' own specialities, I argue that the career advice given by the consultants to the doctors in the study may have been biased with a view to maintaining the class and race hierarchy within the hospital services.

I will now consider the pull factors. Apart from the societal level barriers (structural factors) experienced, most interviewees stated that they were seeking an alternative path to social mobility. They gave a range of reasons for pursuing such mobility, which included: desire for autonomy, job security offered by the vocational training offered (1-3yrs), financial betterment, experience of primary care, working with individuals and communities, the concept of family medicine and applying of a holistic approach, community acknowledgment and the recognition of social status. The majority of the overseas trained South Asian doctors talked about their interactions with the earlier pioneers from their communities in general practice, with whom they had developed strong diasporic networks and who were also looking to inspire others to join them. The interviewees' accounts reveal that, whilst entry into general practice appeared to be the only viable option to get ahead, they had made an informed decision to enter it:

> *I started doing some locum jobs in a GP surgery. One of our friends (South Asian) used to come to see us in the hospital as he was lonely. He told me to do locum jobs with him, which I did and I really enjoyed working with patients and families in their communities. So, I said to myself that I wanted to pursue my career in general practice, 'why am I wasting my time here'?(gp9s).*

---

[3] The first Labour Health Minister

For a majority of the interviewees, being innovative and the desire to do better than others was a motivating factor from the outset. The following response is typical of the responses received:

> *I thought I should do vocational training and go in general practice and do much better than other GPs. I had had years of hospital experience, both in India and the UK, which I thought I could use in general practice (gpm6).*

For nearly all of the interviewees, socio-professional downgrading, as Samers (2010), described it, did not sit comfortably and appears to have been a strong driving force together with a desire to be independent, which was, in part, associated with self-protection from discrimination. The following interviewee described his disappointment when he discovered upon arrival in the UK that discrimination was rife:

> *And then what happened err, here also... grass was not like green that what it was looking from, err, here also it was just like a water tight compartment they always used to prefer people from their own countries you know,[the] other side you know (gpm7).*

His assertion below provides evidence that human capital was not sufficient for him and his colleagues to progress further than to a certain level:

> *...some who did a fellowship, some did MRCP. If they can't progress to the level of registrar or anything then they have got, they have to do something isn't it? For their livelihood, therefore, they join general practice (gpm7).*

The push/pull factors described in the above accounts of the interviewees would appear to mirror the historical experiences of the colonised Indian workers in the mercantile marine industry in the 1920s and 1930s and how they showed resistance to oppression. Tabili (2012) describes how South Asians in Britain have been able to evade and challenge colonisation and recolonisation. The author states that the processes employed by the British Empire, not only drained the colonies of their wealth through flows of goods and profits, but also, through substantial and often 'involuntary labour displacement' operationalised in the form of colonised South Asian being employed as soldiers, merchants seafarers and craftsmen. She adds that the Indian marines who comprised from one fifth to a quarter of British merchant vessels' crews and other colonised people were kept at colonial wage levels, regardless of wherever they travelled. In order to resist the occupational ghettoisation that enforced the colonial 'super-exploitation', the strategy used by these colonised workers was to jump ship in British and European ports.

Tabili (2012) describes this as a system of global empire that was oppressive, whilst at the same time empowering, in that the metropolitan parasitism imposed on the colonised labour force did offer opportunities by which individual or collective agency was able to resist exploitation. The doctors in this study also talked about the opportunities that the system provided as well as a feeling of being entrapped by the structural inequality created by the same system. Their accounts mirror the experiences of those colonised marines, who applied their own agency to combat inequality by jumping off the ships and becoming emancipated. The doctors in the study also talked about exploitation and being sucked into a system that was a dead end, one which blocked upward mobility. They described how they also used their own human agency and seized on the vocational training opportunity to go into general practice to circumvent the structural inequalities.

The doctors talked about how their own social networking provided instant word of mouth information about opportunities and know-how, whilst also offering personal support:

> *... because my friend used to work next door here... and Dr A was a friend. We used to meet in meetings, then he said err, because their practice is a training practice and they wanted to take a trainee, but that trainee had decided not to come here. Then, my friend told me 'there is a vacancy, why don't you go and give your application' (gpm7).*

However, the interviewees described that there was also a glass ceiling in the general practice jobs in certain geographical areas, as explained below:

> *I went for an interview and there were a few of us, all Asian, waiting outside. They (the interviewing panel) told us that neither of us had got the job, but they had one more interview to do next week, because this doctor could not make it that day. We all knew it would be a local lad for whom they were not only prepared to wait, but also, he was to be appointed. Our fear was confirmed later when we asked around (gp9s).*

However, the interviewees described that there was a also a glass ceiling in the general practice jobs in certain geographical areas as stated below,

> *I went for an interview, there were a few of us all Asian waiting outside, they (the interviewing panel) told us that neither of us had got the job but they had one more interview to do next week because this doctor could not make it that day. We all knew it would be a local lad for whom they were not only prepared to wait but also, he was to be appointed. Our fear was confirmed later when we asked around (gp9s).*

The majority of the interviewees stated that general practice jobs in well sought out areas were difficult to obtain, as they would be offered to "local lads" (white UK doctors), who only applied in such areas, whereas the overseas trained South Asian doctors would only be successful, if there were no white doctors applying for such jobs. Whilst the interviewees, in general, were reluctant to explicitly admit discrimination was going on, comments like the above are a fairly strong indication about their perceptions regarding this matter. Reluctance to describe racist experiences is discussed in depth in chapter 5.

Ellis et al. (2007) argue that spatial accessibility to jobs may well be just as significant as social access to jobs. The interviewees had varied experiences in finding jobs; some were able to find work with relative ease, while others described an element of gatekeeping in general practice, carried out by both white and other overseas-trained doctors:

> *When I was looking for jobs in general practice, it was proving to be very difficult. People used to say, 'yes you are a good doctor' and make promises that 'we will give you partnership', but when the time came they [Asian doctors] did not stick to their words. The thing with white GPs was that they would also make promises that we will contact you when we have a vacancy, but they would actually appoint their own. With our doctors, they did not appoint anyone, because there were no rules at that time that you should have so many patients; they were just gatekeeping (gp1m).*

Waldinger et al. (1990a) refer to opportunity structure, which is seen as consisting of market conditions that immigrants exploit, for example, ethnic consumer products. The following account affirms this, where he explains how he was invited to apply for a job in a practice area where South Asian migrants were settling in. It appears from his narrative that alongside his bicultural literacy (acquired by being trained in an ex-colonial country, and several years of experience in the UK), other personal factors, such as being married to an English woman, were considered as additional positive features:

> *This time round, I did not bother applying, but I got a phone call from one of the doctors on the panel asking why I had not applied. I said there was no point, because I knew I was not going to get it. He told to me to come for the interview and bring my application with me, which I reluctantly filled in, but I wrote very little on it; I just said please see previous application etc. I went for the interview and the doctor who rang me said, 'we have all met you, but Mr so and so has not seen you, Mrs so and so has not seen you, therefore only they will be asking you the questions'. One of them asked, 'are you married', I said 'yes', and they said, 'you are married to an English girl?' I said 'yes' and they said, 'in that case you are going to stay in this country'(gp9s).*

The interviewee's account suggests that through repeated negative experiences, he had lost faith in the fairness of the system; however, the informal networks that he had made worked in his favour and was headhunted. It also appears from his narrative that his migrant status was mediated by his marriage with an English wife, which was perceived as a marker for permanence in the country, thus offering stability to the employer.

Social and demographic changes and proximity of residence create a demand for ethnic services (Ladbury, 1984, 107). The following interviewee talks about the dynamics of the opportunity structure and how employment niches were being created in this area:

> *In Sheffield at that time 85% of people from South Asian backgrounds were Mirpuris and there were few Asians, nearly all of these were uneducated and were working in factories. They were just starting their businesses and few went into restaurants and cafes. At that time, even their children didn't speak English, because they had just arrived. I am talking about in the early 60s. I was offered the job, because it was becoming increasingly difficult for locals to manage the language and culture issues (gp9s).*

As some communities and areas in the UK were becoming more diverse, the demands placed on the inner-city practices were growing, and it appears that overseas-trained South Asian were being purposely sought out. Some of the interviewees talked about being recruited by white senior practitioners through previous links, which suggests that since they were known quantities, they were likely to be considered safe individuals from the employer's point of view. Apart from niches being created in areas of high ethnic density, the interviewees also talked about opportunities that had been created by the flight of UK qualified GPs from white working-class areas:

> *Yes, someone was working there before, a white doctor; he moved to Spain, the practice was very deprived, debilitated. He was doing that Spanish practice for almost over a year, neglecting this all together, so it was really neglected. Yes, living in two places, hardly any... there wasn't even a list, only four or five patients. I did a lot you see, that practice you see was in one of those terraced houses and hardly anything there. So then, I think within three years more or less I built up a beautiful purpose built practice in the area, and then it was like jungle mein mungal.* [4] *The result was that in a few years time I got the GP of the Year Award (gpm4).*

The above quote shows how, with determination and the use of his entrepreneurial skills, the interviewee was able to transform a deserted place into something special, even outstanding. Other interviewees talked about what could be considered as utilising structure and agency for the

---

[4] An Urdu language expression meaning transforming of a place from dry woodland into a wonderland.

transformations they undertook, as evidenced in the following:

> *...system is pretty good here, they call them cost rent schemes. That is, when you buy... you take a loan from the bank and that health authority has to pay the interest (gpm4).*

For some of the interviewees, networking with other overseas-trained migrant doctors provided vital links, especially those who were now reaching retirement. The following interviewee's account shows that he was appreciated for his attitude to work:

> *I was offered a couple of other jobs, which I didn't take. One was in Rotherham, they were offering me £11,000 and all the seven were white and senior to me. Another one was similar. I took this one because it offered £14,000 and also, it was run by a Polish doctor who was about to retire. It was my good luck that I bumped into a local doctor in a meeting after completing my training, I did some local jobs for him, he was a Polish GP, and he asked me where I was doing my training, told him I was working in X hospital. He said I was hard working and asked me when I was going to finish that job. He said come and work for me. So he took me as a partner, he was soon reaching 73-75 years of age, and on his retirement, he handed over the practice to me (gp8b).*

This was echoed also by the following interviewee, where another migrant doctor was possibly impressed with his hard work and/or values:

> *I accidently met an Irish GP who was very influential. I did some weeks work with him as a locum. He, for some reason, wished that I inherit his practice. I accepted his offer. I found out from the practice history that there had never been a local doctor in that practice. It was built in 1903, they had had an Irish-Irish-Scottish-Polish-Indian doctor since it was built. After five weeks, he had a massive heart attack and he was no longer able to work.... He talked to the chief executive of the PCT and wrote to Secretary of State in Health and Social Care. They both said you can go ahead with your plans. He phoned me and said it was good news... I worked there for 27 years (gp2s).*

The above narrative suggests that the niches previously carved out by the earlier overseas-trained migrants, such as the Irish and Poles, were now being claimed by this new group, the overseas-trained South Asians.

Logan et al. (1979) point to the existence of an established pattern of dependency on migrant doctors by the North East Thames Regional Health Authority prior to the arrival of South Asian GPs. Cargill (1969) notes a disproportionate number of Irish GPs working in Birmingham and Essex. The interviewees' accounts suggest that the migrant status created a sense of bounded solidarity and also facilitated networking.

Becoming Entrepreneurs and Engendering Resistance

Ethnic entrepreneurship has been an area of interest for social scientists for a long while now and has enthused much research and debate about this social phenomenon. Ballard (1994) regards migration itself as an entrepreneurship activity. Most of the literature in the area of migrants as entrepreneurs has been written based on the experiences of manual or semi-skilled workers, although Ballard, (1994) acknowledges that not just peasants, but people with professional skills have migrated apart from India. However, Zhou (2008, 219) refers to the typical images that are conjured up in relation to who the entrepreneurs are:

> *In the laymen's eye, however, ethnic entrepreneurs often carry images of petty traders, dealers, shopkeepers or even peddlers and hucksters who engage in such industries or business as restaurants, sweatshops, laundries, greengrocers, liquor stores, nail salons, newsrounds, swap meets, taxi cabs and so on.*

Bygrave and Hofer (1991) define an entrepreneur as someone who perceives an opportunity and creates the organisation for its pursuit. This effective strategy of circumventing labour market barriers is employed by ethnic entrepreneurs to move up socioeconomically in the host society (Zhou, 2004). Anecdotal evidence suggests overseas-trained South Asian doctors' entry into general practice to be the result of blocked social mobility within the NHS (Nowikowski, 1984). However, few previous researchers have considered overseas trained GPs as entrepreneurs in their own right.

Apart from some autobiographical accounts, such as that of Sayeed (2006), little is known about how overseas-trained south Asian doctors overcame some of the social, environmental and economic challenges of running practices, which they either set up from scratch or that had been left vacant as a result of local doctors emigrating or wanting to work in less deprived areas. Nowikowski (1984) provides a detailed account of the historical structural inequalities linked with colonisation, arguing that the emergence of businesses has been a survival strategy applied by Asians in the UK aimed at combating the disadvantage they have experienced as a result of inherited positions of structural inequality. In her study of Asians living in a middle-class residential area on Manchester, using survey respondents who were heterogeneous, including GPs, Nowikowski (1984) found that the Asian doctors had also adopted similar strategies to overcome structural barriers in the NHS. For example, where their mobility was severely restricted, they had chosen specialties that were less popular or did not involve hospital work, such as general practice, which allowed them to manage resources independently.

In seeking to understand the contributions of overseas-trained doctors in general practice, it is important to explore their experiences in relation to concepts of entrepreneurship. Using this analytical lens, can inform us about the types of social capital (bonding and bridging) and social relations in which overseas-trained South Asian GPs are embedded, in particular, ethnically dense as well as poor white working class areas.

In the chapter that follows, this entrepreneurial process is explored in depth which has not been done before. Previously, I explored how the doctors in the study navigated their way into the UK system and the barriers that they encountered when trying to integrate fully into the NHS institution. This section has built on their subsequent experiences and examined the empirical evidence that suggests that the doctors in the study underwent an entrepreneurial process in order to integrate into the institution and the communities that they served, as a reaction against racism and perceived social mobility (Jenkins, 1994). I consider this new interpretation of the contributions of overseas-trained South Asian doctors in the context of entrepreneurship.

It has been argued that immigrants have a greater propensity to become self-employed as it provides an alternative path to their blocked social mobility (Zhou, 2008, Ward and Jenkins, 1984) and entrepreneurship is used as a survival strategy (Nowikowski, 1984). A research study in Australia into immigrant entrepreneurship found that there was a diversity of paths that new immigrants take into entrepreneurship, ranging from being unemployed to taking up manual labour and professional labour, including doctors (Collins, 2003). The causes and consequences of ethnic entrepreneurship have been an area of interest in sociological research and a number of theoretical and practical insights have emerged since the 1960s as to why immigrants have a greater propensity to opt for self-employment as an alternative to social mobility as well as why some groups are more likely to do so than others.

The significance of South Asian communities' contribution to entrepreneurship in the UK and how it has been determined has been the subject of much discussion (Ward and Jenkins, 1984, Werbner, 1984, Kalra, 2000). So called 'ethnic businesses' small retail shops, restaurants and take aways, have been associated with the socio-economic mobility of South Asians in Britain and their cultural characteristics, such as being industrious, relying on family and friends for cheap labour and a desire for independence, have been described as ideal for entrepreneurial activity (Mars and Ward, 1984). It is notable that a small scale study undertaken in Manchester in 1970 showed that overseas-trained South Asian doctors' were also constrained by their race and employed strategies of self-employment to circumvent the system that blocked their mobility in the NHS, as they were restricted to the least desirable and poorly paid rungs of the medical occupational hierarchies (Esmail, 2007). As a consequence, it is argued that the overseas trained South Asian doctors entered into general practice as it allowed them to manage resources independently (Nowikowski, 1984).

The following chapter examines a new interpretation of the contributions of overseas-trained South Asian doctors in the light of their entrepreneurial behaviour, which appears to reflect parallels with lower skilled migrants from South Asia (Nowikowski, 1984). The concept of entrepreneurship provides a useful analytical framework for the investigation of their contribution and community activities. I will explore the empirical evidence relating to the experiences of overseas trained South Asian in the study, examining the nature of their contribution as health professionals in the rural and inner-city case study areas. The discussion will identify the factors that determined why and how the entrepreneurial activity was generated and uncover their process of entrepreneurship.

CHAPTER 3

UNDERSTANDING ENTREPRENEURSHIP WITHIN GENERAL PRACTICE

Existing theories on entrepreneurship have sought to explain the causes and consequences of entrepreneurship, with there being general agreement that it is the interactive effects of structural factors (at a societal level), and group and/or individual level characteristics that underpin the phenomenon, while how they interact with each other determines groups' propensity to succeed (Zhou, 2004). Experiences of exclusion and discrimination discussed in previous chapters have demonstrated the impact of structural factors at the societal level. As said previously, it is important to explore the experiences of overseas-trained South Asian doctors' and their contribution in relation to concept of entrepreneurship. Whilst some previous studies, such as that of Nowikowski (1984) and more recently, Simpson (2018), have highlighted the contributions of overseas-trained South Asian doctors' as entrepreneurs in general practice, there is a dearth of knowledge on the actual entrepreneurial process the doctors underwent.

In the previous chapter I examined the push/pull factors for entry into general practice and how the doctors negotiated this entry. In this chapter, I will discuss how the structural factors, group and/or individual level characteristics interacted and facilitated entrepreneurship in general practice.

Jack and Anderson (2002) contend that considering an entrepreneur in isolation does not enhance our understanding of entrepreneurship, but rather, in order to enhance our understanding of the phenomenon it should be regarded as an embedded socio-economic process. The authors use Gidden's view of structuration as a theoretical framework for exploring the link between the entrepreneur (as agent) and the context (as structure), illustrating in their study how social structures affect entrepreneurial activity. They argue that embeddedness in the social structure produces opportunity, enhances performance and enables entrepreneurs to use the particularities of the environment. They add that the role of the entrepreneur conditions both recognition and realisation of opportunity in the social structure.

Hansen (1995) argues that entrepreneurs identify social resources as an essential step in the start-up of their businesses, in particular, the concept of social embeddedness is significant to entrepreneurship. Jack and Anderson (2002) further argue that entrepreneurship must involve drawing upon society, because it is embedded in the social context. These authors contend that the social whole needs to be taken into account when examining the entrepreneur (individual/or "agent") as it is paramount over its individual part (Cassell, 1993). They emphasise the significance of the context (structure) in which the entrepreneurship is embedded and state that the extent to which an entrepreneur is socially embedded and congruent with the structure is likely to affect their ability to draw on the social and economic resources of that structure, thus impacting on the nature of the entrepreneurial process and event. Drawing attention to the dynamic relationship between structure and agency, Jack and Anderson (2002) refer to their ethnographic study in which respondents were providing something that they considered the local community needed and would be benefit from, whilst at the same time rely on that community to support their business.

The interviewees' accounts in this study echoed similarities with the above findings in each of the three case study areas. Their accounts show that viability was produced in ways that involved social factors and embeddedness and their practices were embedded in the locale, in other words, while the interviewees drew value from the local structure, they simultaneously added value to the structure. The interviewees talked about local structures in the form of context, the local environment, and becoming part of the social fabric of the society, for example attending a wedding party in a working men's club and other local cultural and religious events. A detailed discussion of social embeddedness is incorporated into Chapter 4. The interviewees attributed local factors to their success and in the ethnically dense areas, this occurred in the form of locals providing inspiration for the venture. The NHS also appeared to have been keen on recruiting Asian doctors in such areas. For example, one interviewee said he was invited to apply for a job by the local NHS in a pre-dominantly Asian area. Moreover, patients from within the Asian communities were willing to help with the opening of an additional practice, for which the doctors in the study often acted as socio-cultural mediators within the NHS; providing a culturally and linguistically competent service.

In rural areas, the interviewees talked about ways of embedding (at both a social and professional level), for example, through the membership of rotary clubs and golf clubs as well as other actions, including involvement in fundraising in the local area. Together with other innovative activities instigated by their practices, this projects an image of the doctors in the study as individuals who were genuinely interested in the wellbeing of local communities. The scarcity of resources in rural environments went hand in hand with the entrepreneurial spirit of the interviewees and such contexts provided them with perfect places in which to grow.

Entrepreneurship and innovation are interlinked. Determination to improve services for the most needy was stated as the main reason for innovation by many of the interviewees. Many of the overseas-trained South Asian doctors talked about their frustrations regarding how they were unable to implement their vision in the country of origin as a result of financial and governmental constraints. Many in the study had a clear idea as to what an excellent healthcare model should look like, as they had several years of experience in the country of origin working in remote villages with very few resources, as well as in the UK.

Community ties and networks were mentioned as playing a vital role in the start-up process by many of the interviewees:

> *... I had to set up from scratch. I came from a hospital background, I didn't need to even buy a spoon, but when I came here, even the glass of water that I needed to drink, I had to buy. Pakistani community helped me greatly. I got to know some shopkeepers, Asian grocers from whom I used to buy my groceries. When I was looking for a place to rent for my second surgery, they used their networks and got me some premises at a very low rent, £5 per month I think it was. I had patients but no premises. I had to be able to deliver services in a short span of time. With the community's help and word of mouth, I got both the premises and the patients (gp9s).*

The following interviewee talks about continually searching for creative opportunities after some negative experiences of working with other overseas-trained south Asian doctors:

> *I talked to Dr K about my problems. He had had similar experiences, he was sympathetic, he said 'there is a room available upstairs to my practice', he said 'go and start practising'. So, I had a telephone line connected, brought a table and chair and started to practice from there (gpm7).*

He talked about how he gradually built the patient list, which was vital to the survival of his business, and then expanded upon this:

> *Slowly, I built up my patient list. When I used to see my patients from the old practice, they used to ask, 'oh, doctor, where have you gone, they are telling us you have left the area, we miss you' etc. I told them about the practice, then they started joining my practice, one came, another came and with six months I had around 500 patients. The patients were predominantly locals [white]; they developed a good relationship with me. Then, I started looking for premises in a suitable area. I saw*

three shops, one of them was empty. So, I rented and converted it into a surgery, and then there was no turning back. Within a year, I had 1,000 patients, in the next year I had 2,000 patients (gp7m).

His account below shows how he networked with another overseas-trained doctor and continued to aim higher:

After this, Dr K approached me. He said, 'it will be a good idea if we join up our practices and have a bigger practice', which we did (gp7m).

The interviewees talked about what can be described as entrepreneurial behaviours, such as injecting vision, attracting and exciting others along with persistency:

We started to design a project in our heads that we should have a larger building, which should be modern also. This building that we are in now, it used to be a bank building, which had been deserted for a while. After the bank, someone else came, but it did not work for them, so they left as well, it was so dead business wise. We both started exploring how we could materialise our ambitious plans (gp7m).

He talked about the structures that acted as lubricators for their business plans. His account provides evidence of positive institutional networks and support:

At that time, there was a very good person working in PCT; he was a chief executive. He said, 'R.. we will support you with your project and do whatever we can do'. He said, 'we need a good surgery in the area'. The PCT was extremely helpful; they said you can have a lift installed as well. We were so grateful, because we had not thought about that. They said, 'don't worry about finance; we will help you with that'. We raised some money ourselves, me and Dr K and we went to ask for money from the bank. We shared the loan between ourselves and the PCT also gave some development funds. Then, we developed this project. This building that you see now was just a shell, there was hardly anything inside, everything we had was tailor made. We had to work with architects, builders, which was not in our experience before. We asked them to design four, five, consultation rooms, we wanted a spacious patient waiting area, toilets, lift etc. (gp1m).

Individuals and groups can only work with the resources that are made available to them by their environments. Aldrich and Waldinger (1990) state that market conditions shape the structures for opportunity that may favour services to coethnics, and areas where the mainstream market is served. Such structures also pertain to the ease with which access is obtained, which is determined by how much inter-ethnic competition there is and the nature of state policies.

Having experienced the positive interactions described above, the interviewee went on to state how he had been able to integrate into mainstream institutions and widen his contacts. As a result, his business did not just become part of an ethnic enclave, but rather, it was actively involved with mainstream activities:

> *I started to build my contact with other GPs in the area and joined the local medical committee. They represent all the GPs in the area. There was a vacancy for a member and I put forward my name and was selected. I used to attend meetings and meet other doctors in the area. This was a pre-dominantly white area, all the others were white in my area but they accepted me as one of them. I was a member of the committee for three to four years (gp1m).*

The need for proximity to a co-ethnic clientele and ethnic resources has been acknowledged as crucial in the initial stages of development in ethnic businesses as they provide necessary support for survival (Portes and Manning, 1986). It is notable that community ties and networks have also been stated as significant factors in the establishment of self-employment for Jewish people (Goldscheider, 1986). The above account shows that community networks were vital in helping many interviewees becoming established in high ethnic density areas, and this factor may have been important in encouraging Asian doctors to switch to general practice.

A desire to take risks is a feature of entrepreneurialism. The interviewees' accounts show that risk management was a key consideration by all of them, and they used their networks effectively as they offered support concerning know-how; however, each particular context had its own particular issues, which meant that there was risk taking involved. The following interviewee talks about the risk involved in setting up a new practice, which was a typical response in this regard:

> *It was quite a risk taking a job, because you don't know how things were going to map out, whether you will have patients, especially business wise the area was quite run down. You can imagine what it would be like, even the bank had gone somewhere else, because there was no prospect of business in the area. I didn't know if I was going to have good practice partners etc., but I was very committed and wanted to make it work (gp1m).*

The interviewee's account shows that he was aware of the uncertainty of how his patients were going to receive him as a doctor, which is likely to be a big challenge for all GPs as patients can choose which practice to register with. Like many other interviewees, he was not quick to jump on the bandwagon and name it as racism, but rather, he and the others always appeared to make a very thorough assessment of the situation. He believed that there were multiple reasons for these challenges:

It was partly because I was a new doctor; they had never had an Asian doctor, for generations, they were having English doctors. In my practice, three generations had practised, grandfather, father and then son from whom I took over. So, it was understandable, that people will feel apprehensive. They thought, strange person, strange name, strange everything Asian, to start with. To be very frank, there was some of that as well, okay, so quite a lot of them left me (gp9s).

He talked about how he was able to gain the trust of his patients and how the number dramatically increased from within the Asian community:

I established the surgery, even though I was Asian, people, in a few years time, started knowing me. I am not boasting about myself, but they thought I am not rotten, okay, I am as good as they will get anyway. So, they started coming to me and the number of patients started picking up. When I started the practice, around 700 patients were from our own community; when I left 9,500. It increased to such an extent that I had to employ two more doctors (gp9s).

The account below shows how he networked with other overseas-trained South Asian doctors at a local and global level in order to run a successful practice:

My good old friend Dr H... was in Libya, he wanted to come because he had a small boy, who was growing older. He was about to start school and he did not want to send him to Libya and my friend did not want to leave it late . I said, 'look, I have a big practice here, why don't you come and join me'. So, he joined me after I had been in the practice for four years. It then became so big that we were struggling with two. So by this time, I had developed many networks, I got to know where my other friends had gone, some were in Pontefract, some in Wakefield, some in Manchester. The practice had grown so big that we had to appoint a third one [Asian] (gp9s).

Recruitment and retention were described as issues in many of the geographical locales that the doctors in the study worked. It appears from their accounts that resource mobilisation was facilitated by the fact that they were able to draw upon their connections with an instant supply of coethnics. However, the above networking mode would also suggest that the overseas-trained South Asian doctors were almost duplicating the exclusive networking that existed among the white doctors, which excluded the former. Such exclusionary practice runs parallel to the entrepreneurial process that their low-skilled entrepreneurial counterparts adopted in the retail industry in the UK; they relied heavily on family members' labour. That is, the doctors in the study appeared to rely on other overseas-trained South Asian doctors in the same way. There can be a number of explanations for this. To begin with, this exclusion was not likely to affect the UK qualified doctors as these very niches had been created by their unwillingness to work in such areas in the first place. Aldrich and Waldinger (1990) argue that ethnic entrepreneurs manipulate family and coethnic perseverance and loyalty to their own advantage, but they also incur obligations in doing so. The motivation of the above interviewee appears to have been fuelled by the prior trusting relationship that had been built and maintained over the years regardless of physical distance. The following interviewee's account would suggest that this may have been a survival strategy in a hostile environment:

> *When you are forced into a corner, you have to learn these things and you have to do it, otherwise there is no go (gp1m).*

As the interviewees had invested a lot of energy and hard work into their newly acquired positions, trust was likely to be a significant factor in forming new working relationships. Its significance can be evidenced when one interviewee, as discussed above, talked about forming transnational networks with his friend in Libya. In her study on the Pakistani community, Werbner (1990) also found that a great deal of trading was based on long-term trust and personal reputation, which subsequently led to the development of chains of entrepreneurs. Many of the interviewees talked about creating employment opportunities for other overseas-trained South doctors, who otherwise may not have had access to social mobility.

Entrepreneurs exploit opportunities and this was evidenced in many of the interviewees' accounts. Several of them mentioned the importance of seizing additional opportunities to further their own financial strength and enhance health care provision, along with other supportive structures:

> *We became a fund holder*[1] *practice, which meant that we had to do more things; the more you did the less you had to send patients to hospital, OK. So, we had to expand and the FPC [Family Practitioners Committee] were again very good. I have no complaints against them or executive council, they came and asked, 'what do you want?' I said,' give us a grant, we have got an architect; he will do the drawing, so we can enlarge the surgery'. They said , 'you apply and we will give you what is called a special type of loan where the FPC will pay the interest' (gp9s).*

He talked about innovative work in the practice:

> *We modified the practice and moved out to live somewhere else. After that, the practice got bigger and bigger. I got to know a lot of people who became good*

[1] In the 1990s, the NHS reforms introduced the GP fundholding scheme, which meant that general practices received funds annually to purchase designated services on behalf of a specified population. http://www.civitas.org.uk/nhs/download/Civitas_LiteratureReview_NHS_market_Feb10.pdf

networks. I was asked if I would do some occupational work in a hospital. For eight to nine years, I did this work. We bought all the equipment that was needed for a modern practice. All the changes were done, we had ECG machines, respirometry machines, we had a small theatre in which we could do minor surgery, all these things that I could do. It meant that secondary care services were provided on the doorstep of the deprived communities. It also saved money by not sending the patients for secondary care (gp9s).

The above account shows how structure and the agency of the doctors in the study created positive outcomes. It also illustrates how the interviewees utilised networks to secure resources for areas that may not have been able to secure them previously. Reasons for innovation were stated by many interviewees as self-fulfilment, opportunities for broader skill utilisation, enthusiasm for greater autonomy and being able to pursue own ideas. The following interviewee explains how being an entrepreneur became the way to realise his potential and that of others like him:

We [Asian] were very enthusiastic because this [GP job] gave you livelihood, not just increased income, also, we had the skill, because a lot of us had worked long ....time in hospitals, we were over skilled for just writing down a prescription. You know, they are boys who have done MRCPs and FRCS, who have a lot of things, I myself, I think I have done with my own hands 200 appendectomies in the hospital and about 150 hernia operations, all these minor operations, they were on my list of things in hospital, I used to do them all. My chief did not even know that patients came in with appendicitis and had it out and gone home. I was capable of doing small bits and bobs instead of sending them to hospital (gp9s).

The following interviewee, like many others, explained that the transformations they envisioned in general practice was as a result of making the best use of their capabilities (which were greater than is typical for UK qualified GPs) and resources, while offering enhanced primary care services and saving the establishment money:

We came here not to become GPs, we came to become specialists, we had enthusiasm and we had capability. I did around 300 vasectomies on my table (I did a fair amount of circumcision of Pakistani babies, probably 150. OK, in addition, I was the first doctor who started doing vasectomies under local anaesthetic. It's because I was able to do it. We made a huge contribution in that sense. It's only purely because of God's grace, out of those 300, there was no bleeding, no infection, nothing. Others started following me and they were, incidentally, most of them all Asians, otherwise it was the consultants (gp9s).

Using their own agency to improve the provision of healthcare and the specific working conditions they were working under cropped up in almost every interviewee's account. The account below refers to all of the four GPs being Asians and comments on the *drive in us*, which might explain why the doctors recruited others of a similar background. They were a self-selected group of people, who had taken on the challenge of migration to bring about changes in their personal and professional lives:

I had a purpose-built building just before I left. It was a joint initiative, me and my practice partners, the other building was old now, all of the four were Asian by now. We had this drive in us, all of us, were all determined that our practice should be better and bigger and patients should have access to better facilities, e.g. there should be an operating theatre, computerised system, bigger consultation rooms etc. You see here, we felt that we could have access to funds and resources, we could have our dreams come true, we wanted to provide seamless health care to patients, whereas in India, we had limited resources. We wanted to improve working conditions for us as well. You will have heard about the PFI [private financial initiative] government scheme. Most of the practices made use of this initiative (gp6b).

The interviewees talked about having a long-term vision and the need to survive over time, up-skilling in areas where they lacked the experience and skill to meet the needs of all members of society:

I was so much determined to learn that I appointed a locum for two months to do obs & gynae, okay, and so many deliveries, I wanted to be capable of doing things. Half of the patients were women and if I knew how to help them, wherever I felt I needed to upskill myself, I attended every single course (gp9s).

Individual and Group Level Characteristics

Zhou (2008) states that some immigrant groups and ethnic minorities are more likely to be entrepreneurs than others in the pursuit of socioeconomic mobility. In this section, I will describe interviewees' own unique characteristics that acted as a catalyst in the entrepreneurial process. The individual level characteristics refer to imported individual traits and behaviour, such as age, education, job skills, experiences in the countries of origin and in the receiving countries (Zhou, 2004). The doctors in this study were a self-selected group of highly-skilled people, who were fairly young and enthusiastic about enhancing their social status and careers. Many interviewees talked about the postgraduate qualifications that they had managed to obtain in the pursuit of a job as a consultant. One interviewee reported having four postgraduation qualifications in different fields prior to commencing vocational training as a GP.

The above support Smith's (1980) finding that British qualified and overseas-trained South Asian GPs were a somewhat contrasting group in that they were late entrants and more likely to have higher postgraduate qualifications as well as many years of hospital experience. The interviewees talked about a combination of things, such as several years of hospital experience, both in the UK and the country of origin as well as the integration of their own cultural values into their roles as GPs:

Having done different jobs in India and the UK, which gave me, in total, 14 years experience, was very helpful, because you could help the patients in general practice a lot. Then, we got involved with the elderly, we had to do that. There was also community cohesion, so you were much more than others at that time. I could advise the elderly, because I had worked in geriatrics, and that helped me a lot in general practice with people and patients. They were elderly, what to do with them and how to do it, when to get social workers involved or physiotherapists or whatever is required for the care of the elderly... I do think, though, that I incorporated my own cultural values into how I practised. For example, we take care of our elderly much more than in this country (gpm6).

Being trained in ex-colonies where the medical model mirrored the UK model and the ability to use creative thinking skills was described as an asset by several interviewees. As one put it:

... our medical training was based on similar models to the UK curriculum, but because we had limited resources in our countries, we were so used to thinking outside the box and we understood things better. Many medical students appreciated how we were able to explain things better (gpm6).

The interviewees seemed well aware of their expertise and self-worth in terms of their experiences in the country of origin, which Zhou (2008) referred to as an imported individual-level trait:

They [British] did not have the experiences that the foreign doctors brought with them. You do medical training, but your life experiences and professional experiences differ. You see other people doing things sometimes right, other times wrong, then you learn. In our countries we have a lot of hands on experiences, because we have a lot of material, population; you deal with a lot of people both medically and surgically. We see more complicated cases in our countries than here by comparison. The consultants here used to depend on us a lot more, because of our experiences. They used to let their own go and say to them, 'in time you will also learn' (gpm8).

Another interviewee talked about how the experiences in the country of origin and in the UK helped him and his colleagues to become successful physicians in the primary care setting:

We already knew many practical things, taking blood, lumbar puncture, drainage of fluid from lungs. We knew all that, because chest problems are common in Pakistan. You see, over there you see a lot of ill patients and you see a lot of medicine and in one year what I learnt in Pakistan, you learn here in five years, so all that experience that we brought with us. Because, there is so much poverty in Pakistan, no proper organised health system, you mostly work on your own initiative. You see, in Pakistan, they didn't used to go to until they became really ill. I worked in chest clinics and my experiences in Pakistan were so useful here, because we see a lot of chest patients in Pakistan, they had TB, smoked, a lot of patients with cancer etc. I knew what investigation to undertake as I had a lot of experience in this area, the more you do, the better it becomes. In hospital work in the UK, I was responsible for 100 patients in four different wards. Consultants used to be in different hospitals and you did most of the things without them even knowing, because they were not contactable (gp3b)

A few interviewees (3/27) stated they had brought with them the experience of working in the armed forces in the country of origin and that this provided useful management, leadership and organisational skills. Some interviewees reported how they were encouraged to apply for GP posts spurred on by other doctors who believed in the benefits of appointing overseas-trained South Asian doctors in certain geographical areas:

I was invited to apply for this post. Before the interview, one of the panel members said to me, look, 'we need people like you, you are very experienced and highly qualified, we would like to offer you the post, but on one condition that you will remain in the North West' (gp7m).

Group-level characteristics include predisposing factors, such as migrants being a selective, as in this study, culture, aspiration levels, the possibilities of resource mobilisation, the existence of ethnic social networks, capacity for general organising, and government policies that either constrain or facilitate the acquisition of resources (Aldrich and Waldinger, 1990). Culture refers to the cultural repertoire that migrants either import or adopt in the host country. They are group specific, behavioural patterns, distinct group traits, social structures, collective resources, and coping strategies in the form of imported and reactive cultural values (Zhou, 2004). Portes and Zhou (1992) use two concepts to sum up the group-level characteristics: "bounded solidarity" and "enforceable trust". Bounded solidarity is produced by migrants' overseas status and by being regarded as 'culturally distinct', which then intensifies feelings of shared cultural heritage, and reciprocated obligations among coethnics. Rather than having spontaneous feelings of solidarity with other coethnics, bounded solidarity is based on the 'enforcement capacity' of the ethnic community that regulates the individuals' behaviour within the community and its power to use sanctions against anyone who violates the expected norms in that society. The key enforcement mechanism applies to dealing with anyone who violates it is 'enforcement trust'. It means that the community has the ability to honour status to individuals or exclude them. . The abovementioned group-level characteristics are rooted in ethnic social structures that produce social capital that facilitates entrepreneurial growth.

The interviewees, in their accounts, emphasised 'we' when talking about innovations and frustrations. Their accounts showed that they functioned collectively to reinforce values and norms that they derived from their own cultures and mobilised resources to achieve their goals. They also acknowledged each other's expertise and called upon their own cultural resources in problem and creative thinking techniques, such as the collective reciting of poetry, some using idioms from their own languages from which to draw strength. An example is when an interviewee was talking about losing half of his patients' list when he took over his practice from a white doctor. He believed that his race had played a part in this process. He explains how he coped with the challenges involved with this situation, reciting the following verse in Urdu:

> *Baad e mukhalif se na gabra e eqab*
> *Ye to chilti and tujey uncha uraney kaliey*
> *[Translates]: Oh bird, don't get troubled by the strong wind blowing from the opposite direction, It blows only to make you fly higher.)(gp1s)*

Another doctor recited lines from a late 13th century Persian poet that are also commonly used in conversations by Iranians today:

> *There were tensions/conflicts between us [Asian] as there was competition among them and backbiting, but I remembered what Shaikh Saadi had said that you must not backbite and say things about others that you cannot say to their face...(gp8s).*[2]

The above account shows that there were tensions and conflicts among the overseas trained South Asians doctors. I will expand further on this issue in the section discusses the downsides of the ethnic entrepreneurship. The evidence shows that the coping strategies employed originated from cultural resources, such as the following:

> *... that was my philosophy, only when the right time comes, you get what you want. Your own destiny determines what you get...(gp5s).*

Levitt (1998) refers to the role of social remittances in promoting immigrant entrepreneurship. Social remittances are ideas, behaviours, identities and social capital related to democracy, health, and community

---

[2] Shaikh Saadi , full name in English: Muslih-ud-Din Mushrif ibn Abdullah), is one of the major Persian poets of the medieval period. He is recognised not only for the quality of his writing, but also for the depth of his social thought. LEVY, R. 2012. *The Persian Language (RLE Iran A)*, Routledge.

organisation that migrants bring with them from their home countries and then culturally diffuse within the new settings. The author states that the impact of remittances is heightened, if the messenger is a high status individual who is able to give something a new meaning, such that others occupying similar status positions readily adopt them, i.e. following their peers, thus becoming remittance transmitters. This was evidenced in the accounts by several interviewees, who had introduced many new initiatives, revitalising their practices and equipping them with modern facilities. The account below shows how one interviewee became a social remittance transmitter:

> *Others started following me and they were incidentally most of them Asians, but local GPs as well (gp9s).*

The majority of the interviewees described getting involved in poetry gatherings, which served as a forum for reviving strength and enthusiasm. They believed that their experiences of exclusion had created a side to them that was not apparent in their countries of origin. Many interviewees' accounts provide evidence of how they reflected on many aspects of the cultural context of their personal and professional lives. They incorporated cultural values in their practice model, for example, the values of social justice that acknowledge the equal worth of all citizens was mentioned by almost all interviewees, who frequently compared things in the UK, with their country of origin, and felt privileged that they had access to opportunities where they could help the needy. Their narratives also frequently showed the prominence of their professional identities, where emphasis was placed on meeting the healthcare needs of the deserving. Many of the interviewees talked about having had challenging life experiences in the country of origin and thus, appeared to have a heightened awareness of the needs of the deprived.

A positive attitude to work was something that also cropped up in many of the accounts, which is likely to have facilitated the creation of an entrepreneurial spirit. Interviewees also referred to being appreciated for providing pastoral care, which they believed was a vital aspect of their practice:

> *I think the word 'hardworking' had not been invented in the olden times (my time). All we knew was that we had to work and work with passion, not for the sake of it. We treated work with respect and did not count hours or weeks. We had love for each other and regarded each other with a lot of respect, and these things are priceless and rare these days. These things were not taught as part of our medical training in India, but we learnt them from our experiences in the community. It never comes to my mind even today that any of my patient is wasting my time, because I think*

there must be a genuine reason that he/ she is taking time to talk to me. The patients here liked us more than the local doctors. We were more caring; I think it was to do with that (gp6b).

The interviewee would appear to refer to the cultural and experiential learning that as a group the overseas-trained South Asian doctors are likely to have imported. One third of all interviewees asserted that white patients often showed a preference for an Asian doctor, which they believed related to their caring attitude. It is also possible that the white patients, who were likely to be marginalised within the geographical contexts that the majority of the overseas-trained doctors were operating in, found such interactions less threatening and were thus, able to form more meaningful relations.

Once established in their practices, many of the interviewees said that they had become involved in training others, mostly GPs with South Asian origins, which may be related to the fact that the geographical locations often did not attract white doctors. As doctors in the study had more experience and skills than the UK-qualified doctors, their contribution as trainers was likely to be invaluable. One interviewee commented on the contribution that he and other overseas-trained South Asian doctors made towards the development of general practice:

There is the Royal College of General Practice; they lay down the rules for training. A lot of us became trainers; we contributed in its [general practice] development. We took trainers and passed on our knowledge, our experiences on to the new learners by letting them watch us how we do it (gpm5).

Many interviewees talked about being an informal mentor and assisting other overseas-trained South Asians, as well as offering cross-generational support to those who were younger, something that can be regarded as a distinctive contribution to the area of entrepreneurship. The following interviewee talked about how he was motivated by his own previous negative experiences, and passed on his knowledge regarding the know-how and skills he had acquired:

Because my experiences were so bad, I was more determined to be entrepreneurial, now all the doctors that work with me are very happy with me. I make sure that they don't go through the same experiences that I went through.

His account below shows how the older generation of overseas-trained South Asian doctors was involved in making life easier for the new one:

I had a phone call the other day from a young female GP in another borough in Greater Manchester. She is from India, has not been long in the country and was having some staffing problems. I went over and just talked to her in our own language and that alone was so comforting for her, told her some tips and after two hours talk, she said she felt so much better and had regained her self-confidence, whereas before, she thought she could not hack it any more. I told her, 'don't feel you are on your own, come and talk to me whenever you need'. I think overseas-trained doctors take time to adjust unless they are flexible and get into the system, working like people want you to work; it can be difficult. You see GPs are independent and it's like a business, so there are two aspects to it, clinical and business, you have to manage both (gp1m).

The fact that the young female overseas-trained doctor was able to pick up the phone and seek advice from a senior colleague with years of experience in an informal way confirms the numerous benefits of coethnic networking that is not available from the mainstream networks. Saxenian (2001) talks about the value that networking creates and cites Mohan, one of the Silicon Valley's entrepreneurs, who talked about how the presence, in itself, of his organisation (The Indus Entrepreneur) created confidence in the community. He added that confidence provides individuals with a safety net, and a feeling of security that they can approach someone in times of need. It helps with risk management and networks help improve one's ability to manage such risks effectively. The above process turns into a self-reinforcing process as one entrepreneur then creates five or ten more entrepreneurs, who then create another ten. Mohan added that the chances of taking risks are reduced in the absence of role models and confidence builders that one can turn to.

The doctors' entrepreneurship is evidenced by their risk taking attitude, their innovation, and networking with other overseas-trained doctors, which has been co-produced by the very nature of the opportunities available, as well as by the individual and group characteristics and their motivation (Zhou, 2008). The following female interviewee's account shows how networks, support, a sense of one's own agency, and a business-like approach can produce positive outcomes:

We purchased land and had the surgery built. We borrowed money and then paid it off. It was risk taking, the patient list was not long, we were quite young and we were going to work for quite a long time. It was an investment, even if we didn't work, we will get rent paid, it was a business enterprise (gp11s).

The building-up of ethnic residential areas where patterns of chain migration and majority group discrimination manifest themselves would appear to present ethnic entrepreneurs with opportunities. The excerpt below provides evidence of how the clustering of doctors and an Asian community may have occurred on a broader scale:

We started off as husband and wife, then we looked for another partner, then we took another doctor. We had so many Asian patients, I think they were gravitating to this side of the city, because people look at what amenities there would be in the area when buying a house, and having an Asian doctor for somebody who doesn't speak the language is an important aspect and to be frank, an English doctor does not even like to look at such a type of practice, let alone work with Asian patients (gp11s).

She added that both types of the patient population appreciated the service they received:

It's helpful, if the doctor speaks the language and knows the culture, patients were happy to receive the service, they had respect for us, they appreciated as well. The English patient is verbally very appreciative and can't stop thanking you, 'I am grateful', 'so nice of you', 'thank you very much'. Sometimes they would bring flowers, you helped me and brought you flowers, presents at Xmas; they were very good. Our own patients were appreciative, but as you know, they didn't express as much as the English did (gp11s).

As stated elsewhere, both the marginalised practitioners and marginalised patients produced encounters that appeared to be reciprocal in nature. Charlesworth (2000, 138, 284) referred to both white and working class Pakistani people in his study focusing on Rotherham, an ex-coalmining town in South Yorkshire, calling it 'linguistically dispossessed, sensorily impoverished and perceptually deprived'; full of people who consequently were unable to achieve any significant form of self-realisation. The patient population in the case of overseas-trained doctors is likely to fall into the above category and includes those who may be more appreciative of clinical encounters with non-traditional medical practitioners. Beagan (2000, 1254) points out that Western biomedicine has not always done well by patients where there is significant difference between the patient and the physician, the latter being mainly white, upper- or middle-class and heterosexual. She provides examples in this regard, such as the over-prescription of tranquillisers, the criminalisation of abortion and birth control, the use of unsafe medical devices such as IUDs and breast implants as well as the history of medicine's mistreatment of women in the light of power inequality.

The Downsides of Ethnic Entrepreneurship

Entrepreneurial activity is not carried out in isolation in that its dynamic nature requires linkages or relationships between key components of the process (Aldrich and Zimmer, 1986). The success of ethnic entrepreneurship has been explained by individuals' personal willingness to engage in hard work and solidarity. This helps to provide the resources necessary to achieve their economic goals and compensate for the automatic set of resources that the privileged social classes entering entrepreneurship seem to have (Light and Karageorgis, 1994, Light and Gold, 2000).

In understanding the entrepreneurial activity of members of ethnic minorities, the significance of ethnic resources, meaning resources gained through ethnic solidarity and ethnic social relationships, is emphasised in the framework of "ethnic" versus "class". As ethnic entrepreneurs lack access to class resources, including economic capital, education, symbolic capital and access to influential economic and institutional networks (Light and Gold, 2000), the available resources are accessed instead through ethnic solidarity and ethnic social relationships. It is the social embeddedness of ethnic business whereby social relations and acquaintances become networks that generate the trust required for entrepreneurial activity, and also provides support, preventing any breach of trust in terms of economic transactions. Reliance on family members is regarded as a considerable part of the ethnic resource (Light and Gold, 2000). However, it has also been associated with exploitation within the realm of entrepreneurship (Werbner, 1990).

One third of the doctors in this study talked about being exploited by their colleagues, who had taken them on based on mutual trust, but the working relationships had become difficult. As one put it:

> *I found out that a doctor [Asian] was looking for a GP for their practice. I worked with him for a short while, but our own people are also very clever as well; they will step over you to get to the top if they can. There was no prospect there either to have a partnership (laughs). Some people have greed, they want to keep all the money to themselves, it was like that. I was employed as a salaried partner. The practice partner kept saying yes 'you will become a partner', but only verbally; this did not materialise (gpm4).*

Trust was described as a key feature in all transactions; however, it also cropped up when the interviewees were discussing in exploitative relationships, with one commenting:

> *At first, the practice partner made many promises, but afterwards did not adhere to them. I worked for a year and half with him. He was not prepared to give a written contract. He said just work and when the payment time came, he did not give an equal share. He said, 'you will have to accept what I give you'. I told him it was not fair, not to have a written contract plus, salary not being shared out to both of us even though I was the one who was doing more work than him. I said, 'there is no trust here, you are saying to me that just accept what I am getting and do my job. There is no discussion about any decision that needed to be made re work, practice business etc. And you keep all the money to yourself'. One day he came and said, 'this is not working out and I want to end this' (gpm1).*

The above account shows the informality of the recruitment process and lack of adherence to employment rights, which is unusual in professional jobs. It appears from the account below that the PCT had failed to intervene directly with the practice partner. This may have been related to their reluctance to get involved in litigation, which might be perceived as a potential race issue:

> *I went to talk to the chief executive of Family Health Services Authority in PCT. I told them that it was not working out and that it was very problematic for me. They said they had known about this practice's history, they said, 'don't resign from the practice'. She said, 'I advise you to start another single-handed practice adjacent to the other practice; we need more doctors in this area'. I thought about it and then decided to act on PCT's advice. I had not picked up before that this practice partner [Indian origin] had got a negative reputation. I found out later that he had done this before. So, I started my own practice from scratch (gp1m).*

It is interesting to note that the PCT opted to ease the obstacles blocking the entrepreneurial initiative of the above interviewee by suggesting the opening up of a whole new practice that would undermine the business of another South Asian doctor. One explanation for this is that the PCT needed more doctors; another may be that it may have been a far more challenging task for the PCT to challenge directly and deal with the competence issues of an overseas-trained South Asian doctor, as this could have led to potential litigation and race issues. The following account suggests that the doctors felt that the PCTs were selective regarding who they helped and why:

> *I was being treated not equal and was doing more than my fair share of the work and not getting paid for it. I complained to the PCT and even the BMA. They said that it was a private arrangement between me and the other Asian doctor, and there was no contract in place, therefore there's nothing they could do (gp7s).*

Organisations are said to recruit like-minded people. The above account shows that the recruiting of GPs of similar cultural background was based on a similar principle and the qualities that were sought out included the ability to bring the same level of passion as the employer, demonstrate creative thinking, having vision, having expertise as well as being diligent and determined. The above findings lend support for Khan's assertion (2007, 47) that bonding social capital can serve to promote exclusionary practices. The author states:

> *...bonding social capital can work to exclude people; even those who draw strength and support from their existing social networks recognise the potential problems for such networks where they place constraints on group members.*

The interviewees often looked for further opportunities and regrouped with other individuals who had had similar experiences as well as joining practices managed by white British doctors, taking opportunities that were initially not available. Whilst these examples show the negative aspects of bonding social capital and how opportunists within the group were willing to exploit each other's vulnerable position, they also show that bonding social capital played an important role in enabling interviewees to later access bridging social capital, which was not available in the first instance.

Unwin (2001) points out that it is often assumed that racial discrimination means white people discriminating ethnic minority people; however, it can work within such a minority. The author refers to accusations that overseas doctors become 'more British than the British themselves' upon receiving consultant status. Unwin's analysis of such a situation appears plausible as he argues that this behaviour is described as an outcome of a system (oppressive), where one is required to behave in a certain way in order to get on.

Social Entrepreneurship

Social entrepreneurship differs from entrepreneurship in that the former has a social value attached to it and social entrepreneurs seek to address a need that the welfare system either cannot or will not otherwise meet. The test of its value can be taken by establishing the extent to which it would be missed if a particular initiative had not been taken up (Thompson, 2002, 414). Evidence from some of the interviewees' accounts suggests that the roles played by them also merit them being labelled social entrepreneurs. For example, the following GP believed that the Asian women in the area should learn English, and initiated a self-help project in which he used his networks, and status as a healthcare professional:

> *I organised teaching of English language for Asian women in the area. I also felt that by putting English female patients of mine in touch with the Asian women would create an opportunity of volunteering and both will benefit from this group. The Asian ladies could practise learning and speaking English and the English women could learn about the Asian cultural aspects. But I had a lot of criticism, e.g. men said that these English ladies were coming to their homes with skirts on and that was unacceptable to them. I could not understand why they were objecting as the women were supposed to teach women and I don't know what their problem was. Most likely, the men very critical as they wanted to keep hold of the control in the household and did not want their wives to become aware of their rights (gp11s).*

The above example shows that the healthcare professionals may have been involved in both issues of cohesion and conflict in the communities that they were serving. The interviewees also talked about participating in fundraising activities run by their local Rotary and Lions clubs to raise money for equipment for local disabled people. Many of the interviewees (two thirds) talked about their extensive involvement in charitable work in their countries of origin that would be classed as social entrepreneurship. The interviewees described at length activities that they were heavily involved in, and that were geared towards meeting the healthcare needs of the most vulnerable sections of society in the country of origin, by utilising their specialist knowledge and financial resources gained in the UK. The interviewees' accounts confirm that they were involved in the exchange of social remittance and transnational activities, which will be further discussed later. The accounts also show that these health care professionals were in an ideal position to help western countries in offering aid to developing countries.

CHAPTER 4

INTEGRATION AND SENSE OF BELONGING

In the previous two chapters, I discussed the empirical evidence concerning what Bhugra and Becker (2005) describe as the first two stages in the migration process, that is, the pre-migration stage involving decision making and preparation leading on to the physical relocation of individuals from one place to another. The authors also refer to a third stage pertaining to post-migration and how migrants become absorbed within the social and cultural framework of the receiving society. In this chapter, I will discuss the empirical evidence in relation to the identity dynamics of the interviewees, how different aspects have worked to constitute identities for the interviewees and how they have negotiated their identities through some of the above cultural attributes, such as place, ethnicity, Britishness, religion, gender, class and profession. The evidence also relates to how the different contextual factors have impacted on the overseas-trained South Asian doctors' identities and their perception of the surrounding communities.

I will begin by discussing the contextual characteristics of the case study areas which may facilitate or inhibit integration, followed by a discussion as to how ethnic identification intersects with other identifications such as place, class, profession and gender.

Contextual Characteristics of the Case Study Areas

Barnsley-Sheffield-Manchester

As described previously, Barnsley is a predominantly white area, with a significant working class rural community, which in the past heavily depended on its coal mining and glassmaking industries. Since the closure of the coalmines in 1994, the area has experienced a lot of unemployment. It has a low ethnic density in comparison with Manchester and Sheffield and only a 0.9% BME population in 2001, 0.3% of whom were of Asian origin, the largest group being of Indian origin (0.2%)[1]. The 2011 Census shows that these figures for the Asian population remained the same a decade later, although the overall BME population sharply increased. Barnsley has historically had a high density of overseas-trained South Asian GPs - making up 38% of the total GP workforce in 1992 (Taylor and Esmail, 1999). This over-representation of overseas-trained doctors in general practice in the area may be attributed to its contextual characteristics, such as the level of deprivation, which make it a less popular area for UK qualified doctors and thus, less competitive for the former group.

Barnsley council's initiatives regarding ethnic relations are historically not as well established as in Manchester and Sheffield. An umbrella organisation, the Barnsley Black and Ethnic Minority Initiative (BBEMI) was set up in the area in the 1980s to promote good race relations and racial harmony amongst the BME population and the wider community. As the ethnic communities are small in size, the social and cultural events are organised jointly. The British National Party (BNP) is known to have a stronghold in the area. The news of a local mosque being burnt down in the 1980s would suggest that there has been hostility against the borough being multicultural.[2] Barnsley Council Online[3] refers to growing concerns about the increase in racist incidents across the borough, which led to the establishment of The Barnsley Racial Harassment Project in 1997.

Sheffield, in contrast, is a large urban area with a much higher proportion of BME population than Barnsley. The history of settlement for BME communities in Sheffield is linked with the post-war labour shortage in traditional industries, such as iron and steel, which attracted migrants from the Indian subcontinent and African Caribbean countries. Prior to this period, Sheffield experienced the presence of Jewish, Polish, Irish, Somali and Yemeni people in the city. However, the proportion of BME people has been increasing and was 8% in 2001. It included people of Indian (0.6%), Pakistani (3%) and Bangladeshi (0.4%) origin, increasing to 1.1%, 4% and 0.6% respectively in 2011. Sheffield also has a slightly higher proportion of people in mixed groups and Chinese people than the national average.[4] Sheffield also has had a high density of overseas-trained South Asian GPs, and these made up 14% of the total number of the GP workforce in 1992

---

[1] Census 2001.

[2] Lord Nazir's paper Muslims in Europe, Understanding and Responding to the Islamic world at St Antony's College, Oxford on 25-26 April 2003, http://www.sant.ox.ac.uk/ext/princeton/pap_ahmed.shtml

[3] http://www.barnsley.gov.uk/

[4] Sheffield City Council, 2001 Census Topic Reports, Ethnic Origin, Corporate Policy Unit. September 2003. https://www.sheffield.gov.uk/your-city-council/sheffield-profile/population-and-health/2001-census/ethnicity.html

(Taylor and Esmail, 1999).

The city has well established BME religious and cultural organisations as well as mainstream initiatives addressing the needs of its BME communities. The city has had forums, such as the Sheffield Committee for Community Relations, which was founded in 1967 to promote equality,[5] and events to mark Black History Month have been held since 1997 to celebrate the diversity of the city.[6] Despite having sizeable immigrant communities, the city is reported to have had fewer racial tensions when comparison with other cities in the UK and certainly has escaped the race riots that some other British cities have witnessed (Taylor et al., 1996). Following the decline in the steel industry, there was a shift away from employment in manufacturing industries to jobs in service industries, as in other cities in Britain, and the city has affluent as well as deprived areas. Taylor et al, (1996, 205) refer to the particular class dimension of the local structures of Sheffield and Manchester in their research, where new immigrants of different class backgrounds are presented with a different mix of opportunities and problems.

Manchester is a major urban area and differs from Barnsley and Sheffield in relation to its ethnic density. Originally, only Manchester city was chosen for this study, however, due to recruitment difficulties, other boroughs of Greater Manchester were also included such as Tameside and Rochdale, although the majority of the doctors in the sample are from

Manchester is a major urban area and differs from Barnsley and Sheffield in relation to its ethnic density. Originally, only the city of Manchester was chosen for this study; however, due to recruitment difficulties, other boroughs of Greater Manchester were also included, such as Tameside and Rochdale, although the majority of the doctors in the sample are from the city itself. The BME population made up 19% of the total population of Manchester in 2001. The proportion of BME included people of Indian (1.5%), Pakistani (6%) and Bangladeshi (1%) origin, which had increased to 2.3%, 8% and 1.3%, respectively, by 2011. In the 2011 Census, Tameside had 5.9% South Asians, which predominantly included people of Indian (1.7%), Pakistani (2.2%) and Bangladeshi heritage (2%). Rochdale had the highest percent of South Asians (13.5%), including people of Indian (0.5%) origin, a much higher proportion of people with Pakistani origin (10.5%) and of Bangladeshi heritage (2.5%). The GPs who had qualified in South Asian

[5] Report of Sheffield Racial Equality Council, 1 April 2006 to September 2007. http://www.charitycommission.gov.uk/Accounts/Ends34%5C0001112134_ac_20070331_e_c.pdf

[6] Black History Month. https://www.sheffield.gov.uk/your-city-council/policy--performance/how-we-will-deliver/other-strategies-plans-and-policies/equality-and-diversity/events-and-festivals/black-history.html

countries made up 30% of the total GP workforce in the city of Manchester in 1992 (Taylor and Esmail, 1999).

Jones and Snow (2010) provide a historical view of the formation of BME communities in Manchester, pointing out that the earliest migrants to the city were Jewish people fleeing from persecution, followed by Italians, Irish, Poles and Chinese people, who worked in different areas of the labour market, such as in the textile, construction industries as well as being peddlers, hawkers, shopkeepers, cotton and silk merchants. The migrants also included professionals, students and West African and West Indian seaman, other workers and their families. Diversity began to be reflected in the type of restaurants in the city, with African and Asian restaurants starting to cater for the diverse needs of the migrant population. Whilst the Asians mostly arrived after the 2nd World War, the presence of Punjabi traders was evident in the 1930s. The Asians mainly worked in the cotton mills of Lancashire and were predominantly of Pakistani origin. In the 1960s, the NHS appears to have relied heavily on overseas junior doctors in the city's hospitals in that they represented between 30-40% of all of that cohort. Indian and Pakistani-trained doctors were also said to be propping up the city's GP and dental practices. Social and cultural BME organisations have existed in the city since the 1960s. Racial tension/violence has surfaced in the city from time to time, and there have been several racially motivated murders in Greater Manchester, Ahmed Iqbal Ullah, a young Bangladeshi schoolboy, being murdered in 1986 (Jones and Snow, 2010). Manchester is the fourth most deprived area according to the Indices of Multiple Deprivation (IMD), which is likely to place strain on the service sector, especially the NHS.

Place-based Identity

In this section, I will look at how the interviewees happen to occupy particular places, their social and doctor-patient interactions, and their adaptations to fit in.

Settlement in Barnsley resulted via two routes. One involved responding to job advertisements and moving from other cities to gain independence from group practices that the interviewees previously worked in. The second route, as described by two of the interviewees, was to establish links in the area during their vocational training in the area, and then be offered a job following completion of their training. Some female interviewees had existing networks in the area through their spouses, who were working as local hospital doctors. The interviewees' accounts suggest that the tradition of migrant GPs working in the area was well established and jobs were becoming available through departing GPs of Polish and Irish origin, who were reaching retirement. The interviewees from Sheffield and Manchester area also responded to recruitment drives. A couple of those from Sheffield stated that they had had other offers from other ethnically dense areas, such as Leicester and Birmingham, but their preference for the foremost city related to its leafy suburban characteristics. The average length of service for the doctors in the case study areas who remained in the same place throughout their GP career was well over 30 years, which shows a considerable loyalty to patients and communities. In the following section, I will discuss the residential pattern of the interviewees and their sense of belonging to their local areas.

Neighbourhood Areas and Communities

A common assumption held in the causal story of the community cohesion agenda is that different minority ethnic groups actively choose to live in segregated communities (Robinson, 2005). The interviewees in all three case study areas described being part of a pre-dominantly white middle class neighbourhood, where most other professional people lived. The finding in this study is in contrast to the above assumption and suggests that these elites chose to live with other elites in the area. Their accounts show that they had formed a close bond with their neighbours, who had been, like them, long term residents in the area. They talked about memories of raising their children together and different aspects of physical neighbourliness, such as how their neighbours cared for their houses while they were away or helped dig snow from the drive in winter. Their detailed accounts illustrate that they had a fair amount of knowledge of the backgrounds of other residents in the area, for example, one interviewee in Barnsley, described her neighbourhood area as follows:

> *This area, it's all architects, medical, and he's an accountant he's used to be a headmaster, he's retired and the first one is also a teacher, she's a teacher and he's working, he's having some business I think and erm, here is all the retired people except these people, he's an engineer and she's a teacher, and they are… next one is retired, the next one is a young couple, they just bought that house you see, so he's working in graphics and she's doing a part-time job, working for her husband, their children are the youngest children in the area, 17 and 13 (gp1b).*

For most of the interviewees, the contact with neighbours took place over the fence or occasionally their neighbours visited, but this was not always reciprocated, as the following interviewee points out:

> *We do interact with their English neighbours, they come to us, but they don't invite you to their homes much (laughs). The English are well known for being reserved and we don't mind that (gp6b).*

The above interviewee views the behaviour of his neighbours in the context of English culture, while another echoed the above and comments that she too had adapted to that lifestyle:

> *All my neighbours are exceptionally good. We may not go to each other's house for a coffee morning, but I know them well, they know me well. I also like that, rather than chit-chat, I also like that and they also like that, we can talk standing in the driveway for hours, but sometimes, I mean they do invite, if there is any special occasion or for a drink near Christmas, New Year time (gp1b).*

She describes the composition of her neighbourhood and refers to other Asian doctors living in a cluster:

> *I'm the only Asian doctor in this street, here, but, on the other side of it... there are quite a few Asian doctors, all are GP's. I think there are about... at least 12 Asian doctors (gp1b).*

Barnsley is made up of several small remote villages. Some of the villages appear to rely heavily on the services of overseas professionals. Several interviewees' accounts show that it was a norm actively to belong to local and global communities. As one put it:

> *... the people that live nearby, we don't see them very much... they are also professionals, they go home over the weekends, like Belgium, France, They are all international workers. There's a dentist in our village from Belgium, he goes back to Belgium to visit his family every fortnight; goes on Friday and comes back on Sunday. There's a doctor over here from Spain, a doctor from Germany working over here in our village (gp4b).*

Also, close friends described as living in regions other than Barnsley and with whom a close bond was maintained, were mentioned. The following account refers to meeting one's 'own people', which suggests that this was a way of affirming their Asian identities:

> *My friends are always there... they live quite a way from here, I mean I have a friend in Oldham, Preston and Surrey... from 'Madras medical' you see, and so every year May Bank holiday weekend event, we try to attend that, just see your own people and chit chat.... So, it is nice (gp1b).*

Interviewees in Sheffield also described living in pre-dominantly white middle class areas, where they believed they had been accepted partly due to their professional status and social class, which were interlinked. The areas did have other South Asian doctors, to whom the following interviewee refers, thus suggesting that being perceived as middle class along with the presence of a few other Asians may have been perceived to offer a buffering effect in relation to overt racism:

> *My wife (laughs) and I enjoy the freedom we have, apart from a little bit of racism*

which is there, but most of the places it does not matter. When I wanted to buy a house here, which is a predominantly white upper middle-class area, I was the only brown person in this road at that time. Nobody objected to that, there are some ghetto areas, white areas, black areas. If I had bought a house in some ghetto white area somewhere else and if we started living there, the neighbours may start making our life hell. They all came along and they welcomed me here. There's a few Asian doctors here, I think it's about the level of education, I am not saying that the educated aren't racist, they may be, but they keep it under the surface (gp9s).

The gravitation of people with a minority background to form such instances of clustering have been described as a vital resource that offers mutual support and security in the face of hostility from the majority ethnic population as well as being for economic reasons (Johnston et al., 2002, Wilton, 1998). Availability of culturally sensitive services, religious and recreational facilities along with shopping opportunities are also associated with some of the practical benefits of minority ethnic population clusters (Robinson et al., 2002).

The above interviewee believed that the middle-class nature of the area had offered him protection, which a 'ghetto' may not have done. In other words, living with other elites in the area was considered as a protective factor. He did not deny the existence of middle-class racism, instead contending that it was kept 'under the surface. As educated people are likely to be more aware of equalities legislation and the implications of explicitly contravening this, it could be argued that they are more cautious in terms of self-exposure (Blinder et al., 2013).

The interviewee also talked about being part of a middle class close-knit suburban community, where neighbours would just casually drop in whenever they liked:

All these people, they know me and there's no problem. The other day, this guy, Professor of Surgery, he (white) walked in, he goes 'I want money for charity' (gp9s).

Recalling further memories, the above interviewee mentioned that in the 1970s, there was a doctors' club in the neighbourhood where local doctors met up regularly, and where he was the only non-white doctor. He was aware of the exclusion of other Asian doctors in the area, but uncertain why that may have occurred. The fact that he married an English woman may well account for this inclusion, for as Lahiri (2000) points out, those with English wives are likely be more readily absorbed into local communities. According to the exchange theory of Merton (1941), educated African Americans traded on their socio-economic status and endeavoured to maximise their gains through marriage with lower middle class white partners. They exploited their socio-economic status in order to achieve the social status that was attached to having a white partner. The interviewee above went on to explain the reasons that lie behind working class racism, contending that it is based on a different kind of prejudice:

> *I think competition of resources is the main thing, actually, e.g. one household may have a Mercedes and they have 17 children and are on benefits, whereas the next door may be struggling to put the food on the table, they get irritated that he is not getting same as him, working all hours God sends, but here nobody is claiming anything (gp9s).*

The interviewees in all three areas described being accepted by their elite neighbourhoods and were aware that their symbolic capital (professional status) had played a positive role in their integration. A similar observation was made by Rogaly and Taylor (2007, 67), who stated how the Filipino nurses in their research talked about being taunted by white boys in an area where they had recently moved. The strategy that they employed to create physical safety for themselves was to make sure their nursing uniforms were visible, as this symbolic professional identity engendered more value and respect. In addition, Allen (1971) argued that socioeconomic factors play a large part in mediating prejudice based on colour and assimilation of professional Asian people, in terms of speech, dress, ways of living, and expectations for themselves and for their children, thus affording them a higher level of acceptance by the majority. I shall discuss this aspect further in the identities section.

Two of the interviewees of Pakistani origin described their integration in the context of inter-marriage with English partners. The following shows how a predisposition to the British way of life is played out on the ground:

> *Well, you see, I feel as though as I always belonged to Britain. We read about Britain so much and our forefathers had worked with the British. Our parents always said good things about the British, 'they are friendly and honest people, who don't back bite and respect you for who you are'. I have never encountered any bad experiences and I have lived in here for 49 years. I have two daughters, you see they are married to local lads, I mean English boys, who are very nice, we are all happy here (gp4b).*

The above account touches on many issues. It is often assumed that the relationships of post-colonial people to Britain commenced only at the point when they or their ancestors embarked on their journeys to Britain, thus failing to take into account their exposure and conditioning to the British way of life under colonial rule (Sayyid, 2004). It is a well-established fact that the colonial relationship was based on exploitation, where coercion and force were often involved in the creation of the social order (Brah, 1982). However, there is also ongoing controversy over certain aspects of colonial links that are evidenced in the interviewee's account, where it reflected upon on in a positive way. On an individual level, people may well have benefitted from colonial rule, for example, through the introduction of meritocratic procedures and middle-class social structures.

Song (2009) is critical of the assumed relationship between intermarriage and integration, arguing that, whilst intermarriage can entail the transcending of racial, ethnic and religious boundaries, considering them as good indicators of integration, and assuming that social distances are lessened between the minority and majority white groups is problematic. This is because such a phenomenon is much more complex than envisaged. In relation to residential integration or segregation, the author refers to a study by Caballero et al. (2008), which found that mixed couples in Britain do not always live in multicultural areas. The perception of integration may be based on the loss of the minority spouse's ethnic minority identity as researchers use the term synonymously with the term 'assimilation'. In addition, cultural assimilation does not mean structural assimilation. Minority individuals who have intermarried cannot be assumed to be immune from the racism of the wider family network or the wider society and may not feel welcomed or experience a sense of 'belonging' in many mainstream settings. Assumptions are made on the basis of a linear model of assimilation, which suggests that the offspring of a 'mixed race' couple will have a diluted sense of the minority parent's ethnicity and culture. Song reminds us that such assumptions may overlook the re-emergence of the 'melting-pot' theory based on the notion that a minority person will eventually fully integrate into white society.

Regarding the residential patterns of professional groups of Asian origin, Allen (1971, 34) contends that these did not form separate geographical or social units like their low skilled/unskilled counterparts. However, the accounts of several interviewees in all three areas indicate that there may have been residential clustering among the overseas-trained South Asian doctors while living in predominantly upper middle class areas.

Allen (1971) argues that migration of all kinds involve stress for migrants as it involves new circumstances in the form of social organisation. Hence, migrants tend to re-create familiar patterns of life by preserving '*customary social relationships*' in whatever small capacity they can. Individuals draw not only security from such relationships, both social and economic, for they also form part of individuals' self-identification. In all three areas where community interaction with white members of the community was described, it was, interestingly, mostly with individuals with a lower middle class/working class background and interactions with upper middle class white professionals were rarely mentioned.

In Manchester, the doctors talked more about life with other Asian families than did their counterparts in Barnsley and Sheffield:

Asian families want to move upwards but also would like to have a few Asian families in the area, they feel secure that way (gp1m).

The interviewees in Manchester and Sheffield talked about navigating much wider city spaces than in Barnsley. This may be related to such contexts being receptive to BME communities:

My social interaction mostly was with our own doctors, Pakistani and Indian; I was friendly with many white doctors because in my neighbouring area all other doctors were white. We used to visit each other [he mentions a couple of Asian names]. There were around 30 Asian doctors in the mid 70s, but when I took up the practice, there were only two or three. I've had good relationships, used to meet each other socially, used to organise social programmes, used to go on picnics together with wives and children (gp9s).

His account shows that even though the doctors lived in white middle class areas, their contact was mainly with people from similar a race and class background. The interviewees described their areas as being well served in terms of meeting the cultural/religious needs of the Asian community in general. Barnsley, however, does not appear to have catered for the cultural needs of its small sized Asian community, and Asian supermarkets have not found their way into the area as yet. All the interviewees mentioned travelling long distances to neighbouring cities to access relevant facilities, and their comfortable socio-economic status allowed them to combat cultural isolation (Chakraborti and Garland, 2004).

Place Integration

The interviewees' integration in Barnsley can best be explained using a practical model developed by Cutchin (1997, 25) regarding rural physician retention. The author uses the term 'experiential place integration' which places its focus on the connection and interaction between doctors and local communities. The author uses the above concept to determine how strongly a GP feels part of the community, and the degree of integration with the local community, arguing that it is this degree of integration that influences their retention in rural places. Cutchin's practical model proposes three primary principles namely security, freedom and identity, which characterise place integration. The extent to which such dimensions are manifested determines how well a doctor has integrated into the community and feels a sense of place.

Cutchin's dimension of security includes: confidence in medical abilities, commitment to aspirations and goals, ability to meet family needs, comfort with the medical community and institutions, practice group environment, availability of social and cultural networks as well as the respect of the medical community and community at large.

Having worked both in the country of origin and in UK hospitals, all the interviewees talked about their confidence in their medical abilities based on several years of hands on experience related to the specific diseases suffered by their local communities, such as chronic chest diseases. The fact that majority of hospital doctors were also of Asian origin and part of the professional diasporic community, as referred to by many of the interviewees, meant that they were well networked with each other. The interviewees' accounts show that their ethnic links proved highly significant when making arrangements with other overseas-trained South Asian doctors for undertaking Out of Hours Service. The spaces, such as the Rotary Club, The Lions Club, as well as golf and tennis clubs, became those of elite networks that worked to connect interviewees with place and the medical community at-large. The leisure pursuits combined sport with socialising activities, developing social and cultural capital (Valentine, 2001). The following interviewee's account shows how Asian food and hospitability also played its part in forging diasporic solidarity, thus assisting in the integration process (Lakha and Stevenson, 2001):

> *It was mainly Asian doctors when my husband joined the 'Rotary Club', with a few white doctors. They used to come and enjoy the meals that we cooked on a rota basis and spent some time together, 'Rotary' was a good thing for mixing (gp1b).*

Cutchin argues that the interaction between physician and the physical environment of a place presents challenges and responses and within such processes lie the act of integration. The author adds that the physician becomes woven into the social fabric of the place through interacting, over time, with the evolving problems that a place poses. The following shows how specific contextual embedding was achieved by one of the doctors in the study:

> *There was a lot of community activities that I and other Asian doctors used to go to. There might be a dance, there might have been a pea and pie, whatever, small things, you know. I have a reasonably high profile in the community; I have served as a local councillor, well, this MBE was given to me by recommendation of my patients, who are 99.9% white... for my services in medicine. I am involved in charity work, there is the 'Lions club*[7]*. We hold functions and raise funds for local*

[7] The Lions Club is a charity organisation that serves the needs of local and global communities. Its ethos is that working together can lead to the initiation and carrying out of projects that will make the community

> *charity, you know, local causes, e.g. if someone needs a wheelchair in the community and they can't afford it, we buy little things or whatever it takes from the funds. I have been its member for 37 years and have raised several hundred thousand pounds in the past for hospitals and things; that's my contribution to the community (gp2).*

The above account shows the interaction of an overseas-trained South Asian doctor with low and high class strata that includes participation in community activities, such as dancing, and pea and pie parties, which specifically relate to the culture of a working class mining community. The evidence also shows how elites' own privileged position may have enabled them to integrate with all sections of society with ease.

The membership of the Lions Club referred to above can be regarded as a form of class membership, which cannot be gained solely by one's job, but rather, is a way of 'mimicking' a culture of that class, which dictates its terms, as stated by Bhabha (1994) in his Theory of Mimicry. This theory refers to situations whereby some Indians and Africans (the colonised) imitated the language, dress, politics, or cultural attitude of the British (the colonisers). This is seen as an opportunistic pattern of behaviour in which an individual copies the person in power so as to have access to that same power within the context of colonialism and immigration. The findings also support Lahiri (2000, 62) assertion that the mimicry theory can also be reworked in specific contexts such as how a middle class Indian student attempted to take on a white working class identity in order to be accepted.

Lahiri draws on a historical case in 1899, where an Indian student, Wagle, apprenticed himself with a factory in Britain to study the glass industry. In combating enormous hostility based on race and his middle class status, Wagle learnt that the greatest hostility he faced was due to his class and from the factory workers, rather than from the factory owners, with one of the former telling him that 'We hate all gents the same'. He, therefore, decided to integrate 'not in gentleman's clothes but as a fellow workman'. By adopting a cosmetic change and using phrases, such as 'old chap' 'chappie', shaking hands, acquainting himself with the workers' home lives as well as making himself aware of what was acceptable and unacceptable in that distinct working class culture, which eventually led to his become accepted. Lahiri (2000, 62) comments on this outward assimilation:

> *Wagle camouflaged his appropriation of imperial knowledge by adopting a mask of assimilation. But this time mimicry is relocated, away from the colonial periphery to the metropolitan centre, Britain, and the new class dimension causes Wagle (the colonised) to mimic British working class, metropolitan culture rather than middle-*

a better place. http://www.lionsclubs.org/EN/our-work/index.php

class, colonial culture.

It would appear from the interviewees' accounts that their interactions with the subsets of pluralist British society reflected both Bhabha and Lahiri's approaches.

The combination of place and person influences the integration process and leads to variation within the integration experiences (Cutchin, 1997). The interviewees' narratives show that their own characteristics, such as exposure to western education in the countries of origin, professional status, and the specific characteristics of the place, including the rural context and the need to sustain healthcare provision, may have facilitated the integration process.

The challenges of working in rural practices included dealing with complex chronic diseases as most of the patient population were described as ex-coalminers. The interviewees' accounts show sensitivity and empathy to the social context and realities of the majority of white working class patients when they described how the occupation of mineworkers affected the life chances of those patients, thereby exacerbating the demands placed on the doctors. It appears that the ethnicity of the doctors was also a resource here, as many talked about the usefulness of their expertise gained in the country of origin. As one put it:

> *They [the miners] would invite us, just to get an idea of how people are working inside mines... sometimes they had to really, you know, crawl through small places, [pause] people were getting more neck pain, sickness, chronic chest diseases, fortunately most of us [Asian doctors] had ample experiences of those illnesses from our own countries(gp1s).*

The empathy described in several of the interviewees' accounts towards the miners' circumstances shows they were aware of the significance of engaging with the social contexts of their patients:

> *I was aware that paperwork needed to be completed there and then. I mean like any compensation, because people with mines…there were lots of people with pneumoconiosis [lung disease acquired in mines] and for pneumoconiosis, they had to give compensation, people were suffering a lot really. We had to write letters in a particular way and as quickly as possible. Sometimes you have to do more details... he [patient] cannot breathe properly, he's out of breath like that he needs medication, and again these are those things, because they were really working very hard, and in very adverse circumstances. You know they have to be inside a long time, and they were getting this disease, because of the... mine dust (gp1s).*

Ability and opportunity to achieve a vision and develop something of their own in the form of providing enhanced primary care services, thereby reducing the cost of secondary and tertiary care, was seen as offering the freedom to practise holistic medicine and continuity of care by many interviewees. Two of the female interviewees talked about focusing on offering enhanced primary care services for pregnant women and their newborn babies; services that did not previously exist. They were proud of their achievements, as previously, female patients had had to travel long distances to attend hospital ante-natal appointments, whereas these services were brought to their doorsteps, as a result of the doctor's entrepreneurship activities, as previously discussed.

Networking with local people on an individual level was instrumental and a reciprocal relationship appears to have existed in several of the interviewees' accounts. For example, one described how networking with a local woman, a retired tax officer, had helped him to become familiar with tax affairs, whilst another mentioned how an ex-senior council manager, who subsequently worked for him, expanded his local links. Several female interviewees talked about networking with local women for childcare arrangement purposes. Such relationships appeared deeper and warmer than simply instances of networking:

> *I came to know this lady through my hospital clinics you see and so she was quite willing to do the full time nanny post. She was not a professional, you know in those days, just a word of mouth, you know you. I got on well and she got on well and that's it and she was in the age group, like a grandma to the children, so everything fitted fine (gp1b).*

In relation to the 'dimensions of freedom' in Cutchin's model of place identity, the interviewees talked about the freedom to practise holistic medicine and continuity of care, being able to socially interact, have the ability to develop healthcare provision, become involved in community affairs, personal and family activities as well as developing perspective on self and place. Regarding the dimensions of identity, interviewees talked about being able to work with like-minded practice groups (often with other overseas-trained South Asian doctors), being able to fulfil aspirations in their place of practice (for example, being able to access government funds to modernise practice buildings) and being able to see themselves as belonging to communities.

At the time of arrival, having an *awareness of self in time and place,* relating to the identity dimension of the integration model, the interviewees described experiencing a feeling of social isolation. Ethnic minority households in a rural context do not privilege notions of 'community', because of the small population and their sparse spatial distribution (De Lima, 2004). There was evidence of the duality of roles in the interviewees' accounts, that is, healthcare professionals as well as becoming community leaders advocating for the needs of the Asian communities in Barnsley. Some interviewees described how by so doing they maintained their self-esteem and a sense of identity. While some interviewees talked about directly integrating with the local communities, others reported how they got involved in community development activities in order to engage with rural minority ethnic groups and thus, their maintain cultural identities. The majority of the interviewees, both of Pakistani and Indian origin, described their political mobilisation in seeking to set up a legitimate place in a public space for the provision of their specific cultural needs (Vertovec, 1997). This resulted in the emergence of the Barnsley Black and Ethnic Minority Initiative (BBEMI) in the 1980s. The aim of the organisation was to raise local people's awareness of diversity issues as well as tackle the social isolation experienced by BME communities. The interviewees' accounts provide evidence of intra-group cohesion among the interviewees of both Pakistani and Indian origin, in relation to joint working and creation of a collective space for the Asian community. This could have been due to the communities in and around Barnsley being very small and thus, collective action was the only viable way to proceed, if they wanted to engender a sense of belonging.

In addition, interviewees of Pakistani origin also talked about their involvement with charitable work, managing to raise sufficient funds to purchase a building for the use of a local mosque, congregational prayers being considered an important element of their religion. The interviewees adhering to the Hindu religion talked about worship as a private matter, rather than collective. This could be attributed to the differences between religions and within religions, for example, temples based on caste, regions, background and settlement history (Vertovec, 2000) or where the differences between them have their origins in language and nationality (Bilimoria, 1996).

Cuba and Hummon (1993) contend that place identity concerns significant affiliation of self with place, using in their study an eight dimension conceptual framework for the measurement of such affiliations, covering: friend-related (people, neighbours) dwelling-related (home ownership, personal possessions), self-related (feeling comfortable), family-related (reared family in the place, work), amenity-related (natural environment), community-related (sense of community), and prior experience-related aspects. Many of the interviewees' affiliations in Barnsley appear to have been rooted in economic and status concerns, which resonate with the friend-related and family related categories above, as evidenced below:

> *Barnsley has been my home for the last 37 years and my attachment is basically with the place because it gave me my living. The attachment is mainly to the family not to the place, but to the place my attachment is because it gave me my daily bread.*

> *You can go anywhere and its fine, but if you have never even been anywhere 'there is pie in the sky'. You can go to London to live, but what's the point, if there is no work, we all may have dreams but that's not the reality. This place has given me, as I say, my daily bread. I have been happy, I have been recognised, what else more can I ask for? (gp2b).*

The interviewee makes passing reference to the popular aspiration of working in London. Regarding which, many of the doctors previously mentioned they had come to the UK thinking that they would work in prestigious hospitals in the capital. Nonetheless, he is content with the place he has worked in for nearly four decades, for it has provided him with his livelihood. It is noteworthy that the interviewee uses English idioms, such as *pie in the sky* and *gave me my daily bread*, with the latter coming from the Lord's Prayer.

The interviewees in Barnsley were more likely to talk about national attachments than local. For example, one female interviewee talked about her regular trips to the Chelsea Flower Show and Royal Ascot, as well as visiting her network of friends up and down the country. Others also referred to place as a context that provided a secure base from where they could interact with the wider world. A common expression that was used by many interviewees was '*this place provided us with a space to grow*'. Much of the social participation tended to be in neighbouring cities and towns, where people from similar backgrounds lived. The fact that the interviewees did not refer to an extensive involvement in the local community is not necessarily related to a desire not to integrate, but rather, this should be seen as the product of the homogenous social context in Barnsley, which does not reflect the multicultural aspect of Britain, as found in the other two focal cities.

Place was experienced differently in Sheffield. The interviewees' accounts show that their involvement in local communities was with a much wider range of activities than in Barnsley. This included being involved in a local school mentoring project, equality work with the Community Relations Council, working closely with the police regarding community relations, membership of the rotary and sports clubs and other community involvement. The interviewees also talked about being directly asked by white patients to participate in community activities, for example, involvement in boxing matches as a doctor, boxing being a local working-class sport.

Since the majority of Asian people in Sheffield migrated to work in the city's blue collar industries, their education level was generally not very high. This meant that people like the overseas-trained South Asian doctors were in demand by them when it came to representation at the institutional level. The interviewee (of Indian origin, Hindu) quoted below, explains how he happened to become a representative for the minority ethnic community:

> *I have been involved in community cohesion for the past 25 years; I'm respected as one of the persons who has done that. I used to join all these... African-Caribbean's and others, the Pakistani community. There was the Living Art from India. Indira Ghandi and Margaret Thatcher, they called together a few artists from there: painters, decorators, sculptures etc. I think it was '82 in the Millennium Art Gallery, there I was [link] the person, my wife was a voluntary English teacher, and the woman that worked with her... her husband was the curator of Millennium Art Gallery, so that's how we met. He said 'look I don't know anybody involved in the Indian community, so you can lead that part, and link up with the Indian High commissioner etc', so, we organised that. After that we had a cultural programme as well, that was an exhibition I think for two weeks, the artists came and did the casts there (gp5s).*

He adds how one contact led to the other and he became embedded in local structures:

> *...so then somebody called me 'Look there is no Indian organisation, there is nobody like you, I thought you are the person who can do it', then I was involved in the community. So, from the beginning, I was involved in the general cohesion work. So first approach was from there, so I represented everybody at that level. I was closely working with the Chief Constable on race equality matters for many years and represented on the local Race Equality Council (gp5s).*

Several of the interviewees talked about local iconic buildings, such as the Millennium Art Gallery and local people who they could relate to and thus, feel included. There was also evidence of cohesion within the South Asian community, for example, the interviewees of both Hindu and Muslim origin described how they pooled their resources to make charitable donations to Pakistan during the earthquake crisis. The interviewees in Sheffield were much more explicit about their concerns as to how they may be judged by their patients, than were those working in Barnsley. The former group was constantly striving to improve their image in the face of having to deal with the competitive nature of urban GP practices.

The Manchester interviewees' accounts suggest there was more intra-group cohesion there than in Sheffield and Barnsley, with most interviewees describing their social interaction with people of a similar cultural and linguistic background. This may be related to the fact that the city of Manchester provided the context for such opportunities, given that the Asian community is much larger in Manchester than in the other case study areas.

The interviewees mentioned being involved in literary events (*Mushairas*[8]), and interacting with lay members of the Asian community, though mostly with other elites.

McPherson et al. (2001) argue that people choose who they wish to associate with. Often, such preferences are based on cultural similarities and the sharing of origins, customs and values, which bring about better understanding among people. Kalmijn (1998) argues that, apart from cultural compatibility, people also choose to interact with others who are as socio-economically successful as themselves, the implication being the subsequent sharing of similar activities and social circles. However, Martinović (2013) adds that the determination of such choices is only one element of the story, as the context in which individuals are located also dictates the extent of contact with others of preferred characteristics. Regarding which, the opportunity for inter-ethnic contact is determined by the size of one's own ethnic and other groups as well as how segregated/integrated the ethnic group is in the area (Blau and Schwartz, 1984). Martinović (2013) adds that ethnic groups that are bigger and more segregated provide greater opportunities for intra-ethnic contact, whereas smaller groups that are spatially dispersed are more likely to have inter-group encounters.

For a community identity, social participation in the local community is essential (Cuba and Hummon, 1993). However, many of the interviewees from the Manchester area focused less on social participation in the local community and more on their involvement in the business of professional bodies, such as the Local Medical Committee (LMC) and BMA. Rotary Clubs did not surface in any of the conversations with interviewees from Manchester. Less social participation may be related to the fact that these roles were being taken care of by other members of the Asian community, as the city has a much larger one, when compared to Barnsley and Sheffield.

In addition, almost all the interviewees talked about their elite networks based on alumni relationships and how they maintained close contact with their friends and colleagues, meeting up annually as a group where information was exchanged. Interviewees across all case study areas talked about sending remittances for charitable work to the country of origin. Four of the Manchester interviews talked about their extensive involvement in social entrepreneurship activities in the countries of origin, thus showing that the concept of community is much wider for this cohort in that it was seen as transcending national borders. Some of the interviewees mentioned that they did not wish to be pigeon-holed and work solely with their own community, actively seeking out areas that provided wider opportunities for

[8] Mushaira is an Urdu word for a poetic symposium, where poets gather to perform their works, this being a much-loved elite cultural activity in Pakistan and India.

There is class distinction here, and a vast majority of doctors in this country tend to be from the upper middle class, and I am not sure if a middle class doctor from here would take an interest in what his/her [patient] family are up to. These little things go a long way to building a trusting relationship between me and my patients and trust is so important in our doctor-patient relationship (gp1m).

Evidence shows that the elite professionals incorporated their religious/spiritual beliefs in their practice. Regarding which, the following interviewee stated:

I found myself often working with poor people for whom sometimes I could do little as a doctor to change their social circumstances. But I remember what one of our poets had once said that 'Dard ke dawa na sehei, dard sun he liya hota', [if you cannot cure pain, at least you could have just listened to it]. So there was a lot of that. I could relate to some of the things, coming from Kashmir, where I had seen deprivation and poverty directly in the communities that I had worked with (gp8s).

The doctor-patient relationship in Sheffield and Manchester was described as more of a mixed nature. Working with marginalised communities both white and Asian as marginalised practitioners and the challenges this entailed were raised by several of the interviewees:

The English patients that we had were actually the ones no 'local' doctors wanted to keep, as these patients were very demanding (gpm1).

Another interviewee explained in detail the challenges involved:

I started [the] practice single handed. I used to write to my patients and telephone them to remind them about immunisation for their children as the children should have had their immunisation. The drawback for us was that we did not get paid, if the children did not have their vaccination. So, I used to visit around eight to ten patients daily in the evenings. The ones who agreed, I used to give injections to them in their own homes, as they did not want to attend the surgery (gpm5).

The interviewee described in detail how one young 18-19 years old white mother had missed three immunisation appointments for her baby, but he managed to track her down after several home visits. Below, he provides evidence of the vulnerability of migrant doctors trying to provide a service to socially excluded communities:

By the time I managed to get round to her, it was late evening. She said the child was asleep. I said, it will not harm the child, it's just a prick and that the child will go back to sleep again. She agreed and I gave the injection. After a while, she made a complaint to the PCT that I went to her house late evening. PCT did not pay any attention to the fact that I had gone to give an injection. They took a different view.

They said that the woman was young and was not ill, why did you go to her house? I had to collect all the evidence of my whereabouts on that day and how many patients I gave injections and how I had left her a note earlier that I would call back etc. It took about three to four months and I had to appear before our medical committee (gpm5).

He added that the structures were less supportive than patients and that it was the intervention of a lay person, the girl's mother, who eventually saved his name:

Her mother found out that she had reported me to the PCT. Her own mother said to her that she must withdraw the complaint, otherwise she will break her [daughter's] legs. 'He only came to give your child an injection, what else did he do?' The daughter said, 'He came at night-time', the mother said, 'so what? he only came to give an injection to your child'. The mother said, 'Did you not ask him to visit you at 2am when you were in a refuge?' I did have to talk to her mother at the time as she [the daughter] was half dressed [when I visited her], which I did not like and had to tell her mother that she should behave properly, if she would like a doctor to visit her; the mother had told her off then as well. She withdrew her complaint and the PCT dropped the case against me (gpm5).

His account below provides evidence of a possible shift in individuals' attitudes:

The same young woman wrote to me one year before my retirement and said, doctor, my children have grown older now, I have matured, my mother has died, I have not received the kind of service that you provided me, I want to come back to your surgery and be your patient, will you accept me?(gpm5).

The above story of a young woman who came to appreciate the services for which her mother saw the value from the start may be related to her maturity as well as evidence of how the presence and perseverance of overseas-trained South Asian doctors may have contributed towards the transformation of attitudes in UK society. The narratives of the doctors in the study show that the nature of doctor-patient encounters had been shaped by the historical colonial context:

...some would show their arrogance by their body language that they were superior than us. You see they feel superior because they have ruled over you for hundreds of years or more, you know, they feel they are superior than all over the world not just us, they have colonised every part of the world. We did not think of the white working class as coming from lower strata, because before us, they were English first (gp10s).

Another interviewee's account points to the hierarchies that exist within the UK social class system. He adds that being migrant doctors, their focus was on performing their duty well:

> *We had no concept of demanding/ non-demanding patients, we saw ourselves as the provider of the service and that we had to do our duty. These patients were very appreciative of our services and they had a lot of respect for us. In fact, we often used to give their examples to our own community patients, who were sometimes yelling for more help and we used to say, 'look at these patients who are so content with so little' etc. These English patients were rejected by others, but for us they were still better than our own in terms of their demands (gp5m).*

The above refers to a number of aspects, such as the incorporation of cultural values that emphasise a sense of duty and the issues of working in deprived areas, where patients are classified as demanding. The experiences of the marginalisation of overseas-trained South Asian doctors within the NHS may have better equipped them to empathise with patients from disadvantaged backgrounds and their accounts provide evidence of insight into the symbiotic relationships that occur between marginalised practitioners and marginalised patients. The excerpt below would suggest that due to the perseverance of overseas trained South Asian doctors, marginalised white working-class patients may have been the beneficiaries:

> *At that time, if you were not happy with a patient, you simply wrote a letter for the patient stating that you were not happy to continue providing a service for them and then, they had to find another one from the NHS list. I remember some patients used to say that they did not have a problem with me, why was I de-registering them? So I didn't in the end, and they were the ones who stayed in my surgery until I retired and were forever grateful for the service they received (gpm5).*

Interviewees talked about the diverse healthcare needs of their patients and the demands placed on the Asian doctors. In ethnically diverse areas, such as Manchester and Sheffield, the interviewees' accounts appeared less sympathetic to the issues confronting the South Asian patients, which may have been related to the complexity of their healthcare needs:

> *They [the English] used to come with complaints like, 'doctor, I have a headache since yesterday'. So, I did certain checks, checked blood pressure, checked temperature and mouth. With Asian patients, it was like this, 'doctor, I have severe headache, and my ear aches as well'. Ok, I check for this. Then I am told, 'oh, my foot hurts and I cannot walk, I have a boil on it', so I examine this. And then I am told, 'I have a stomach ache, so we were asked to write 3-4 medicines on one prescription. It took us longer that way as we had to explain things. Then I used to be told, oh doctor, I have had a letter from my sister, can you please read it and reply to it accordingly. In comparison with the English patients, we had to spend much more time with our own [Asian] patients (gpm5).*

The interviewees stated that being part of the same cultural group as the patient was both a benefit and a hindrance:

> *The Asian patients, when they do have appointment, instead of one patient, you get four, because they want to see me. I think communication is crucial and patients find it very satisfying when they find that I can communicate with them. When I go to visit other GP surgeries and in some English doctors' surgeries, there is a notice placed, one patient, one complaint, one appointment, one patient. When I have an Asian patient before me, I cannot say to them just one complaint or one person (gp1m).*

Ahmed et al. (1991) found a prevalence of less favourable attitudes among Asian doctors towards Asian patients. This can relate to a number of issues. Ethnic inequalities in health and health care is an area which has been well researched (Bhopal, 2008, McAvoy and Donaldson, 1990). Meeting the linguistic and cultural needs of such patients in deprived locales must have placed a disproportionate burden on overseas-trained South Asian doctors. Scaife et al. (2000) argued that South Asian patients are more likely to be frequent attendees at a GP practice. These patients may regard Asian doctors as a member of their own community and make unrealistic demands. The Asian doctors, on the other, hand may not have wanted to be pigeon-holed in the roles that were ascribed to them, that is, to work with pre-dominantly Asian patients, as some interviewees pointed out in earlier accounts. The difference in class identity of overseas-trained South Asian doctors and Asian patients may have acted as an additional barrier.

Interviewees in Manchester talked about the ever changing demography of inner city practices, and having to meet the needs and expectations of diverse communities, such as Irish, Chinese, Polish and Nigerian. They described the transient nature of the population in an inner-city practice. It is interesting to note how the following interviewee refers to the new migrants as an 'influx', thus taking on dominant societal values:

> *When I started, we never had any of this, err, we now have lot of immigration from, err, Nigeria, Romania, Poland, Czechoslovakia and from Pakistan too. There was a lot of influx in between, err, year 2002 to 2006 when a lot of people came. We have got even people from Africa... sub-Saharan Africa. There is lot of migration, even Portugal. There is lot of influx, even a lot of people from France, they are sub-Saharan Africans, they are migrating, then we have got Somalis (gpm7).*

Evidence of perceptions of the doctors in the study regarding their doctor-patient interaction shows that different elements of both the doctors' and patients' identities intersected differently in different contexts. The findings of this study show that standard theories concerning the socio-cultural dimension of western medicine do not fully reflect the experiences of overseas-trained South Asian GPs. This is because the asymmetry in power relationships that is said to exist in clinical discourse is reversed in their interactions with white patients, whereby both bring an overlay of imperialism to the encounter.

The narratives show how the interviewees constructed their own identities in relation to their perception of white identities, which they experienced differently in different geographical and class contexts. The marginalised positions of both overseas-trained South Asian doctors and certain group of white patients led to the forming of symbiotic relationships, i.e. the insights have shown that they are more of a reciprocal nature than fuelled by medical dominance on the part of the professional.

British Identity

All the interviewees expressed a strong affinity with a British identity, although the reasons for this were complex. As a post-colonial people, already primed, they had a pre-disposition towards a sense of belonging to Britain; a nation they held in high esteem. The interviewees chosen were a select group of individuals, who has experienced pre-migration exposure to British education from an early age, a medical education model mirroring that of the UK, and positive reception in the UK, that had had a long lasting effect. The interviewees felt a deep affiliation with the UK, despite the fact that they experienced some level of exclusion. They constantly attempted to justify why Britain needed to prioritise their own medical graduates over the needs of overseas-trained doctors. There was a tendency to look at the bigger picture rather than dwell on individual experiences. There was also a sense of gratitude among all the interviewees towards Britain, whereby they could relate to the opportunities that Britain had offered. The following interviewee explains how he interprets his sense of belonging to Britain:

> *There is a saying in our culture that you should be' namak halal', which means one should be loyal to the benefactors, even if you have only had a pinch of salt from them. When I came, I only had £8 on me and now, with God's grace, I have achieved so much. My children have done well, I have a nice house, status in the community; medicine and Britain have been good for me (gp7s).*

Almost all of the interviewees used their own cultural interpretive framework to reflect on their experiences of being in a country that offered opportunities extending to the future generation:

> *When we came, we bought £3 with us... and there is a man here, his house is here, his whole family is here… he has got house everything... so, obviously for our children it is less struggle, so to establish... you built a house from £3... you achieved*

something, so you had to establish you can't get anything without struggling..., one good thing is there was opportunity here to do... if you worked that hard in India or Pakistan, it is not necessary that you would achieve, both of my sons are doctors, one is a consultant (gp5s).

With another interviewee stating:

I have been here so long that the question of belonging does not cross my mind anymore; I belong here and feel part of the society. My children were born and brought up here, they very much feel British. There are better facilities, no corruption, no dishonesty; life is as organised as I had heard about when I was in India (gp6).

For many of the interviewees, their daily encounters with society at large were different from those of their less privileged counterparts, as the former were perceived as being privileged as a result of their particular type of social and cultural capital that held them in good stead. It would appear from the interviewees' accounts that Britain had provided them with the distinct social status that they aspired to prior to migration. Several of the interviewees mentioned attending elite social events:

I love going to the Chelsea flower show and Royal Ascot every year (gp1b).

Positive individual experiences in comparison with the country of origin were cited for their attachment to Britain. The following interviewee talked about his deep pride when he received his OBE from the Queen:

In 2009, I was given an OBE.[9] *Yes, this is the picture at Buckingham Palace, you feel very proud, out of the whole country, including Wales and Scotland, I was the only GP in this year given an OBE. I was the community hero for my contribution to public services (gpm4).*

Others talked about their admiration of the ethos of the National Health Service, and also adapting to British values in their lives:

I think queues are good, whether it's queuing in the railway station or cinema or wherever, a queue is a queue it doesn't matter. There are a lot of things that are good about Britain and we all need to learn from it, and adopt those values, in particular, the National Health Service, which I think is admirable. Other nice things, punctualities and discipline generally, it used to be. It's all breaking down, err and they used to be very proud about their environment, the streets and so on so forth, now it's, it's as bad as any other rotten city anywhere else in the world. I do feel British, I feel happy that I have learnt a lot of good British values, and that doesn't mean I don't feel Indian. I know I'm an Indian I feel Indian, because I

[9] Officer of the Most Excellent Order of the British Empire (OBE)

grew up, my whole formative years were in India, but of course, I do feel British as well (gp2m).

Fairness and tolerance were referred to as British values in many interviewees' accounts, which one can argue is ironic given that they did not always experience them according to their own reported narratives. However, it suggests that the doctors in the study reflected on their experiences in comparison with either their countries of origin or others. For example, the following interviewee talked about discriminatory practices in other parts of the world, making Britain a better country:

There's good and bad things here. Good thing is if you came from Pakistan Bangladesh etc, or anywhere else, or from Wales or Scotland, the pay is the same, If you go to Saudi Arabia, there is a hierarchy, if you work in the middle east, Arabic speaking doctors get the highest pay and then other foreign doctors and then, the Indian Pakistani doctors. It's not fair, but they can do whatever they like, you see (gp3b).

The above images of Britain being fairer and more tolerant are partly based on the conditioning that people from ex-colonies have been exposed to, as previously discussed and partly due to personal positive encounters with individuals. The above findings support the assertion of Modood (1992, 273) that, despite Islam preaching for people to be valued for their virtues rather than their colour and race and while most Muslims contend that their religion is a genuine multi-ethnic one, Pakistanis' experience of Arab racism is such that they would rather work in Britain for less income than in Saudi Arabia for a higher one. The author refers to racial humiliation becoming a regular feature perpetrated by shopkeepers, taxi drivers and catering staff, experienced by diverse Islamic ethnic groups while performing a pilgrimage to Mecca. The interviewees' accounts showed a great deal of respect to British people for their adherence to the laws and procedures of the country. As one interviewee explains:

I had more problems with my own people than white people. You meet people who exploit you. When I used to do locum jobs, the practice partners used to make a big fuss when it came to payment. They would say, 'oh I am not running away somewhere, why are you in a hurry, I am here'. They did not appreciate that you have done work and you want to be paid on time. You see, the white doctor will never treat you like that, they adhere to the procedures. Many of our own doctors didn't follow the local procedures on employment; he will implement what he knows works back home (gp1m).

For some, Britain also offered a sense of security that they did not have in the countries of origin, because of cultural, religious and linguistic tensions:

> *My brother had already been to the UK, he said, 'go to Britain, the living conditions there are good, there is no discrimination on class basis there, if you are clever, you will make it' (gp6s).*

The account below shows that integration is a topic that is actively talked about among overseas-trained South Asian doctors:

> *I think when we sit with our own people, at times, you feel that [integration] missing, and somebody when talked to like this that we got to contribute to British society, then you are considered as 'oh what is he talking about?' I think that feeling ought to go away. We are here all my life and I came here when I was 25 years old, I'm now 61, so all of the good times of my life they have been spent in this society, good and bad, and who knows in India or Pakistan that 30-40 year time period, how these will have been spent, but this society has given me so much. I should be grateful to this society, which I think I am. We should as a community also, become a part of it, this is what integration is and these are the kind of values we want to give (gpm4).*

The interviewees were often keen to point out that they did not believe they had to give up their Indian or Pakistani identities to become part of the British society:

> *...that doesn't mean for even a second that where my warmth to my own country is concerned is lessened. That is even more, I would really want to do something for my society as well, but my duty to this society is perhaps as good as paramount, as... absolutely. I came voluntarily here, nobody forced us to come here, and this society, despite what you say, has given a lot to us. We just can't say that 'oh we've been treated as rubbish and slaves and exploited' and all, yes every society does, Indian and Pakistani are no less. When it comes to exploitation, the amount that happens there, there is no comparison, so we have to accept those things, then become a part of UK society (gpm4).*

Another interviewee who previously had said that his reasons for migration were related to political instability in India explained that Britain valued his abilities, which may never have happened in India:

> *Recognition, of my work, recognition of me as an individual is something, and perhaps I would have struggled getting that recognition back home. So in a way you see that, as I keep telling you, cream rises to the top, so when cream rises to the top everybody recognises that. So recognition, identity, whatever it is, they are still a lot better here and I'm proud of my British identity (gpm4).*

The interviewee's reference to *cream rises to the top* suggests that Britain in his view accords opportunities on merit. He explains that exposure to the British way of life has made him into a better person and that British society is not as corrupt as that in his country of origin:

I like to think, and this is again I'm not a 'hundred percent judge' of myself, but I like to think I'm a better person. I have something in me which I want to give, rather than taking anything. So I think in my view, in 30 years it made me a better person, erm now go back to our sub-continent I think the biggest thing, which is now hitting both India and Pakistan, is the societies' fabric has corruption in it. You can't get anywhere without really giving something to somebody. Our society is totally, is that a part of this society, answer is yes corruption is everywhere, but it's not to that level.

He compares the everyday reality in the country of origin and the UK:

... you can really still get on with what you really want to do in Britain; here you have no problems... not with milk, sugar, electricity, water or gas. How many times you would have gone to even the income tax office, you wouldn't have known where your income tax office is. Would you ever know who your super-intendant police man was? Would you? In India or Pakistan you will even know who the constables are, leave that, you would even know who the electricity man is... things are very very different and I think those kinds of positivities, we should appreciate of this society (gpm4).

His account below provides evidence of how he very much feels part of British society and is involved in the grassroots politics of the NHS, being committed to the enhancement of universal healthcare:

I'm very much involved in that looking into particularly public health issues, prevention and cure. If we really look into public health issues, even the expenses we were talking about in NHS, we can't afford it anymore, because of so many reasons, obesity related, respiratory related... alcohol related, these are preventable problems. We have to really concentrate our efforts on that, if we want universal healthcare to be sustained (gpm4).

The significance of the role of the media was apparent in several of the interviewees' accounts regarding a sense of belonging to Britain. It was often mentioned in a negative way, and associated with a detrimental portrayal of overseas-trained South Asian doctors. However, a couple of doctors mentioned contrasting experiences:

I got on very well with the local patients; I was often in the newspaper. Once, I was able to diagnose meningitis very quickly with a small baby and sent him straight away to hospital. After a couple of weeks, I was surprised to see the parents; they came with the Star newspaper photographer and wanted my photo with the baby. They said that the consultant had told them that, if I had not diagnosed and treated the baby quickly enough, the baby would not have survived and they were so grateful for what I was able to do for them. In another incident, a patient was operated on quickly, because I made an immediate referral. The patient came to the surgery with a bottle of wine after he recovered and said he was very grateful; he did not think of me as an Asian (gp4s).

His comments about bringing a bottle of alcohol as a gesture of gratitude was mentioned by several other doctors, who interpreted this experience as acceptance rather than being offended that their cultural identities had not been acknowledged. This act, for them, confirmed their professional as well as British identity.

Integration into the social fabric of the local community was evidenced in numerous accounts, which showed that despite, having multiple identities, often human relationships took precedence over any other social hierarchy:

I had a patient [white male] who was always cleaning the outside area of my medical centre. I did not even know this until one day, he came in to see me, his hands had scratches all over and were bleeding. I said to him 'what have you done to your hands?' He said, 'oh nothing much' and it was then that I found out that it was him. He said, 'I was just cleaning the bushes; actually, I want to keep your place tidy'. He died two weeks after and his wife was struggling a little after he died, I employed her as a cleaner, she became very friendly with my wife, it was like a mother-daughter relationship. I had many more positive relationships with local patients. I had 30% our own patients and 70% English patients (gp4s).

Beider (2011) argues that in much of the literature, individuals belonging to white working-class communities are variously portrayed as perpetrators of racial harassment, antagonistic to immigration and with fixed views. However, the account above and others in this study show that there can be a bond between individuals that is not always shaped by racialised experiences. The interviewees mentioned such positive encounters with patients with some passion. These were memories that they continued to treasure several years after their retirement:

Ability to understand one another, I think. Just by close contact and caring about them you see, interest in their family, their welfare, and that's how, I mean I'm just not gone there as just their doctor and come out. You go into details about how they're coping with their lives, their welfare, their next of kin, I mean their children. They get enough support from them or are they getting into any trouble with anyone else like social services... and so and then ,people, the elderly people living on their own and you feel sorry for them looking out for the 'meals on wheels' (gp1b).

The interviewee below talks about how she became 'bonded' with the families of patients:

So you go there and see all your patients and then, they tell you what goes on in their family. So by going, by talking to them, yes... yes, by talking to them they will tell me everything, what goes on in their family you see. So I would help as much as I could, whatever the system I needed to approach so that's how I became well bonded to the community. Even now when I go there, the little ones... 'Doctor, do you remember me? (gp1b).

Almost all the interviewees were able to recall occasions where they felt moved by having pleasant encounters with patients, which strengthened their sense of belonging to Britain:

Yes, one fella [fellow] really caught my... I mean it was so... it… really brought tears in my eyes. He waited for me, you know you see something, in the corner of your eyes, something is not... somebody is watching you.. so, this guy was just... I saw him.. he was.. in Meadowhall. I went into the shop, he stood right outside the step, outside the store.. so he stood there... he waited until...I came out, then he... ermm… he said 'excuse me... Aren't you doctor...?' he said… I said 'yes' and the minute I saw the face I knew that family, yes because I didn't see him eye to eye when I went into the shop... although I knew that... then he said 'Don't you remember, you... you looked after me "all" my childhood days, now I am working now'. It's a definite family..[mentions name], you see, then you see that face, everything comes back in your head, all that grandparents, mother... mother's name, father's name, and this child's name, everything. So, it was a nice gesture that he could remember me, and appreciate the service that was offered to him, as a doctor and as a family doctor. That family doctor was there at that time that bond was there, between the doctor and the family, so he was so grateful and he... family doctor, values were there more than I think nowadays (gp1b).

Notwithstanding the loyalty each individual felt towards Britain, one third of the interviewees also raised their concerns about the sheer inequality that they had personally experienced, mostly by the establishment, rather than the British people:

...45 years I have been living in this country. I have a British passport, in general terms, yes, I feel British. In real terms I also say 'yes', because local people also like us, the majority have worked in India and Pakistan… and Ethiopia. They are used to seeing the world population, and they do like us, the majority of them, but when the matter of your other things concern, we feel that there is somewhere some distinction, for example, we get reported too readily, why is it that we have more complaints than the locals? (gpm5).

He adds that that the duty also lies with the responsible bodies, if there are competency issues, especially when overseas doctors have stayed in the UK for a considerable length of time:

> *... we have British [professional] experiences, because we have been here for a considerably long time. We have got our postgraduate education in this country, so if we are failing to meet the standards then why are we failing. Local doctors have far fewer complaints. It is our view that, I will give one example, only one. There was someone [a white GP] who was alcoholic, living on drink, he would drink a bottle of alcohol and then, he would work. If any of us ever did that, we would not have been allowed to get away with that. He was reported, they called him, and said to him, 'don't put the alcohol bottle in a visible place'. He still continued drinking, he used to be so drunk that he would fall over, but nobody held him accountable. Not all of us can do that, if we get reported, it goes right through to the GMC direct. Then they investigate, if it's local doctors, they sort it out between themselves on an informal level. We feel under pressure, and to be honest with you, I have taken retirement for this reason, it's not my retirement age yet; I could have continued (gpm5).*

His account makes reference to 'we', which suggests that the above experiences are widespread, but individuals may be suppressing them, especially those who remain in employment:

> *I often felt that someone is peeping and seeing over my shoulder. I was extra cautious whenever I was prescribing. I was cautious in Pakistan too, but over there I didn't have this fear that I am being watched all the time, that somebody is watching you, what you are doing. I was investigated once for no valid reason like many of my friends and colleagues, but they did not find anything (gpm5).*

Migrants navigate or negotiate social pressures in the countries of settlement. They may face different social pressures from within their community either in the country of origin or country of immigration and in a variety of different settings (Bhabha, 1994). The following interviewee's account would suggest that the doctors negotiate identity both within the community and across communities:

> *I personally think that the problem lies with us. We Indians and Pakistanis are very very slow, culturally we are so much conscious of the other man or what will the neighbour say; he says what he says and let them say, For example, when we came here to live in this area, my friends, who I regard as very learned men, they were shocked as to where I was going to go to live when I said I am going to live in this area. They said, 'oh, you are very brave'. My friend said that I will be better off in an area where there are apne [own] people, plus you can buy a large house for £40,000 etc. I said it's a personal choice, if you want to stay in your area, you stay there, I am happy to stay here. I was not happy for my friend to be critical of my choice (gp8s).*

Interviewees' accounts suggest that some of them were directly caught up in community cohesion issues. For example, one interviewee believed that Asian women must learn English in order to integrate into the wider society, so he set up an initiative where his English female patients were linked up with Asian female patients. This was met with some resistance from Asian husbands, who objected to the inappropriate code of dress of the English women teachers who came into their homes. The interviewee being from a different religious background did not think there was any merit in those objections. Similarly, an interviewee talked at length about how he also resisted a suggestion made by the PCT for his practice sign to be translated into one of the South Asian languages and erected outside his practice. The gesture made by the PCT seems to suggest that, with such a gesture relating to an explicit inclusive practice in the area, it was not perceived in the same way by the interviewee. This may have been related to his personal prejudices towards a community that was different from his own in terms of class/culture/religion/linguistic background. The example shows the complexity of the issues involved in such dialogue.

Diaspora and Transnational Identity

In this section, I will discuss how interviewees constituted diaspora identities in the UK. Diaspora identity, as discussed previously, is based on a common ancestral homeland, one dispersed with a sense of marginality in the country of residence. The accounts of the majority of interviewees confirm that the bounded solidarity among them developed as a result of surviving in a racist environment. Two thirds of the interviewees, of both Pakistani and Indian origin, stated their interest in poetry and were actively engaged in collective poetry readings. The poetry verses they recited were from the South Asian poets of their era, in particular, Faiz Ahmed Faiz, a well-known Pakistani poet who wrote extensively in protest at the post-colonial conditions afflicting South Asia, such as continued poverty, the neglect of the poor, inequalities, injustices, hunger and oppression (Zulfiqar and Husein, 2011) . The type of poetry they recited would suggest that they used their love of literature to help overcome racism. One of the volumes of autobiography of African-American writer and poet, Maya Angelou (1997), *I Know Why the Caged Bird Sings,* in which she metaphorically refers to a bird that is struggling to escape its cage, illustrates how she turned to her literary work and seized upon the power of words to help her cope with racist oppression.

The poetry readings highlight the significance of the role of South Asian languages (Urdu/Hindi) and social spaces in promoting inter-group cohesion, which appeared fundamental for individual and group survival. Language appears to have played a significant role as a form of social capital in intergroup cohesion, and in the Urdu/Hindi medium poetry has been used to become revolutionised as well as to revolutionise others.

The view that shared experiences of being an immigrant enables diasporas to develop a sense of belonging to each other that may never have otherwise developed, is also supported by Saxenian's (2001) study of South Asian engineers in Silicon Valley. Their accounts in relation to how they integrated into the medical world, as well as into British society can also be described using the concept of 'professional diaspora', a concept applied by Neiterman and Bourgeault (2012) in their research study with immigrant physicians residing in Canada. The accounts of the interviewees suggest that they formed professional diasporas based on ethnicity as well as professional identity. Almost all talked about supporting other colleagues and friends who had had personal and professional difficulties. The following account shows how one interviewee was able to help another member of the diaspora, despite the fact that he held stereotypical views about Indian origin Hindu doctors:

> *I have Hindu friends, but I never ask them for help, because they never help their own, some of them come to me for help. Dr X [Hindu] was having problems getting into the local golf club, so he came to me and I introduced him and he managed to get in (gp2s).*

Many of the doctors were affiliated with professional networks and associations, some of the organisations being based on the country of origin, such as BAPIO and Pakistan Medical Association (PMA), whilst others pertained to overseas professional status, such as the Overseas Doctors' Association (ODA).

Ethnic clustering has been observed to occur among highly-skilled migrants in parallel with low/unskilled migrants. Bornat et al. (2009) draw attention to such clustering in geriatrics which was the result of an intersection of a number of factors such as discrimination, professional hierarchy, geography (the least desired hospitals) and client group (older people).The authors argue for the need to investigate the implications of such ethnic clustering. The process of ethnic clustering in general practice mirrors that of the above. Such diasporas served to support overseas-trained South Asian doctors in the study, helping them deal with contextual challenges, as seen above. The interviewees talked at length with regard to avoiding the formation of tight ethnic networks in their early years in Britain; however, the experience of racism appears to have contributed towards cohesion among them.

Brah (1996) argues that one subtext embodied in the diaspora is that of 'home', which continues to be a mythical place of desire in the diaspora imagination, that is, it remains a myth and hence, place of no return. On the other hand, 'home' is also about the 'lived experience' of a place, a locality, being deeply linked with how the processes of inclusion or exclusion operate and the subjective experiences that occur in particular localities. The findings related to place identity in this study support Brah's assertion. As the local structures in Barnsley were less inclusive when compared to Manchester and Sheffield, the interviewees from the foremost locale articulated a sense of belonging more to Britain than to the place itself. However, the interviewees in Manchester were more likely to experience overt racism, as the changing demography of the patient population did not appear to foster the same close bonds with patients and community that the interviewees from Sheffield and Barnsley talked so passionately about. The fact that they were the only group who mentioned their extensive involvement in transnational social entrepreneurship activities in their country of origin may be related to achieving social recognition elsewhere, as argued by various scholars, such as Vertovec (2002), Glick Schiller et al. (1992), and Vertovec and Cohen (1999) who refer to attachments that migrants maintain with persons, customs and interests which do not relate to the interests cultivated in the place of migration. Basch et al. (1994) also add that the racialisation of migrants in the USA that labels and disciplines them as such, leads them to seek alternative identities by means of cultivating transnational ties. Huynh and Yiu (2012) on the other hand, point out that realities at the ground level, prevent any interest and concern for the home country; such an assertion would certainly hold true for Barnsley.

Class Identity

Weedon (2004) states that class as a category of identity is significant in social contexts, in terms of ways of speaking and dressing, exclusive forms of education, cultural pursuits and membership of particular organisations and clubs. The author argues that class remains a key component of subjectivity and identity, with people certainly knowing the classes with which they do not identify, even if they do not explicitly acknowledge them according to how they are ascribed by social theorists Weedon (2004). Others have argued that, whilst this was once an over-riding aspect of identity, it is now in decline. However, in this study, the evidence suggests that this might not be the case among the South Asian communities as the majority of interviewees appeared to have a strong identity derived mainly from their own occupations. This can be evidenced by the following interviewee's account, which was echoed by many others:

There are very few of our own people here, but there are Asian doctors. You will probably know that doctors usually socialise with other doctors; they don't socialise with the general public (laughs). So, I never really felt isolated, because we had daily interaction with other Asian doctors, either in Barnsley or Sheffield (gp6b).

Class identity was also reflected in their attitudes towards investing in private education for their children as this was considered vital for class mobility. Rex and Tomlinson (1979, 15) argue that the class structure of British society provides opportunities for some sections of the Asian community that are not available to other immigrants. For instance, Asian professionals have choices open to them to either stay in the state system or send their children to private schools, whereas such choices are not available to working class Asian immigrants (Rex and Tomlinson, 1979, 160). In general, the interviewees were appreciative of the fact that they had been able to invest in their children's futures by enrolling them elite expensive schools and also having the the resources to pay for higher education, The majority of the interviewees were appreciative of the fact that their children had also made the choice to go into medicine. Such experiences facilitated their sense of belonging to Britain as it offered opportunities not only to them, but also, to the next generation. The following interviewee talks about the sacrifices he made to achieve his goal of investing in his children's education:

> *My children went to Wakefield School; [Independent] I had to do an 80 mile trip every day for school. We sent them to private school, because as you would know, we want our children to become professionals and a good education is a vehicle to fulfilling your dreams (gp3b).*

A number of interviewees talked about the negative experiences their children had experienced at school. However, only one identified it as racism when the child had been called a 'Paki', whilst others regarded it as bullying:

> *When we came back from Pakistan, we decided we would stay in this country. It was affecting my daughter's education She had been to a school already, but when she came here she went to a school in Chesterfield, she had some bad experiences, other children used to call her a dupper [stupid], they thought she didn't know anything (gp3b).*

There was a tendency among many interviewees not to accept racism as a possible explanation in similar situations. This seems to suggest that the external experiences were not validated by the internal beliefs held about a privileged identity. This denial may be related to protecting a system, which offered them the class privileges that their unskilled counterparts were denied. Cole and Omari (2003) argue that individuals actively shape class as they engage in different class practices across time and context. The majority of the interviewees were affiliated to organisations that are well known to perpetuate a more segregating than integrating role, for example, service clubs and private schools.

The interviewees may also have sought to shore up a privileged elite identity in order to compensate for an insecure racial one. Apart from membership of the Lions Club, one third of the doctors in this study said they either had been or were continuing to be Rotarians. One interviewee mentioned being invited to join the Rotary Club by a headteacher of a local school in the area where his practice was located. Farmer et al. (2003) point out in their study, how physicians were often associated with social groups that they perceived as being on a par with their professional standing. Very few of the interviewees' said their children attended state schools. They had the same goals for their children as they had for themselves and viewed education as the primary vehicle for upward mobility. This would seem to suggest the practice of closure and reinforcement of upper-middle class solidarity; however, the following account implies that this may also be an indication of the doctors navigating safe spaces through membership of BME communities, though this interviewee also highlights cultural difference:

> *Lot of my friends were involved in rotary clubs and this club and that club, but I was so involved in my practice and family that I didn't have much time on me. They wanted to integrate themselves and obviously they were not going to go to local working men's clubs, because they find that the education system was not there, they did not have the same habits, for example. All Asian don't drink that much, even if it's a Hindu doctor, he might only have a little bit, but not mad, like taking 17 pints every day, you see (gp9s).*

He adds that the working class male may not be as sophisticated or polite. His account shows the fear of being subjected to racial harassment:

> *They [Asian doctors] may have wanted to go to working class men clubs, but they might have been scared that people in those clubs may not have been so receptive. When people are drunk, they might be babbling and say something of a racist nature. You see, what soberness conceals, drunkenness reveals They may not be so nice, you know, they may be a bit abrupt, they may have not got the educational level, they don't know, many of them, how to behave sometimes, many of them are perfectly nice gentlemen. I have been to one or two working men's clubs, because some patients invited me, one was a wedding party, it was the first time ever I had the experience of going to a working men's club, they were perfectly alright type of people, you know...(gp9s).*

Social identities and differences are also constructed around bodily differences, such as race and gender, which can open or close spaces of opportunity (Laws, 1997a) .

Rich (1986) draws our attention to the fact that our experiences of everyday spaces are based on our material bodies. Whilst altering the mode of speaking and dress cropped up in many accounts, being undertaken to fit in, the above interviewee refers to being conscious of the embodied experiences of himself and the 'other', in this case the working classes and their social capital (manners and speaking), which was not appreciated by the middle class respondent.

Almost all the interviewees talked about meeting the complex healthcare needs of the Asian patients and communities. While there was evidence to show that many of the doctors in the study had tried to address their cultural and linguistic needs, there was also a tendency to describe the BME patients as challenging and more demanding than the white patients, in particular, Asian ones. One third of the interviewees referred to violence and oppression within the Asian community, as though it was epidemic and something the communities brought with them (Keskinen, 2009). The following shows that the interviewee believes in the existence of homogeneity in the culture of the women that she was dealing with, whilst asserting that they can change their position by refusing to be coerced:

> *Asian girls were being forced into arranged marriages and women were not allowed to take contraception by their husbands. There was this girl who came to me one time, her parents wanted to arrange her marriage and force her into it, even though she was born and brought up here [UK] and if she didn't want to get married there, why should she? I told her, 'if you don't want it, then no one can force you, you are an adult'. It took quite a lot of time to explain to the victim that the solution was in her hands, the control was within her hands and she had the power to do what she wanted and not be a victim, (laughs), and to stand up for yourself (gpm3).*

The interviewee's assertion that the girl was 'born and brought up in the UK' takes no account of the universality of violence against women, making the assumes that this is a land that has already achieved gender equality (Keskinen, 2009). The class identities of the interviewees were exposed in their accounts regarding Asian people, in particular Asian women, as evidenced in the following quotes:

> *I've seen women from lot of other Muslim countries, they really I think they are much more conservative here or have become over the last 10 years, than people in your Pakistan or in India. Even Muslims there in India they don't dress like this here and that's why you feel more different. I think you have to; you just can't have a very rigid appearance or your ideas, so you'll never mix up with anybody. Sometimes I get female patients and it's really difficult to even examine their ears as they are so fully covered (gp3s).*

Ballard (1979) and more recently Ang (2003) contended that a powerful strategy adopted by those who are marginalised or excluded from white structures or western hegemony is that of claiming one's difference and turning the readopted cultural identity into symbolic capital. Cultural resistance has long been an important part of Indian history. For example, the use of cultural symbols was utilised during the independence movement to combat the denigration and devaluation of their cultures experienced by Indian people who were perceived as 'uncivilised and uncouth' by the coloniser. This included Indian elites, such as Gandhi, who started wearing the traditional dhoti instead of western attire (Brah, 1985). The above excerpt illustrates that the interviewee had little comprehension that this adaptation of Muslim women may be a coping strategy, and a reaction to the rejection experienced in British society. The evidence suggests that the interviewee's strategy revolved, instead, around adopting a symbolic identity of their medical profession, rather than their cultural identity. It shows how elites' strategies differ from those of non-elites in dealing with racism. Class identity was also reflected in the interviewees' reluctance to talk about elite racism, which may have been related to their tendency to stick together with people from an upper-class background to convey upon each other rank and privilege (Evans, 1988). In addition to adopting the cultural elite practices of the mainstream British, many interviewees demonstrated their elite status within the South Asian group by reciting refined Urdu poetry during our interview. The interviewees' accounts reveal almost enclave living among the doctors in the study, which may have been used as a survival strategy while operating within a racist society. Survival by drawing on cultural capital in the form of class-based power and identities may have consequently contributed to the strengthening of class identity for its maintenance. Whilst caste did not crop up in any of the interviews, except where one interviewee commented that he believed that Asian educated people living in the UK had grown out of it, further study is required to explore class-based identities and how they intersect with the caste-based identities practised in the countries of origin.

Robinson (1986, 52) argues that differential access to political power and an unequal position in economic production as well as other markers produce cross-cutting affiliations that consequently lead to stratification in societies. The evidence in this study confirms such an assertion. The author draws attention to the fact that concepts, such as 'assimilation to the host society' or adoption of its values are problematic, given UK society is an amalgamation of sub-groups with varying attitudes, values, aspirations as well as political and economic power.

Hybrid Identity

It is often assumed that the relationship of post-colonial people to Britain commenced only at the point when they or their ancestors embarked on their journey to Britain, thus failing to take into account their exposure and conditioning under colonial rule (Sayyid, 2004). As discussed previously, the interviewees talked about being educated at the English medium-stage schools and their medical education being based on the British model. The interviewees' frequent code-switching between English and their first language is one example of their sociolinguistic hybrid identities (Bhatt, 2013). Almost all talked about the ease they felt with their hybrid identities and as one put it:

> *I am proud to be Indian of my roots, but I am equally proud to be British and to be in England. I am a Hindu, but not a strict one; I pray at home and celebrate our festivals (gp2b).*

The following poetic account shows an awareness of hybrid identity:

> *Hum Log Sumandar Ke Bichrey Huey do Sahil hein*
> *Is Paar Bhi Tanhai Us Paar Bhi Tanhai*
> *[Translation: we people are like the two separated seashores that feel apart from each other]*
> *The people from there [India] say you live in England now and become Valaytey [Westernised] and the people from here say we are Hindustani or Pakistani... (laughs) that feeling is there. Yes that is there, love for home country (gp5s).*

Another female interviewee talks about how she chooses what to wear in different contexts. The layout of a consultation room in Britain differs to that of in India and she decides on the appropriate code of dress in the context of her professional conduct in the UK:

> *I never wore a sari to general practice, because I felt sort of very conscious about it, because I think this Indian sari is not right. It's not practical, although you have to, you don't cover yourself, every part of your body, it is open here and there and particularly when you are dealing person to person in a consulting room that's not on; so I never wear saris (gp1b).*

Similarly, she chooses to assert her middle-class identity in a different context:

> *... but in all the social functions, I wear only a sari. Even now, I am thinking of going to Royal Ascot; I will wear a sari (gp1b).*

For some, Britain has provided a sense of security that they did not have in their country of origin and they seemed able to integrate both aspects of their identity in their daily practices without any conflict. The following interviewee, in his previous narrative, had acknowledged the negative aspects of being in Britain and talked extensively about his experiences of racism, whilst also formulating a balanced view of Britain:

> *... this government is good in some respect. There is some good points about this government as well and we must appreciate, you are free to worship, whatever faith you have, it does not matter, your faith is with you, your job is separate, it does not matter, okay, also, I go to bed hoping that, God forbid, if I have a heart attack or stroke, I will wake up in the house and not in a prison or somewhere. OK security is there, in India or Pakistan, as you would know, security is not there and most of other countries as well. So, I am thankful to God that we are where security is, so, yes I do belong to England and I have had a British passport and nationality since the 1970s (gp9s).*

His account below also shows that the media only portrays a stereotypical image of mosques in the UK:

> *Well, I belong to England now. I have no qualms about it now. I tell you I celebrated her majesty's jubilee fantastically, the mosque I went there, we put hundreds of bunting all over there, British flags both sides, union jacks and a big picture of the queen. We had a big dinner there, OK. I belong to a community called the Ahmedia Community. You have got to, my own belief is that you believe in Allah, Mohammed, his prophet (peace be upon him) and beside this you follow other duties placed on you. For example, give charity, observe Ramadan and so on. After this, you must also be loyal to the government in which you are living in, this government. (gp9s).*

Regarding identification with British identity, the interviewees frequently evaluated new situations through their old frame of reference, which was their own cultural/religious value system and they drew meanings from what they already knew:

> *Adaptation...that question is very debatable, very hot question. If you take the religious point of view, there is a story that Umar Ibn Khattab [the second Caliph of Islam] was going from one city to another and was wearing silk that day. People objected and said to him, 'hey, how come you are wearing silk when Islam forbids men to wear silk?' He said, 'the area that I am going to go, they wear silk there'. So, my learning from that is that 'jaisa desh waisa bhais' [equivalent to 'if you are in London, do as the Londoners do'].*

As discussed in Chapter 1, the motivation to come to the UK was to advance their knowledge of western medicine; however, several interviewees from both Muslim and Hindu faiths talked about how they incorporated their own religious identities into the medical professions and strived to become good doctors.

For example, the following interviewee makes links with the deliberate instructions of Prophet Mohammad:

For me, it's[being a doctor] a form of worship. It's sunnah[10] *to treat others, our prophet often treated sick people (gp7b).*

Another interviewee explained how he integrated his religious teaching into his work:

I also believe in spirituality alongside the bio-medicine model of treatment. I would often write a verse from the Quran on prescriptions, which was a prayer for healing and was appreciated by white patients too. You see, we all walk separate roads in life, but we have a golden bridge called duas [prayers] that link our lives together. Once a white patient came up and asked me what this Arabic verse meant. I explained it was a prayer from me that may he be granted good health. He was very happy to hear that (gp7s).

The above accounts lend support to Parekh's (2007-133) assertion that religious identities constitute the axis of one's life and that such identities provide an overarching framework within which individuals define and relate to their other identities.

Dadabhoy (2001, 63), a British born South Asian GP, refers to the pressures from both the white and Asian community concerning integration and describes how he experienced a culture of 'all or nothing', where his white friends had stereotyped him as an 'extreme misogynist' for his wish to adhere to Muslim religious observance, and where he was conscious of being labelled a 'coconut' by his Asian friends, if he mixed in predominantly white circles.

A few of the interviewees described some aspects of their everyday life that would fit with Mimicry Theory. That is, they could be classed as 'mimicking', for example, membership of rotary and golf clubs. One interviewee proudly stated how they call their daughter by the English name given to her by an English nanny, who could not pronounce her Indian one. This could be interpreted as an integration attempt by some or within the context of mimicry by others.

Many of the interviewees appeared to be conscious of cultural racism, believing that one should not make oneself appear too conspicuous in the UK which may suggest a coping strategy or a personal choice to integrate into British society:

In my opinion, Indians and Pakistanis are keeping their culture in this country, which I don't think is proper, because the culture is different; the dress is different. You have to adapt to the way of life here (gp8s).

[10] The teachings of the Prophet Mohammad (The Fiq of Medicine, 2001)

The above views were shared by two thirds of the interviewees, who believed that one should adapt to new ways of life and not impose their own way of thinking on others. They believed that adhering to a cultural code of dress can be overbearing for 'locals'.

The interviewees' accounts show that they negotiate belonging discursively and by the repositioning of self. Many talked about playing a role concerning the unmet needs of their own communities, whilst also contributing to the enhancement of community cohesion by connecting individuals with institutions:

> *I used to teach Asian children the Quran, because there was no proper system for religious teachings. They were children of Indian, Pakistani, Bengali Muslim families. I have been a chaplain for a long time and I visit patients in all of the hospitals in the city. Sometimes when someone dies and there is no relative for Muslim families around, I also organise for a Muslim burial (gp7s).*

For many of the interviewees, the construction of social belonging involved the freedom to be able to maintain their multiple identities:

> *... if you can be Indian you can, you can work in Britain, you know if you are, if you are okay... your language is alright, your language ability... if you are you know good in your job, you know, if you do it err, what is the word? Conscientiously… and you keep a relationship with your colleagues, your friends you know professionally as well as erm, I don't see any problem or any. Why should you have to lose any identity or anything? You can be an Indian, you can be a doctor, you can be a you know, a student, you can be a psychologist and you can maintain a relationship. You don't have to lose, you can still you know you can still celebrate your Eid, Diwali whatever, you know in your own time and place and you can still be a very good professional (gp3s).*

He places emphasis on 'work' as a medium that enhances his sense of belonging:

> *I feel that I provide, I contribute to the community, you know in whatever way little way I do and I feel part of it, yeah,. I think my work is important. I'm working here of course and...the relationship I've developed and the knowledge I have gained over the years (gp3s).*

The interviewees' accounts show how their personal and social identities have been formed in the UK. They talked about how they were able to navigate their multiple identities on a daily basis with relative ease. As one put it:

> *I am Indian and Hindu. I go to Sheffield sometimes, because there is a Hindu temple. I also go to Leeds, Bradford. No problem, it does not bring any conflicts to*

my daily life. I bring my grocery and meat from Asian grocers in Sheffield, even though I don't have to have halal meat (gp6b).

Brah (2007), however, argues that there remains a failure to recognise that identity work is never complete, being always in flux. The following interviewee's account supports such a view:

Britishness? That was the question asked by my accountant, because I wanted to emigrate altogether to India, because of the tax situation, purely that. I raised this question, what are the things I have to do? If I want to emigrate to India... and then she said 'Oh you should not have any property at all here', I said when I come here where can I stay, she says 'You stay with your daughter', I said 'That's not on, I'm not going to lose my independence after all these years, I've got to have a property'. Then she asked me, 'Which is your home? Is India your home or is England is your home?' I told her I have lived in this country longer than I lived in India; England is my home. Then she said 'You are not going to go to India to settle'. I just left it like that (gp1b).

Her account below shows that one's phase of life also has an impact on one's identity. For example, her retirement and being a widow brought new challenges for her:

We used to do all our shopping from Asian grocers, I'm not so bothered now because I have to go to Rotherham. So I mean, when we were family, my husband used to go to the Indian shop, but now I rarely go... I still have Indian food, yes.... I make my own chapattis, rice, daal, and I go to an Indian shop, but I get a big packet, which will last for one year, so that is there and err vegetables, I don't miss much. Maybe when I go I get that Bhindi (Indian vegetable], yes, yes, spinach I will get it, coriander and surprisingly that Indian shopkeeper, she was asking me, 'Why you want to buy coriander, don't you grow coriander at home?' you see... It put a shame on me (laughs), I could have done so; I'm going to make some effort (gp1b).

Her account shows how she negotiates her cultural identity and the choices she makes in terms of the type of food she can do without. It also shows the social aspect of going to an Asian shop, where she has a rich cultural encounter with the shop assistant, who appears to know her well. She talks about experiencing the social isolation that has been created not only by the context (pre-dominantly white), but also, its intersectionality with other layers, such as gender roles, being a widow, and being single within Indian culture:

I miss social gatherings, yes, I miss quite a lot. That's right, it's not like that, even then, those days we used to invite all the doctors here, we used to have just a great time but now it's all stopped. I don't know why, even I haven't invited all those. I

> *mean, when you are in the profession, once my husband passed away I didn't want to do that, that is the main reason for me, because being single, I don't, but one thing I miss are the social gatherings like so many weddings, so many functions we used to go to, my brothers and sisters [In India] full of praise for all the functions, which I miss it, very much so I really miss that part of... family social gathering. Yes I miss it, we have friends, lot of friends, at the end of the day we are all friends, but that family gathering is zero here, no one… which I miss quite a lot (gp1b).*

The empirical evidence shows that the individuals in the study have a strong sense of linguistic, cultural and in many cases, religious identity, but identities are not in competition with each other and in fact, different sources of identity are seen as mutually reinforcing, rather than mutually exclusive.

Identities are Plural

This chapter discussed empirical evidence related to socio-cultural integration and explored the post migration experiences of the doctors in the study. The first part of the chapter described the specific contextual characteristics of the case study areas as well as the demographic characteristics of the doctors in the study, looking at how the interviewees came to settle in their respective areas and develop a sense of place. The interviewees' residential choices showed integration with the local populations, including the white population with a similar class background. However, in the majority of the cases, this included people of similar ethnic backgrounds and the formation of clusters and networks for mutual support.

The impact of migration on the racial, cultural, religious and linguistic aspects of the doctors' identities was examined in terms of how such identities evolved and were expressed in the context of changing needs and opportunities. The findings highlight how the doctors in the study had adapted to new environments, embedding themselves in local structures. However, the degree of involvement varied, according to how inclusive such places were in relation to their acceptance minority communities. All the interviewees strongly identified with a sense of 'Britishness', evaluating their experiences in the context of their own cultural/religious interpretations together with positive experiences in the UK. Where the local structures were less inclusive, transnational identities were more salient than in more inclusive places. The empirical evidence has shown that, while many interviewees referred to dealing with pressures from both white and Asian communities concerning the extent of integration, their own cultural, religious and linguistic identities posed no competition with their newly constructed diasporic identities and British identities. The discussion in this section has shown the complexity involved in the formations of identities, with the notion of one national identity (British) being challenged. The exercise of separating identities under subheadings was a challenging task in itself, given the fact that they are inter-related and experienced simultaneously. The evidence shows that multiple identities appear to have reinforced the interviewees' overall sense of belonging to Britain and being British, but with a sustained attachment to their country of origin.

CHAPTER 5

EXPERIENCES OF RACISM AND COPING STRATEGIES

Evidence suggests that all migrant workers are exposed to some form of prejudice by individuals and institutions. Discrimination experienced by black and minority people in the housing, education and employment sector in the UK has been well documented. Whilst the literature is sparse on the mundane experiences of elite migrants, various scholars have drawn attention to the structural inequalities embedded in the NHS that overseas-trained South Asian doctors encounter. Esmail (2007) describes the inequalities experienced by overseas-trained South Asian doctors whilst working in the lower status 'Cinderella' services of the NHS. Earlier studies have had a tendency of perceiving the problems in the context of structural inequalities, rather than institutional racism.

In this chapter, I will provide an exploration of the doctors' own perceptions and experiences of racism together with an analysis that is grounded in their own accounts. The doctors were asked whether they had ever experienced any overt or covert instances of racism in their personal or professional lives. In order to elaborate upon what constitutes racial harassment, I adapted examples from Collins (2001, 171) in *Racism in Medicine* (See Appendix)

Initial responses were interesting as almost all the doctors in the study denied experiencing overt or covert racism, appearing to believe that racism did not impact on the doctor-patient relationship. Their responses seem to fit in with what Beagan (2003, 612) refers to as 'professional socialisation', which aims to produce neutral doctors for neutral patients with a belief that one must, as a standard of clinical practice, treat everyone neutrally, and objectively, as if they were cultureless, classless, raceless and genderless. Denial may well also be related to the high level of confidence that they possessed and their middle class status (Shaw, 2010). I challenged this belief of social neutrality by sharing of my own experiences as a social worker, which allowed the interviewees to open up.

In Barnsley, a common belief among the interviewees was that professional identities mediated ethnic identities and that the low-level ethnic density was also a protecting factor:

We had a lot of respect here because we were professionals; the patients had a lot of respect for us. I think this will happen where you have more Asian community; here in Barnsley, it was only the Asian doctors here. They [public at large] did not see us as threats in the same way that they will, if it was someone, for example, a general public person from the Asian community (gp6b).

Many of the interviewees' accounts suggested that professional identity predominates when the area has no minority population. Ethnicity in such contexts also created social capital, mitigating the hostility that many black people may otherwise be subjected to:

In the village the community is very close-knit. The only non-white persons in Barnsley in the 1960s were Asian doctors and if the locals saw you in that time, they will think that you are a doctor and would respect you (gp3b).

The interviewees' own analysis as to what encourages the development of prejudice was the competition for welfare resources in ethnically dense areas, such as housing, employment, healthcare, education and benefits, a view also supported by Bonnett (2000, 132), who refers to the 'white backlash' against multiculturalism. Vaughan and Robinson (1986) refer to the responses of white middle and working-class people to immigrants. The former ensured that the pre-existing colonial relationship with Asians was maintained, with the demand for cheap labour, while offering little social acceptance or resources, whereas the latter perceived immigrants as direct threats to their identity. The white working class was forced into situations where they had to share jobs, houses, neighbourhoods, schools, and other scarce resources with immigrants, who they had been told to regard as inferiors. The white working class, as a result, engaged in exclusionary closure to both the middle class and immigrants. Exclusion towards immigrants took the form of prejudice and discrimination. Tyler (2012), in her ethnographical study, explored the entwining of discourses of race, class and coloniality within Leicester, a multicultural city and a suburban English village in the countryside of Leicestershire. The author asserts in her study that white working-class people were able to make distinctions between non-respectable white racists and Asian doctors, who they perceived as respectable British Asians. The following account would suggest that although not being directly subjected to racism, these experiences took place within earshot:

I think, odd ones sometimes do, you know, people say you are a Paki and you are something, but we never had any problems (gp6b).

Some of the interviewees seemed to have a very simplistic view of what amounted to discrimination. For example, a female interviewee stated:

> *Well, I mean once I got the job, you see, there was no question of discrimination. I mean it's as simple as that. I mean, I didn't have it; maybe other people have had it. No, it didn't happen to me (gp4b).*

This apparent lack of awareness of diversity issues may be related to the culture of the NHS at the time when such issues were not actively promoted. The interviewees also tended to make constant comparisons with their experiences in the country of origin, where it was difficult to secure jobs. In her account, the previously cited interviewee had earlier described an incident where she was threatened by the white boyfriend of a female patient, who was adamant that his girlfriend should not be hospitalised even though she was miscarrying a baby. She describes the incident, in which privilege and marginality intersect:

> *It was in the middle of night when I visited this female patient [white]...her boyfriend took a gun out from his pocket..., I said, 'What are you doing?' He said, 'If you don't do what I want you to do, I will shoot you.' I calmed him down, spoke to him, I said, to be on the safe side it would be best, if she could be admitted in hospital, but he wasn't letting her go, because his idea was probably who was going to cook him food but when I closed the door I was really quite worried and afraid, at the time. I didn't know it was a toy gun; I thought it was a real gun (gp4b).*

She talks about the response of the police:

> *The next day the police went to check and they said the family are in a mess they don't know what they're doing, their house is filthy, and then that man showed the policeman what kind of gun it was, it was a toy. I dropped the charges, because you have to work with the same community and it goes against you, the word gets round, you see...(gp4b).*

It appears from her account that the approach she adopted was more of a coping mechanism in a context where there was little acknowledgement of race issues. She was aware that she had to continue working in that community without the police holding her hand, and that *the word gets round, it goes against you* suggests anxiety about possible victimisation. The police in this incident appear to have taken a lenient stance, even though the incident as described above, seemed to be a serious criminal case with aggravating features, such as a female public servant being threatened with an offensive weapon (regardless of it being a toy or real gun, the perception of the victim at the time is paramount), gratuitous degradation of the victim, and the time of the offence. However, the police's failure to take any action was not seen as a major issue by the interviewee, which suggests that she may consciously or unconsciously have lower expectations of the police, like many of her counterparts within the Asian community in the UK. It is a well-known fact that the criminal justice system operates differentially towards racialised groups (Kalra, 2006). The above lends support to Ahmed and Mukherjee's (2012) argument that privileged South Asians, despite class difference, share not only cultures, religion and languages but also their sub-ordinate status as colonised subjects with their working class counterparts in Britain. Vaughan and Robinson (1986) emphasise the significance of considering the causes of prejudice in the context of colonialism and the type of social contact it produced with the colonised. John and Rex (1979) stress the need for adopting a historical approach when analysing such encounters. Lahiri (2000,xii) argues that:

> *Imperial/colonial relations are no longer located exclusively in the context of a colonial backdrop; Britain also serves as a 'space of colonial encounters'.*

More recently, Tyler (2012), in her own ethnographical study, argues that older white people have memories of working in colonial institutions, which confirms that *relics* from the empire remain dormant in the UK landscape. This was evidenced in the following interviewee's account, when he was taken by surprise to meeting a patient in a remote British city, who had visited his hometown. He states:

> *Many of my patients were ex-service men who had served in India back in the colonial days. I was quite surprised when one of them [patients] told me he had been to my home town Mirpur; finally we made some connection. We had a good chat; he told me about our shortcomings, I mean what[he believed] was wrong with our countries (gp8b).*

Whilst a definitive interpretation of the conversation described above cannot be made, it can be argued that the fact that the interviewee could only recall the conversation in that context is a strong indication that of how it happened and that the perception of the interviewee was that the patient believed the fault lay with the developing countries rather than the process of colonisation.

Two doctors mentioned that they had heard that some Asian doctors had had negative experiences at the hands of patients, remembering the publicity it attracted and the pressures placed on the doctors as a result. It is possible that the interviewees found it difficult to discuss their own experiences and instead, talked about colleagues' experiences. This may have been due to a number of things, such as their own denial, discomfort, gender and age issues impacting on the interviewee process, as well as social desirability.

One interviewee talked about the experiences of a doctor who was a neighbour. A common approach when such incidents were described was to emphasise that the wider public was not intentionally bad and the doctors choosing to self-distance from such experiences. The interviewee below did not wish to elaborate upon his experiences:

> *By and large, people are not bad, this is my sum up, but some who are; they are very cunning and very clever. I never had any untoward response from patients, but you never know what's inside people's mind. Others do experience it. My neighbour, a Sikh doctor was put in trouble. He was accused of sexual harassment and was later acquitted after 18 months, because it was never there in the first place. Another Pakistani doctor had to close down his surgery because of problems (gp8b).*

Experiences of racial prejudice from other professionals and establishment bodies were only mentioned by one out of eight doctors, who explicitly talked about experiencing racial prejudice from a member of staff in the practice. The doctor quoted below explains the differential treatment he and other Asian partners at the practice received at the hands of their own practice manager:

> *There were three of us Asians, and one English partner. The English partner was very good, like a father to us, we never had any problems with him, but the practice manager [English] was very bad to all us Asians. She would treat us badly, sometimes not issuing cheques, like our salary. The pay wasn't very huge anyway that you couldn't save for the next month. So, you needed the money and whenever you asked for it, she will say,' oh I haven't got time to do the cheque' and here we are suffering because of it. So, we all decided that her behaviour was not reasonable and we sacked her. We had taken advice from the BMA and did it properly. We gave her advance notice etc., but she took us to an employment tribunal. In the tribunal, the same representative who was supposed to support us actually supported her (gp6b).*

The interviewee's account would suggest that as a group the Asian doctors were vulnerable and experienced victimisation on the basis of their race. As the perpetrator of the harassment was white, she was supported by institutions, such as the trade union and media. Even though another interviewee stated that he had had a positive experience from the BMA concerning his pension benefits, the role of the organisation was criticised for its discriminatory practices when it came to supporting its members in race discrimination cases. For example, in 2002, the BMJ[1] reported that the BMA had to pay £815,000 in damages for indirect racial discrimination. The interviewee cited above described being subjected to victimisation from the

[1] BMJ 2002;324:1541.2. http://www.bmj.com/content/324/7353

aforementioned complainant, to which the media also contributed; however, the good relations that had been built with patients and the community over a lengthy period were sustained:

> *She won her constructive dismissal case, not only that, the newspaper published stories about our practice, that we mismanaged the practice etc. She told the press many things which were not true. It was very embarrassing, the real issue got lost and our practice issue became the focus. We were going to sue her, because she had spread rumours about our practice and got the media involved; she had to pay back the compensation that she was awarded because she breached her agreement. Fortunately, we had a very good reputation in the community and patients did not take much notice of it (gp6b).*

In general, the interviewees in Sheffield were also reluctant to talk about racism. Instead their narratives tended to centre on constructing themselves as successful professionals. The majority were of the opinion that white patients, having made an informed choice to join their practice, did not have any negative attitude towards them. However, when probed further, a few could recall some incidents where the ethnicity of the physician did matter. In general, it was often the positive experiences that interviewees described at length.

The realities of working in a rundown urban area, in which fear of racism, was real were described by several of the interviewees in Manchester and Sheffield:

> *I am not conscious of racism usually, but I used to keep some verses from the Quran in my pocket to ward off danger. It was s rough area, drug dealing, prostitution, pimps, domestic violence, child abuse, you name it, it was everything....I once went to visit my Hindu doctor friends in their practice, what did I see? Both husband and wife were hiding under the table, because they were being physically attacked by some white drug users (gp2s).*

The above account is interesting in that the interviewee denies being 'conscious' of racism, however, his described action is contradictory, as keeping Quranic verses in his pocket as a protective shield is a pre-mediated action. Two other interviewees also mentioned incidents during which they were physically threatened by unknown drug users, who had barged into the practice and demanded drugs. These incidents were only casually mentioned and it appeared that the interviewees expected to be able to take these in their stride.

Many of the incidents described often involved people not known to the interviewees and occurred during evening home visits in deprived areas known for criminal activities. The following interviewee refers to the unease of some of his white patients and having faith in God:

When I was working in the deputising services, because I was Asian, sometimes I sensed that people were worried about the quality of their treatment, but it was OK with God's grace. An example is when a patient had had an attack at home and I had to see them before hospital admission. You could tell by their body language, their eyes, their one or two remarks, that they were anxious and may be thinking what is he giving me as a treatment. When they felt better with the medicine I had given, they were equally glad and happy as well afterwards (gp9s).

Interviewees also noted that white patients often seemed to have a preference for an Asian doctor:

I noticed that English patients, once they had had an Asian doctor, they were likely to have an Asian doctor even though they had moved areas. On their medical record, you get a history of their GPs and you only see Asian names. I think we gave them better pastoral care, we did not tell them off, we were not patronising; we gave them good service (gp11s).

While the majority of the interviewees when further prompted acknowledged experiences where they may have been subjected to racism, one interviewee was adamant that he had never experienced it:

There was no such thing. I did not experience any racism myself, neither had I seen any discrimination nor did I contribute towards racism. I did have some difficulties, but I got there, as compared with India and Pakistan, there was a different atmosphere. There was all money and there was all officers asking this, asking that and they were catching you on little things (gp8s).

The same interviewee later stated that a white patient had told him off for arriving later than he had anticipated and that he had called for a home visit on a trivial matter, which did not even need one. The patient had also told him that people like him had taken over their [British people's] jobs. Upon further probing regarding experiences of discrimination, it appeared that he had somewhat internalised racism. The concept of internalised racial oppression pertains to racial beliefs and stereotypes of the mainstream society shaping how individuals think about others of a similar racial background (Pyke and Dang, 2003). This participant stated that he had been a president of the local BMA branch and was critical of the role of the Overseas Doctors Association (ODA):

...those things do happen, in a nutshell those things do happen, but we must also look in our own graban [means 'neck', a common Indian expression meaning examining our own actions]. There was ODA, it was their duty to remind them that it's also your job to be vigilant, to be fair to their job, to uphold the medical

profession. I remember I was also framed in a case; all I had to do was that I am sorry, I did it. I was told by someone that I was set up and I should defend my case; I didn't want to use the race card, I was so ashamed that I was capable of doing what I did, I immediately said I am sorry that I did it (gp8s).

In the above account, his use of language such as 'framed' and 'set up' would suggest that South Asian doctors may have been targeted, which in itself, would be classed as a racist practice. His criticism of the role of the ODA also evidenced his allegiance to the BMA. The BMA has been openly criticised for lack of support by its black and minority members in race discrimination cases. For example, in 2002, the BMA were ordered by an employment tribunal to pay £815,000 compensation to an Asian surgeon after the association refused repeated requests to assist him in race discrimination claims (Dyer, 2002).

For the above interviewee vehemently to deny any existence of racism when he was also an ex BMA branch president implies him playing a tokenistic role within the organisation.

There was a tendency among the doctors in the study to search for almost scientific levels of proof for experiences that could be classed as racist in nature. This may be related to their individual coping mechanisms, which may have been provoked by their particular professional background and class position becoming entwined:

I never experienced racism from anyone. There was one time that a male English patient came to register with the practice, he asked the receptionist who the doctor was and the receptionist pointed towards me. The patient walked out and said he did not wish to register, and that was that. But I cannot say he was being racist as there could be many reasons as to why he did that. He maybe wanted someone that he could relate to in terms of language and culture just as we do. Based on that experience, I think that the patients who were registered in my practice did not hold prejudices as they were free to go elsewhere (gp11s

Interviewees in Manchester and Sheffield were more likely to talk about negative experiences with local NHS bodies. The following interviewee talks in detail about how a campaign was instigated against several of his colleagues of both Pakistani and Indian origin, in which they were subjected to racial harassment leading to their dismissal:

I know there was a time when they were getting at Asian doctors, most of them were single handed and they got rid of all of them one by one. I can name all of them…all of them were single handed you see. What they used to do was that everything they (PCT) did was done in such a way that you could not put a finger on it. What they will do you see, in the case of Dr W, I know, they sent this girl whose job was to monitor a few things you know and what she was doing basically was trawling through the notes and finding out. He might have done it, but he has not recorded it, so these small things, they accumulated the evidence and said you are not competent enough. You are not looking after patients; you should be going and they made a reasonably strong case (gp9s).

He provides detailed information about the case of a friend, who he had accompanied in such procedures:

When his suspension ended, he came back to his practice; they said to him, 'look before you take the practice, we want to see you at the FPC office'. The meeting started, the chief executive went straight into options, he said, 'Dr Y, I give you two options, one is either you resign now, if you don't, I have got these 25 cases, while you were away for two months where you have lagged behind'. You see, I would say that if you take me to a practice today and ask me to find cases, I will give you 25 cases, you go and see the patient in the middle [emphasis] of the night, you don't always remember every bit of it in the morning to write down. OK, yes, you come in the morning and you might even forget the diagnosis (gp9s).

He goes on to explain that the treatment of Asian doctors differed in different eras with similar incidents taking place in different cities:

There was a time when we were desperately needed, e.g. I was asked to apply for the job and then came a time that they did not want us. It was because we grew in numbers. Racism exists and you cannot deny that; it's present in every stage. But it is often underground and sometimes it erupts like a volcano; it comes to the surface, ok and then it subsides. Within one year, one by one, they got rid of five to six Asian doctors in Sheffield. I know this because I was involved in helping them out. They might have got rid of me too, but what happened was one doctor asked me to take him to the GMC. He escaped from there, but his health deteriorated and then the poor fellow retired. But after that they (the PCT) slowed down in their vindictive campaign. I got a phone call from a friend in Glasgow, he was experiencing the same thing in the same way at the same time, they got rid of nine Asian doctors, who were running single handed practices in one year (gp9s).

His account appears credible for its detailed nature. He mentions the names of individual doctors who experienced enormous difficulties and suspension. The individuals mentioned in his account include both Pakistani and Indian origin GPs, some of them interviewees in this study. However, they did not discuss such issues at length and their initial reluctance to be interviewed might have been related to such negative experiences. The interviewees who had been subjected to such humiliating experiences may have found it difficult to talk to a researcher. One other interviewee also talked about ongoing difficulties with the PCT, while the remaining nine did not mention experiencing any particular problems. Two others (Indian origin, Hindu) mentioned a disproportionate number of complaints made against Asian doctors going through to the GMC, rather than being dealt with at the local level.

The majority of interviewees in the Greater Manchester area described being subjected to racist experiences while carrying out deputising services, where they often felt threatened by the white male partners of patients. Many of the doctors recalled being asked to do home visits for trivial matters. Two of the interviewees also felt that complaints against Asian doctors were sometimes based purely on cultural/linguistic differences, rather than poor practice, and they felt at a disadvantage when defending themselves, in comparison with white doctors. Cultural identity was also said to be a bonus in some circumstances. One interviewee explained that he had received preferential treatment from colleagues and patients:

> *...they very often used to be very appreciative that err doctors from the Indian subcontinent is... is taking so much care and giving them so much more attention and to... to their needs, their... their health needs and so on, in their view more than their own kind (gpm2).*

The account below shows how one GP chose to recall positive experiences rather than dwell on negative ones, and while he acknowledged the experience of racism, he did not see it as part and parcel of the wider society. Rather, he sought a clinical diagnosis:

> *So the question of, in my experience, the question of being an, an Asian and getting discriminated against by white patients didn't happen. Yes, it did happen once or twice, through people with personality problems, but they're not reflective of white people generally. Occasionally, I can't even think how many... less than two or three times, the converse has happened, erm, sometimes when we've had locums the, the patients who've seen... they were white doctors, and then they will come back within a few days and say 'I don't want to see another white doctor ever again'; that sort of thing (gpm2).*

The interviewees' responses exposed the discomfort involved in sharing experiences of racism. Their reflections showed that they had to work through several layers of professionalism and class attitudes. In several of the accounts, reference was made to the possibility of making one's own life better, and that hard work would cancel out any negativity, which shows the prevalence of a middle-class attitude.

Experiences of racism from colleagues or other professionals have been documented anecdotally by South Asian doctors. For example, Dadabhoy (2001), a second generation South Asian doctor, describes in depth his experiences during his medical training in the UK, doing hospital rounds and his general interaction with the NHS staff, where he was subjected to hostility and intimidation. However, the majority of doctors in this study chose to remain silent; it was a subject either not commented on or described as not problematic by most of the interviewees, except for the following interviewee, who stated:

> *I had a good relationship generally speaking with local [English] doctors, but I have also felt with some that there was some negative undercurrent, some bias. Some seem fine (gpm8).*

The doctors working in the inner city area practices were more likely to say that they had had occasions in their practices when white patients had specifically asked for a white doctor at reception. Experience of racial harassment in city areas appeared more common for these interviewees. Interviewees generally talked about lessening visible differences to protect themselves from the racism arising out of cultural difference. The participant quoted below appeared to think that effective communication mediates any other negative attitudes, whilst previously having talked about experiencing racism when he was undertaking deputising services:

> *No racism. I don't think, as a doctor, if you can communicate with them, you can talk to them and they can understand what you are saying, you don't experience much difficulty. Most of my patients are white, they understand what I am saying and I understand what they are saying, If I don't understand, I say to them, 'please speak slowly' and then I understand (gp1m).*

However, his account below shows the extent of the abuse and pessimism that surrounds such behaviour. It also shows that many of the interviewees had suppressed their memory of racist experiences:

> *I am not saying that everyone is good. No, there are people who will treat you as a Paki, because when your skin colour is brown, this is inevitable, you have to take it in your stride, you can't change that, they will swear at you. If that happens, I say to them clearly, 'if you don't trust me because of the colour of my skin, you are free to join anywhere else' (gp1m).*

Perceptions of the key medical organisations differed among interviewees, with one interviewee who is a chair of the BMA stating:

> *...me being chair of the BMA, 40% of the GP colleagues here, they are from Indian subcontinent, so I have been dealing with them for about 25 years. Very good, as a matter of fact, I have always tried to sort of educate them, that's fine, we accept it, that racism does play a part, it has a role, but your own mistakes, your own short-comings... this been done to me. This has happened to me because I'm Asian, look*

at it... yes what wrong you have done. Try to rectify that then, if something is left there, then we could yes..... broaden your horizon a bit, yes that is there and we will look into it (gpm4).

The above accounts raise a number of issues. Firstly, they provide conflicting perceptions of experiences of racism. It is possible that some overseas-trained black and minority ethnic doctors may have played the race card, as has been suggested. Organisations such as the BMA, which was accused of discriminatory practices, may well have been appointing likeminded people, thereby simply providing lip service regarding equality matters. Without the support of the majority, and appropriate training, black and minority officers in positions of power may also collude and act as gatekeepers for the organisation.

Some of the interviewees showed limited understanding of race relations acts and did not have a clear understanding of what constituted racism or racial harassment. The strategy employed by them in relation to their move from a hospital career into general practice appears to correspond to that described by Lykes (1983) as *purposeful indirect coping*, one of the four approaches that black women in her study applied in dealing with racism. This means that individuals respond to the situation deliberately, but in such a way that they change their goals and acquire solace in a different pursuit, rather than solving the original problem. In spite of the fact that most interviewees were able to articulate their experiences of institutional racism on an aggregate level, there were silences in the majority of cases when it came to experiences of it on a personal level. Some gave brisk replies, while others diverted the conversation away immediately and instead, gave examples of oppressive practices in the country of origin. Conversations became emotionally charged and the interviewees' unease was evident. This denial may have been a mode of resistance. Apart from a denial strategy, there was also obvious pessimism around discrimination issues and a common approach, where racial discrimination was seen as being a 'fact of life' and nothing could be done to change people's attitudes. Many of the interviewees were quick to state that discriminatory practices also take place in their communities of origin. The following accounts were typical responses in this regard, with one interviewee stating:

There is no solution for discrimination; I don't know… what I'd say. In India and Pakistan, if there is a Sanwali [dark skinned] girl, she will have a tough time to get a man. Discrimination is right through; it's human nature. I mean, if you're going for an interview and one of your relatives comes in, you are bound to be favouring him or her. So, as far as discrimination goes, it is human nature. Discrimination is an ongoing thing, but on a national level, institutionalised racism etc., that's wrong. I can't imagine that there is no discrimination anywhere. It is everywhere (gp5s).

Another interviewee (Indian origin, Hindu,) also echoed the ingrained nature of racism and the way it permeates all societies:

> *Discrimination is a story. Doesn't it happen in our own country and don't people from our country here do it? Pakistani doctors' practices take Pakistanis only, or vice versa, that is discrimination too, isn't it? It is human nature... basically. I think this is where you have to accept that discrimination will always be there. There is a glass ceiling, as in, they will let you get up, but it is possible that they may prevent you from rising further... it is possible (gp2b).*

The above interviewee shows his awareness of institutional racism; however, he shows little comprehension of how racism impacts on individuals. The growing body of research on stratification by one's skin colour shows that differentiation by light or dark skin tone is an issue that remains of sociological significance in the lives of black women even today, being described as a lasting imprint of European colonisation and slavery.

Hunter (2002) argues that beauty is highly racialised and informed by ideals of white supremacy that date back to slavery and colonialism. It operates as a tool of white supremacy and patriarchy in that it elevates men and whiteness in importance and status. Hunter refers to her study analysis showing that skin colour continues to affect the major life outcomes of African American and Mexican American women, with light skin tone conferring privileges in education and income for both groups as well as a higher spousal status for the former. Hunter emphasises that it is crucial to examine the intertwined history of these focal groups in order to make sense of any racialised process. This means exploring how colourism is located in South Asia. Whilst Black scholars in the United States have traced colourism's internalised racism back to the history of slavery (Parameswaran and Cardoza, 2009). Hall (2003) contends that there is little work that can explain the historical origins of skin colour discrimination in India as affirmatively. However, Parameswaran and Cardoza, (2009, 12) state that:

> *In the absence of research that conclusively locates colorism in India within the histories of British colonialism, the Aryan conquest of the subcontinent, or the evolution of the caste system, we can only speculate here that social distinctions of skin color may be related to interwoven beliefs about light skin's signification of superior racial, regional, and upper caste/class identities.*

Marya Axner (an online resource) *The Community Tool Box*, in *Healing from the Effects of Internalised Oppression* refers to such a phenomenon as the internalised oppression that occurs among members of the same group as a result of being oppressed over a period of time. The author explains how it functions is that people internalise the myths and misinformation communicated to them about their group by society. Instead of addressing global issues, people turn the oppression on one another, the implication being that they treat each other in ways that are less than fully respectful, adopting attitudes and behaviours that undermine, criticise, mistrust or hurtful. The author refers to Spike Lee's 1988 film *School Daze*, where light-skinned African Americans at a prestigious black college look down on their darker-skinned fellow students as a result of internalising beliefs that being black is bad. Several of the interviewees' accounts showed symptoms of internalised racism and there was a tendency to discredit fellow doctors who had made complaints about discrimination. The following interviewee is able to relate to the institutional racism element, but nevertheless, equates his situation and others to 'beggars', thus raising a number of questions, as doctors are far from being beggars, regardless of country context:

> *...beggars can't be choosers, simple as that. Errmm, quite a few specialties, not only in general practice, in the hospital sector as well, like geriatrics, ENT, psychiatry and those kinds of specialties was manned by people coming from the subcontinent, there is no doubt about that (gpm4).*

It is interesting to note that, a report in 1996 stated that each recruited overseas doctor saved Britain £28,000.[2] Since racism operates in different ways and according to the specific history of a society (Castles and Miller, 2003) coping strategies can also be culturally specific. There was some ambivalence among the interviewees concerning the impact of colonialism, with some believing that British society, by and large, is not racist, whilst others felt that they did not want to fall victim of a self-fulfilment prophesy, so would rather focus on having faith in their own abilities. Social class also played a role in the doctors' survival strategies, as can be evidenced by the following interviewee's response. This is situated in the class context within which she was raised, with both parents being highly educated:

> *... if you have confidence in yourself, then you are capable of anything, that's what I'm trying to say... so, our role should be to bring that confidence back and say why not? Because it is in our hands, we are only limited by our thinking... nothing else limits us. If we only think within certain limits, then we won't be able to see beyond that, ...I don't think that we should adopt the victim role and we should... we are what we are... what we make ourselves (gpm3).*

A study conducted by Shorter-Gooden (2004) investigating the coping

---

[2] Roots of the Future, Ethnic Diversity in the Making of Britain **published by Commission for Racial Equality (1996).**

strategies of African American women when confronted with racism, developed a useful model regarding these strategies. It describes the ongoing internal and external strategies that individuals call upon as well as those that are conjured up to deal with specific situations. Ongoing internal strategies include *resting on faith*, *standing on shoulders* and *valuing oneself*. While the first is self-explanatory, the standing on shoulders strategy refers to where individuals place importance on the connection with their heritage, culture and ancestors, who had once engaged in emancipatory struggles. Valuing oneself implies actively engaging in ongoing self- development and providing a positive view to resist the prevailing negative stereotypes.

An external ongoing strategy is described as *leaning on shoulders*, where individuals rely on social support, for example, their family. The strategies to deal with specific situations are referred to as *role flexing*, *avoidance* and *standing up and fighting back*. Role flexing relates to altering one's behaviour, such as speech, dress or appearance, to fit in better with the dominant group and to minimise the impact of bias and negative stereotypes, which takes the form of acting more 'white' or appearing less 'black'. Avoidance strategy pertains to staying away from places, people, or subject matter likely to prompt biases and prejudices (Shorter-Gooden, 2004).

The evidence that directly and indirectly emerged in the interviewees' accounts in this study would suggest that they employed multiple resistance strategies in dealing with the impact of racism. The interviewees in Barnsley were more likely to apply a role flexing strategy, whereby they tried to fit in with the local community by appearing more white than black. The majority of them made reference to the inappropriateness of the dress code of Asian Muslim women, believing that migrants should not publicly display their distinct cultures as it would make them stand out when they should be minimising the impact of negative stereotypes, thus implying the employment of an avoidance strategy. Several of the interviewees referred to adaptation that included mode of dress and speech according to the wishes of society:

> *I don't have to lose any part of my identity; I don't think so. The only aspect which you probably lose is how you dress and how you talk. Other than that, once I'm inside my house I'm in my own environment, maybe I've accepted things that a lot of people don't accept. There is a void; there is a social gap, for all of us who are immigrants. But you have to accept that and then take it from there and once you accept that, you are not thinking about it, worrying about it, whatever, but inside my four walls I do what I want to do. When I'm outside, I have to do what the society expects you to do (gp2b).*

The interviewees in Barnsley also appeared to make reference to navigating fewer city spaces in comparison with those in Sheffield and Manchester, which suggests that their approach involved employing an avoidance strategy. Central coping strategies described were within the domains of an ongoing internal strategy, i.e. *resting on faith*, *standing on shoulders and valuing oneself.* Specifically, interviewees' accounts show that they relied on their faith as well as their cultural resources and spiritual beliefs, such as destiny and fate. Evidence suggests that specific cultural values were incorporated by individuals who referred to cultural proverbs that emphasised optimism rather than pessimism:

> *We have a saying in our culture that Jis thali mein khao, us mein ched mat karo (translation, don't make holes in the plate that you eat off of), which implies that you take care of it, because it is providing you with food. There are good and bad aspects of every person and my personal philosophy is… what is he or she to you?... there may be 99% bad in you and 1% good in you, if there is even 1% implied by me then you are excellent for me, I should not concentrate on your 99% (gp5s).*

Nearly all the interviewees stated how much they appreciated that they had been allowed opportunities for their achievements and that they owed Britain as much as they owed the country of origin:

> *We only had a few pounds in our pockets, we owe to this soil and people (gp1s).*

A few of the interviewees mentioned that they had become more engaged with their religious identity than they were prior to migration, with their thus believing that this new side of them had been created in the UK. Reference to God was a recurrent theme in several of the interviews:

> *I was safe not by virtue of British people, God saved me from trouble and I was lucky (gp8b).*

A significant number (two thirds) of interviewees talked about their exposure to South Asian poetry and how they utilised its power of communication as it provided psychological resistance and facilitated hope. They combined this strategy with the ongoing external strategy of *leaning on shoulders* in the form of garnering social support from their diasporic links, with a significant number talking about regularly attending poetry readings. These collective gatherings were attended by interviewees of both Pakistani and Indian origin, providing not only a cushioning effect against adversity, but also, promoting cohesion between these groups. This coping strategy may have been particular to their relatively elite class and educational background.

There was evidence of the family being the first port of call from which to seek emotional support when the interviewees encountered racial experiences; however, two contrasting accounts came to light which add the dimensions of race, gender and class. In one interviewee's account there was no mention of any experiences of racism until his wife entered the interviewing room to offer some tea and asked whether the husband had shared his experience when he had been physically assaulted by a white drug user, with an Asian taxi driver having saved his life. Whilst this prompt provided cues to recollect this memory, it also raised questions about the gender difference between the researcher and the interviewee.

In the second interview, the wife (English) also joined the interview and the discussion about racism. Despite the interviewee having talked about his experiences of racism at length and how he kept Quranic verses in his pocket and a golf club in the boot of his car as a defensive shield, his wife was adamant that there was no racism in the hospital where they both worked. She accepted that the overseas doctors were kept on a lowly pedestal, but her explanation for this was that this related to uncertainties about their overseas qualifications. She talked about class difference and how she as a nurse observed social distance among consultants, doctors and nurses. She also mentioned how overseas-trained South Asian doctors found solace in making alliances with the nurses (white), in some situations. She added, this relationship often became personal, as their own had done; however, she appeared unable to relate to or validate any experiences of institutional racism. Family may not have been a site of much support in such situations. The least desired personal style strategy *standing up and fighting back*, involving physical confrontation, was only mentioned by one interviewee.

All the interviewees in the study appeared to have employed an avoidance strategy at some stage. They were uncomfortable in describing people in racial terms and constantly used terminology such as 'local people' and 'Caucasian' meaning white British or English and 'our own people', referring to Asian people. One interviewee explicitly stated how he and other doctors avoided places that were likely to bring them into difficulties, such as the Working Men's club, where he believed that people, having drunk an excessive amount of alcohol, may be overtly racist. In general, the specific coping strategies that transpired in this study match up fairly well with the framework developed by Shorter-Gooden (2004).

Feagin and Sikes' (1994) study found that middle class black men and women referred to overachieving as a strategy for proving oneself. In this study, each one of the interviewees talked about innovation, entrepreneurship and the extensive work undertaken to modernise their practices, which could be classed as overachieving.

Despite the evidence suggesting that the interviewees employed a wide range of strategies to overcome oppression, their tendency to be dismissive about their experiences of racial discrimination on a personal level is a cause of concern. The interviewees who had retired were more likely to talk about racism than those who continued to work, showing perhaps that the former group has had more time to reflect on their lived experiences, whereas the latter group, in addition, may have continued being constrained by an organisational culture where such experiences are not validated. Such a strategy may not only cause harm to the employee, but also, cost the employer and affect the provision of quality healthcare. A small study conducted by Krieger (1990) in California using a random sample of 102 black and white women and a telephone interview methodology, found that the coping strategy of 'not talking to others about it' may be ineffective. That is, it emerged that those adopting this strategy were 4.4 times more likely to report hypertension than women who acted and talked with others about their experiences. Many interviewees in their accounts referred to their colleagues' sudden deaths, which is something that needs further investigation

CHAPTER 6

DISCUSSION AND CONCLUSIONS

I set out to investigate the perception of structural and socio-cultural integration experiences of an elite group of migrants, that is, overseas-trained South Asian doctors in the UK, in order to contribute to contemporary community cohesion debates. In order to gain a greater understanding of how different environmental characteristics impact on the social interactions of migrants and their sense of belonging to Britain, a multiple case study approach was employed across different parts of the UK, including: Barnsley, Sheffield and Greater Manchester. In sum, the empirical evidence has included analysis of 27 interviews with overseas-trained South Asian origin doctors in these three case study areas in England, comparing areas of relatively high and low ethnic diversity.

The interviews with the doctors explored the motivations and adaptations involved in the migration process of overseas-trained South Asian doctors and how they overcame numerous obstacles in their struggles to establish themselves as UK medical professionals. Their career aspirations and realities were examined as well as how they used entrepreneurial processes to enter into general practice as a practical solution to the limited opportunities offered in the hospital sector. The findings have illustrated how they rebuilt their lives in the UK by setting up GP practices as viable entities. They did so in order effectively to serve the needs of marginalised patient populations and were simultaneously able to develop close relationships with diverse communities. Several of the interviewees talked about handing their legacy on to their children who had also begun medical careers. The evidence shows that the interviewees had a positive perception of their migration trajectories and a strong sense of belonging to Britain alongside an ability to maintain their cultural identity and transnational links. The findings discussed in Chapter 4 have shown how these doctors' own elite positions positively influenced their social integration. In chapter 5, I examined the experiences of racism and coping strategies the doctors employed to address these.

This concluding chapter is aimed at relating the theoretical elements of this study with the empirical findings. In this chapter, I will revisit the research questions as outlined in the introduction before drawing the findings together. The limitations of this research study will be discussed, as well as presenting the implications for policy making and recommendations for future research.

The main research question that this study set out to explore was what insights the 'lived experiences' of highly-skilled elite labour migrants, namely overseas-trained South Asian doctors, add to our understanding of community cohesion. I discussed the doctors' own perceptions of their social mobility in the NHS in terms of working conditions, structural constraints, career development and of their contributions in chapters 2-3. These chapters revealed how poor working conditions in the NHS, inaccessibility of training posts, and the perception of a glass ceiling had led to the doctors' departure from hospital jobs and subsequent entry into general practice. Whilst the term 'institutional racism' was only used by a few of the interviewees, their accounts identified several ways in which structural factors served to disadvantage them and confirmed that the phenomenon of geographical concentration in deprived and remote areas documented in the literature was not accidental. Instead, it was as a result of what the interviewees perceived as systematic structural inequalities embedded in the NHS.

These findings raise questions concerning the functional aspect of the integration of overseas-trained South Asian doctors. The interviewees' accounts relating to entry into general practice and unequal geographical clustering, clearly demonstrate that they were denied equality of opportunity. The spatial distribution pattern of overseas-trained South Asian doctors shows that, despite being an elite group of migrants, there are parallels to be drawn with the experiences of low/unskilled South Asians. Nearly all the interviewees referred to what Samers (2010) describes as 'socio-professional downgrading', which stimulated a desire for independence, and to be protected from discrimination, despite the fact they were often ambivalent about describing any actual experiences of being discriminated against. In chapters 2 and 3, I summarised how the doctors engaged in entrepreneurial processes and how their experiences bore a resemblance with minority ethnic entrepreneurs, in general.

This finding lends support to Robinson's (1988, 467) assertion that the concentration of Indian GPs in deprived practice areas following the departure of UK qualified GPs migrating overseas in search of more conducive environments, can be considered a replacement labour force, although in 'different economic sectors and at different levels in the occupational hierarchy'.

As discussed previously, Navarro (1978) illustrated how deep seated class inequalities in UK medicine have persisted, leading to a division between hospital medicine and general practice, the latter being perceived as an inferior specialty. Despite Navarro's analysis having acknowledged race inequality, he does not convey equal attention to race inequality issues as he does to class inequality. The overwhelming evidence from the interviewees in this study suggests they experienced race inequality and that the career advice given by the consultants to the doctors may have been biased, with a view to maintaining the class and race hierarchy within the structure of hospital services, also that racism within the NHS is merely a reflection of racism prevalent within UK society more broadly.

Based on the empirical evidence, the overall finding concerning structural integration is that the experiences of the elite migrants in this study are not dissimilar to those of their low/unskilled counterparts owing to their also being constrained by their race. There was, however, a reluctance among these elites to cite racism, in particular, elite racism, (for instance, reluctance to describe their experiences with individual consultants as racially oppressive), which may be linked to their class affiliation and professional allegiance. I argue that the white consultants acted as mechanisms of institutional racism and became what Massey et al., (1975, 10) describe as 'the reluctant instrument of the establishment' as they failed to challenge the inequalities in the system. The authors point out that institutional racism can persist without 'racist villains'. The interviewees' individual stories as to how they secured work in their early years expose the informality of the system and the power that the consultants wielded when they travelled all the way to India to 'cherry-pick' overseas-trained South Asian doctors, as described by one interviewee. While these consultants appeared to appreciate individual doctors' skills and experiences, the available evidence suggests that they colluded with the system, rather than questioning the oppressive practices that operated to pigeonhole overseas-trained South Asian doctors at the time in certain specialties of lower status. The Macpherson (1999) this collusion and inaction was as a result of the collective failure of organisations to challenge the institutional racism embedded in their processes, attitudes and behaviour.

The findings in this study confirm what Oikelome and Healy (2013, 557) argue, that the human-capital protection of qualifications, profession and status is not sufficient to equate the experiences of overseas doctors with those of UK-trained doctors owing to the cumulative disadvantage of the intersection of race and place of qualification.

Heath and Cheung (2006) refer to studies confirming that ethnic penalties often remain for highly qualified migrants. The interviewees' accounts provide compelling evidence that they were channelled into general practice intentionally, despite the fact they aspired to become specialists. In addition, the doctors experienced further structural constraints in the form of spatial accessibility that resulted in their geographical clustering, which Ellis et al. (2007) argue is just as significant as social access to jobs. This finding aligns with that of Raghuram et al. (2010), who contend that it is crucial to explore how non-migrant networks may reproduce privilege and shape labour market opportunities for migrants. This was exemplified in the ways in which interviewees described their accessing elite networks, such as rotary and golf clubs, in order to gain elite membership.

The empirical evidence relating to the perceptions of the impact of contextual factors on the identities of overseas-trained South Asian doctors, the insights of their lived experiences, type of social capital they utilise, their entrepreneurial behaviour in order to circumvent perceived blocked social mobility and experiences of transnational identities were discussed in various chapters. I will discuss how the findings add to our understanding of community cohesion.

Firstly, I will discuss the findings relating to the impact of contextual factors on the identities of these elite migrants. There was variation in the characteristics of the case study areas, as discussed previously. However, the interviewees in all three areas described being accepted by their neighbourhoods and were aware that their elite status had afforded them symbolic capital that had facilitated integration. The interviewees' accounts showed that personal experiences, such as exposure to western education in their country of origin, had also contributed towards their integration in British society. Moreover, they were more likely to be accepted by the wider society than their low/unskilled counterparts, being a member of elite clubs is one manifestation of this. The specific characteristics of the place, such as rurality and the need to sustain healthcare provision, may have also facilitated the integration process. By contrast, doctors in urban areas were more likely to report an experience of racism.

Social contexts influence how immigrants' identities are expressed in settlement countries (Khan, 2007). Experience of marginalisation and exclusion within the structures of white or western hegemony leads to minority ethnic groups forming diasporic trans-national links. Determining factors for social integration for the doctors in this study were their own elite position in the form of a professional identity, which served as their social capital, the receptive nature of local contexts, support from professional diasporas and length of service in the area. Their ability to adapt to new situations proved effective, whether that involved applying the theory of (acquiring membership of elite organisations, such as rotary and golf clubs) as well as reworking this theory, including being at the level of patients from lower socio-economic backgrounds in their interactions (such as attending private functions held at working men's clubs). These elites also integrated their own cultural and religious values which they frequently evaluated in new situations, drawing meaning from what they already knew.

Chapter 4 provided empirical evidence concerning how the doctors in the study came to inhabit places, and how place impacted on their sense of belonging. It also showed the cross-cutting affiliations of individuals for social and historical reasons, and how the doctors simultaneously experienced several identities. The assertion made by several scholars such as Tyler (2012), Brah (1985), and Cox (1948), that there is an entwining of the discourses of race, class and coloniality is confirmed by the empirical results of this study. The doctors here are a self-selected elite group of individuals who have been predisposed to a British education and formed hybrid identities as post-colonial people prior to migration. Their accounts showed that they had multiple identities in process, and the findings support Brah's (2007), assertion that individuals are situated across various processes of identification, which change and lead to configuration into a specific pattern in a particular set of both social and psychological circumstances, making a particular identity prominent at a given time. Examples of evidence include the practising of various identities such as religious, cultural, linguistic and professional identities, as well as how one's phase of life impacts on identity.

As previously stated, the specific UK contexts served as spaces where the identities of doctors and patients were simultaneously negotiated against a backdrop of the legacy of Empire. For example, the interviewees described how some patients in urban areas showed their arrogance through their body language, which the doctors perceived as not wanting to see an Asian doctor. The doctors did not perceive white working class patients as coming from lower strata, but rather saw them as *English first.* Numerous examples were provided in which brief encounters with such patients left long lasting and positive emotional impacts on the interviewees, even several years after their retirement. One doctor described his patients as 'extended family' and another stated with pride how they called their daughter by an English nickname given to her by an English nanny because she could not pronounce the Indian name. In all three areas, where social interaction was described with white members of the community, it was, interestingly, mostly with individuals from a lower middle class/working class background. Interactions with upper middle class white professionals were rarely mentioned, apart from through membership of elite clubs, which may be an example of the interviewees' class affiliation. The evidence shows that the doctors in the study were able to reach out to certain social groups that are generally inaccessible to low skilled migrants, for example, Rotary Clubs and prestigious sports clubs because of their elite positions based on their professional identities. It can be argued that their class position helped mediate their ethnic identity, implying that racism operates in a particular way, and that there are factors that act as mediators. The evidence in the study shows that the doctors' professional identities were more salient where local structures were described as less receptive and reflective of diversity, for example, as in the case of Barnsley. In Manchester, although the city is diverse, the evidence from the interviewees suggests that they were more likely to experience overt racism here than in other case study areas because of the city's unique urban characteristics, including a relatively high ethnic density (associated with low levels of trust) and a higher level of poverty, possibly leading to competition over scarce resources (Bonnett, 2000, 132). Working conditions here were described as less rewarding than in other areas and this may have contributed to doctors adapting transnational identities which offered the opportunity of being valued elsewhere. In Sheffield, the interviewees appeared to have strong local and national attachments; may be due to the local structures being more reflective of, and valuing of, diversity than other areas, as well as the city's environmental ability to offer safety, peace and a more middle class lifestyle.

In relation to British identity, a strong identification was evidenced by all the interviewees, though they combined it in different ways. For many, this identification did not simply start on their arrival in the UK; it was something they had been exposed long before. Many had retained the belief that Britain was a fair country, and a place where they had been able to achieve better futures for themselves and their children without being exposed to the specific forms of oppression experienced in the countries of origin such as those related to caste and the social standing of their family in the community.

In relation to integration into British society, the responses of this elite group of migrants were distinctive in that the majority of the interviewees believed in having a 'public conforming identity' with few distinguishing aspects, and did not approve of some of the visible performative acts exhibited in the behaviour of other Asians, in particular Muslims dressing in so-called ethnic clothes. A general consensus was that some aspects of ethnic identities should not be shown in public and instead confined to the private sphere. This was rationalised because visibility brings out an implicit claim of identification, which suggests that the doctors were aware that maintaining an ethnic identity in public negates the socio-cultural conformity expected by UK society (Antonsich, 2012).

The phrase '*When in Rome, do as the Romans do*', was only mentioned by a couple of interviewees, nonetheless, it captures the general attitude of many doctors in the study, across the three case-study areas. While many Asians in the UK may affirm their ethnic identities symbolically by way of dress, the elites in this study achieved this by means of belonging to diasporas which positively affirmed their ethnic identity. They also frequently used their professional identity to shield them from any potential hostility, which in my view, relates to the coping mechanisms of elites, and possibly by their professional socialisation that emphasises the neutrality of doctor-patient interaction as referred to by Beagan (2003).

There was some evidence of challenges arising out of such expectations, for example, one doctor described how his residential choice to live in a predominantly white area was frowned upon by a fellow South Asian doctor. This example shows that, although the class position of the doctors afforded them the privilege of making residential choices, this was perceived as lack of conformity to own community by a fellow doctor. This strongly indicates the shortcomings of the existing community cohesion theories which need to consider other processes of integration because they often approach the process of cohesion as simply two-directional.

The qualitative evidence exposes the heterogeneity that exists within British society due to individuals' differential access to political power, and their differential location in relation to the economic production that generates stratification in any society (Robinson, 1988). For example, the doctors in the study had a perception that their doctor-patient relationships were of a reciprocal nature rather than asymmetrical, as such interactions involved marginalised patients and marginalised doctors, thus exposing the complexity of whiteness, class and cohesion, and the fact that not all white identities are privileged (Beagan, 2003).

The findings also show that the majority of white working class people were perceived very positively by the doctors in the study, rather than being pathologised. These findings also challenge the conventional theories on the doctor-patient relationships in which those with the possession of medical and scientific knowledge have been described as powerful groups that are privileged over others (Lupton, 2012).

Cultural difference is perceived as a threat to national identity as it is assumed that there is cultural homogeneity within the UK society (Castles and Miller, 2003, 248). The language and culture of the migrant has become symbolic for 'otherness' and are 'markers' for discrimination. The interviewees' accounts do not indicate that retaining one's own cultural/religious/linguistic aspects is an aspiration towards separatism. Rather, they show that such attributes were, as argued by Bhatt (2013) as a mode of resistance and an act of decolonisation rather than an aspiration of separatism. The type of poetry (revolutionary, and written by poets who took on a literary campaign against colonialism) recited collectively by the interviewees can be seen to strongly relate to the mode of resistance adapted in the post-colonial context.

Opposition to different languages and cultures is justified on the basis that as the official language, English is crucial for economic accomplishment, with the migrants' own cultural and linguistic attributes proving insufficient for success in a modern secular society Castles and Miller, 2003, 248). In contrast, there is qualitative evidence clearly demonstrating that the main Asian languages of Urdu/Hindi played an important role in the strengthening of bonding social capital and offered culturally sensitive coping mechanisms. The findings in this study show that all the interviewees expressed pride in their ethnic/religious and linguistic identities, alongside their British identity. Their accounts showed how they integrated their own cultural values positively in their work ethos and adaptation to Britain, and drawing strength from the revolutionary writings of poets from their era. The empirical evidence shows that their own cultural/religious/linguistic identities posed no competition to their newly constructed diasporic identities and British identity. However, being British was only one of a range of identities experienced by the doctors in the study and supports Parekh's (2007) assertion. The interviewees' sense of belonging to Britain was described in relational terms. In other words, it was based on Britain's ability to offer better opportunities than the interviewees' countries of origin and the freedom to practice cultural identities. This shows that the concept of Britishness needs to be re-defined and broadened to encompass the views and experiences of its minority communities.

I will now turn to how the experiences of overseas-trained South Asian doctors relate to the existing theories of migration, social capital, entrepreneurship and transnationalism. The discussion in this chapter has already covered the empirical results regarding transnationalism, therefore, in the following sub-sections I will discuss what the empirical results of this study add to the existing theoretical concepts of migration, entrepreneurship and social capital.

Migration and the Elites

Empirical evidence relating to the migration process and the role of broader social structures in shaping migration patterns alongside individual agency was discussed in Chapter 1. The findings showed an intertwining of macro- micro- and meso-level structures involving a complex set of social, cultural, political, historical and religious factors shaping the migration pattern of large numbers of overseas-trained South Asian doctors into the UK. It confirmed that people display different migration patterns according to their occupational class and context (Andall, 2000).

The role of the family has been stated as central in migratory movement from the Indian sub-continent countries (Castles and Miller, 2003). However, this was not always the case for elite migrants in this study. Similarly, the driving force for migration was described as the obtaining of post graduate qualifications, acquiring a fellowship and gaining professional experience in UK hospitals, with a view to enhancing career development, rather than for economic reasons. The doctors mostly utilised institutional networks that they had relatively easy access to such as the GMC, rather than relying on traditional kinship networks as did their unskilled counterparts. Several of the interviewees came to the UK as part of a couple which shows that temporary highly-skilled permit holders were once allowed family migration, contrary to the mass migration of low/unskilled people from South Asian countries where men arrived first. The creative use of religion was clearly evident in the doctors' accounts, not only in their decision-making processes, but also with regard to its provision as a spiritual resource. Their accounts show that the psychological effects of religious values resulted in their commitment towards enduring the hardship of their migration (Hagan and Ebaugh, 2003). The evidence shows that aspects of their culture, language, religion and values, became integrated in the organisation of the migratory process.

The findings show that the kind of reception they encountered differed from that experienced by low/unskilled migrants and in comparison, the doctors had more positive experiences. The exemption from strict immigration control, and the availability of clinical attachments with relative ease, job opportunities in Britain including vouchers and work permits, all facilitated migratory movement and was intentionally designed to overcome the shortage of medical labour in the UK, factors from which the majority of other non-professional potential migrants from these countries were excluded.

Entrepreneurship, Social Capital and the Elites

The empirical evidence relating to the entrepreneurial behaviour of the doctors in the study was discussed in depth in Chapter 3. Nearly all the interviewees described experiencing 'socio-professional downgrading' as paraphrased by (Samers, 2010) which stimulated a desire to be independent and protected from discrimination. The empirical evidence shows that apart from blocked social mobility in terms of hospital medicine, spatial accessibility to jobs to General Practice was a further structural barrier as they were not able to access jobs in well sought-out practices.

The evidence showed that the entrepreneurial process was greatly facilitated by collective interests, strong personal ties that led to the pooling of labour, and financial resources showing similarity with the processes experienced by other ethnic entrepreneurs. Ethnic entrepreneurs use family as social capital, whereas for the interviewees, it was other overseas-trained South Asian doctors who provided their social capital.

The detailed accounts of the interviewees show how both the values and norms on which social capital was based and social capital itself, were socially remitted by them in the new settings (Levitt, 1998). For example, specific individual-level and group-level characteristics such as 'bounded solidarity' and 'enforceable trust' were sources of social capital that the interviewees utilised as a resource. Another distinguishing aspect of their contribution was that their collectivist perspectives were embedded in bonding social capital that produced positive outcomes for them in a society which is highly individualised and less likely to reproduce a similar form of social capital. Such approaches also facilitated resource mobilisation in the geographical locales that had struggled to recruit GPs in the past as the interviewees were able to instantly draw on their connections with doctors form similar backgrounds. The evidence in the study shows that the interviewees were able to combine resources in novel ways so as to create something of value and were able to build special relationships with a wide range of people and communities to whom they provided enhanced primary care services. The interviewees' accounts show how they employed strategies to meet the needs of a diverse population which varied according to social context. Examples are, the application of the *theory of mimicry*, acquiring membership of elite organisations such as Rotary and golf clubs, imitating the cultural attitude of the upper middle class British, as well as reworking this theory, including being at the level of patients from lower socio-economic backgrounds in their interactions such as attending functions held at working men's clubs.

Evidence in the study also suggested that the roles played by these elites merit being cast in the role of a social entrepreneur. That is, some interviewees were able to leverage the prestige and professional status they had acquired to their advantage not only within the UK but also to their countries of origin by setting up various initiatives within state run hospitals.

A key component of the community cohesion framework, as discussed in the introduction, has been the application of the social capital framework in its ethos, where bonding social capital refers to social ties within various community groups, and bridging refers to social ties across social groups. Emphasis is placed on 'bridging' social capital to achieve cohesion among communities. Chapters 2-4 discussed, in depth, the experiences of doctors from migration to negotiating entry into general practice, with how bonding and bridging social capital came to bear on their experiences being explored. The findings show that the doctors came from different cultural and religious backgrounds and thus, were not a homogenous group of people. They had to deal with internal conflicts as discussed in section headed The Downside of Ethnic Entrepreneurship. In other words, what may be perceived as bonding social capital can also be simultaneously interpreted as bridging social capital, whereby the doctors were bridging social ties across social groups within the South Asian communities.

The findings showed that the doctors in the study came to the UK to invest in their human capital by acquiring a western education, which would promise them social status in the prestigious profession of medicine (Husband, 1982). While the interviewees appreciated the opportunities the UK offered, in reality, they also they found isolation and ghettoisation in the NHS, which mirrored the experience of many other migrants in new settings (Laws, 1997). The process of migration and the negotiation of entry into general practice shows that ethnic social networks previously considered insignificant by the doctors became significant in combating exclusionary/marginalising practices by the UK-trained GPs, which led to the strengthening of ethnic identity. They subsequently developed exclusionary practices in their own recruitment procedures and mostly appointed other doctors of a similar background, which shows the negative side of bonding social capital, as stated by Khan (2007).

The evidence in this study shows that the majority of the interviewees had initially wanted to make a bridge with individuals and institutions, rather than rely solely on friends' networks that constituted bonding social capital. However, the entrepreneurial process described above shows to the contrary, with the findings lending support to Khan's (2007, 46) assertion that individuals are more likely to seek social ties among fellow members who are unable to participate in institutions of power and are discriminated against by those who profess to include them.

The findings of this study lend support to Khan's (2007) assertion that bonding social capital eventually allows individuals to participate with increased confidence and engage with institutions of power. This was true for several of the doctors in the study, who were only able to penetrate the system by means of networking with other overseas-trained South Asian doctors. The interviewees acknowledged that they drew strength and support from the existence of such social networks. However, they also recognised that such links reproduced oppressive practices and that this form of social capital also contributed to exploitation. The finding that can be derived from this empirical study is that community cohesion be seen as an issue that is purely white versus BME communities. For, Britain's BME communities also need to strengthen their social ties within before seeking to create bridging ties across wider social groups. There is some merit in Khan's recommendation that bonding social capital is a positive resource for migrants, which this study has also established and given the government's own interest in equal participation for all, it should invest in supporting bonding social capital. The oppressive practices, I believe, stem from the outcomes of lack of responsibility on the NHS's part as articulated by the interviewees (being informed that PCTs could not intervene in the GP practices' affairs for their self-employment status) and possibly cultural aspects, such as religion, the region one comes from and status in the country of origin. Further research needs to be undertaken to establish the causes of intra-group exclusionary practices. The empirical evidence highlights how the doctors in the study were excluded from mainstream networks, which pushed them into utilising networks with other overseas-trained South Asian doctors. The findings strengthen the assertion of Raghuram et al. (2010) that further empirical research needs to be done to explore the process of how these networks operate relationally between migrants and non-migrants, rather than focusing entirely on migrants' networks.

Limitations of the Study

Like any research this study has limitations, which should be taken into account when considering the conclusions. The sample consisted of overseas-trained doctors of Pakistani and Indian origin only, therefore, the empirical evidence only relates to these groups. Also this study is of a qualitative, case study nature and so there are limits as to what can be generalised. Moreover, the researcher's own identity has played an important role in the research process. Regarding which, Chew-Graham et al. (2002) refer to their own study, which involved peer-interviewing (a GP researcher interviewing GPs) and list the advantages and disadvantages of the duality of the researcher role. The authors emphasise the significance of transparency in reporting and discussing results. I have described in detail how I minimised such limitations through reflexivity in the research process and personal reflexivity. Despite this, a researcher's voice is always implicated in the research process of qualitative methodologies in one way or another, but this does not mean that valuable insights cannot be gained.

The use of convenience sampling also means that the data volume was not sufficiently randomly chosen to make conclusions representative of all overseas-trained South Asian doctors in the research case study areas, other cities or other countries. In addition, the responses of the doctors in the study are based on their own recall, which may have lapse in its accuracy over time. Moreover, as patients' perspectives were not incorporated in the analysis, the findings could not be triangulated.

Policy Implications and Ways forward

This study has consistently shown that, whilst the elite positions of the doctors in the study as healthcare professionals placed them in a privileged position, they often simultaneously had similar experiences to their low skilled/unskilled South Asian counterparts. Next, I will draw the findings together and discuss a number of key policy implications stemming from this research.

The empirical evidence relating to social capital showed that the creation of bonding social capital was an important approach for the doctors in the study as it provided them with the necessary resources to overcome blocked social mobility. This finding lends support to Khan's (2007) assertion that the fostering of social ties within homogenous groups is linked to the failure of institutional support and that such ties allow them to participate as equals and with more confidence in UK institutions. The findings support the view that the 'social capital cure' underpinning the community cohesion policy detracts attention from the implications of the politics and practices of racism and discrimination, which are often underplayed in initiatives that promote social capital (Cheong et al., 2007). I strongly agree with the above authors that it is important to have an alternative conception that takes into account understanding the immigration process and the contexts of migration. This is because it is these contexts that equate the experiences of overseas-trained south Asian doctors in this study, who are elite migrants, to the experiences of unskilled migrants with South Asian origins, rather than their human and social capital. What this means is that overseas-trained South Asian doctors experience structural inequalities in relation to the context of their migration, rightly described as 'indentured labour' by Esmail (2007). For example, the doctors in the study talked extensively about their poor working conditions that involved employment in temporary positions and being kept on the lower rungs of hospital posts.

Bridging social capital is championed over multiculturalist policies in that the latter is said to have caused residential segregation, and the former is associated with cohesive communities (Khan, 2007). The evidence in this study suggests that, whilst the doctors did not live in ethnic 'enclaves', they did mention living close to other South Asian doctors for the purpose of mutual support, rather than in order to self-segregate. The interviewees also described privileged white people who also tended to live in a secluded way. They described how their negative bonding social capital is rarely seen as problematic in comparison to disadvantaged ethnic minorities, who tend to be pathologised (Khan, 2007).

Linked with bridging social capital is 'contact theory', which as discussed in the literature review chapter, proposes that bringing people from different groups together for purposes of collaboration can reduce prejudice. The findings from this study suggest that such a view is over-simplified, as what appears to matter most is not the quantity of interactions, but rather their quality between people of different backgrounds (Allport, 1979). The evidence in the case study areas illustrates this, in particular, in relation to Barnsley. As Barnsley's social structure lacked culturally appropriate opportunities for social interaction for the interviewees, they expanded their spatial radius to neighbouring cities/towns by going on regular trips to mingle with friends from similar cultural and social status backgrounds. Zones of contact with local people tended to be supermarkets, and encounters were brief. What was deemed important in these encounters was the type of pre-existing relationships they had and which made the contact meaningful leaving such lasting effects that the doctors remembered the incidents despite having retired several years previously.

According to Hewstone et al. (2007), contact between groups with strong identities can produce two types of outcome, one where there is an increase in prejudice and competition, and the other where the diametric opposite occurs, leading to increased positive attitudes and lessening of conflict. The authors drew attention to the significance of a power relationship for achieving positive outcomes between groups. This is illustrated in the empirical evidence. The doctors in remote areas and inner-city deprived ones were able to do their jobs as professionals and win over the trust of individuals and communities, because their professional background subdued other aspects of their identities. They reported how local PCT structures enabled their entrepreneurial processes, thus being able to set up practices. This, I believe, happened because there were shared goals, because the PCT had an obligation to provide a service in areas that had been abandoned by UK doctors in pursuit of better opportunities elsewhere. The findings lend support to the views of Hewstone et al. (2007), who contend that having a co-operative task and shared common goals in environments where cooperation, rather than competition is encouraged under circumstances of scarce resources, is crucial. The authors add that this contact between groups needs to be legitimated by means of institutional support. The empirical evidence showed that the fact that the GP practices were being managed by these doctors implied that the doctors did have institutional support, which contributed towards positive outcomes in terms of social interactions. This may not be achievable by a migrant who is economically disadvantaged. Conditions under which group encounters occur are also argued as being crucial, with different kinds of contacts being likely to bring about different kinds of solidarity (Phillips, 2007). The evidence in this study has shown that the doctors had a perception of a close bond with their white working class patients. Apart from the overlay of imperialism that both the patients and the doctors brought to their encounter, the asymmetry in the power relationships, in my view, was partly owing to the overlapping experiences of marginalisation and as a result of increased contact under difficult, but shared circumstances, as stated previously. In his study of ethnic relations in prisons, Phillips (2007) observed that 87% of prisoners held a positive view of relations between ethnic groups, while interestingly, only 59% the British population shared that view. The author concludes that this may be related to the fact that prisons offer much more intensive contact with members of other ethnic groups than outside that environment. The findings from the current study highlight that what was significant for the interviewees was the creation of the conditions for a cohesive and fair society (which led to an interviewee referring to his patients as extended family). This was advocated in a foreword by Bhikhu Parekh in Modood et al. (1997), although in this case, it was the institutional support and co-operative tasks at hand that were highlighted. However, there is no reason why such intimate relationships of trust evidenced in doctor-patient relationships cannot extend to other situations provided supportive conditions are created.

This study has also evidenced that community cohesion is a phenomenon that cannot always be measured by indicators prescribed by the government. Parekh (2002) advocates for contact and meaningful dialogue, whereby people can communicate with each other and in places where this kind of dialogue can happen, such as across 'cultural playing fields' and the right conditions. There were numerous examples that the interviewees were able to recall where there was an element of experienced cohesiveness despite race and class differences. For example, one doctor described how a white patient undertook gardening work at the back of his GP practice building without the interviewee's knowledge. Another doctor reported how an encounter with a patient brought tears to her eyes, because he had waited for a considerable length of time outside a shop to be able to talk to her, although she had been retired for several years. While another doctor repeatedly referred to his white patients as his 'extended family' and these are only a few of the examples described by the participants in the study. Community cohesion, in my view, should be, as Wetherell (2007, 4) argues, about fostering such casual exchanges as pleasantries in shops and pubs, with regular contact that strengthens what, at present, remain weak ties for many people.

Discussions around identities revealed that while the interviewees showed strong association with the British way of life and values, they also positively incorporated their own cultural values into the mix, and drew new meanings from them. The evidence in this study strongly supports the view that the meanings of the term 'British' will need to become more inclusive of the experiences, values and aspirations of ethnic minorities. By achieving this, migrants can become citizens with equal rights and an integral part of the national culture, in the implementation of the community cohesion framework. While there is some mileage in Putnam's assertion that bridging social capital requires that we 'transcend our social and political identities to connect with people unlike ourselves'(Putnam, 2000), policy frameworks need also to consider the psychological aspects of one's identity. In addition, policy makers need to bear in mind that ethnic identities are far from being 'pure' or 'static'. Indeed, the interviewees in this study referred to spaces of negotiation both within and across groups, supporting the point that Hall (1992, 252) makes, whereby sharing social spaces with others from different cultural backgrounds inevitably leads to transformations of identity. For example, many Indian origin interviewees of Hindu background talked about dietary changes, such as moving from being strict vegetarians to purchasing halal meat. The dress code of a female interviewee was also adapted to what was considered more appropriate in a confined consultation room in Britain.

Language is another area to be considered. The findings of this study suggest that community languages played a significant role in the cohesion and entrepreneurial activities of the overseas-trained South Asian doctors. Bilingualism was somewhat acknowledged and promoted in the old multicultural policy, whereas this has been diluted by the community cohesion policy framework, with more emphasis placed on having one common language. The findings of this study have shown that languages contain social values and attitudes, cultural practices and social norms that the interviewees called upon in times of adversity, which they drew enormous strength from. It is useful to have one national language, but English does not need to be the single predominant language of communication. Similarly, other languages do not need to be confined to their own language communities, for as evidence in this study has shown, they have much to offer to a wider learning community.

This study has highlighted that there are a number of areas where greater recognition of the role of overseas-trained South Asian doctors is vitally important. For example, the extensive contribution that they have made in the provision of healthcare services in the UK, as well as their commitment to meet the needs of the most marginalised UK communities needs to be more widely acknowledged. In sum, there should be greater recognition of the much wider roles of overseas-trained South Asian doctors, instead just pigeon-holing them as culturally competent professionals.

The discussion on how racism is experienced by overseas-trained South Asian doctors highlights the need for the NHS to develop ant-racist strategies, policies and practices for the future. The findings strengthen Coker's (2001, 2) argument that the NHS needs to understand the language, philosophy and practice of discrimination, their relationship with the underlying ideology of white supremacy and power, and then, translate such awareness into their policies.

Policy development needs to take into account that professionals from BME backgrounds also need awareness-raising regarding diversity issues. A common assumption is that all BME staff have a high level of awareness regarding diversity issues, whereas the findings have shown that lack of institutional support around diversity issues can lead to individuals' internalising negativity. It is important to recognise that they need to be supported before they can support themselves. One way forward is that more awards should be made available for individuals to undertake innovative work and enhance current equality and diversity training, with the aim of inspiring the creation of positive role models. An example is the Mary Seacole development award that Pamela Shaw successfully used as the basis of a DVD to enhance current equality and diversity training. Specifically, this is from the angle of celebrating the contribution BME professionals have made to the NHS, with the intention of making these individuals more visible and showing how they felt good about themselves and their service contribution (Shaw, 2010). Overseas-trained South Asian doctors, including those who are retired members, as well as a variety of other BME professionals from different occupational backgrounds could be approached with a view to getting involved in enhancing the delivery of Equality and Diversity Training, as they have a wealth of experience in areas such as dealing with adversity, empowering others, and working with marginalised groups. This should not just target BME groups, for it should also include people who lead from the heart, have passion within themselves, determination, and are also able to access opportunities. It would be helpful for them to provide others with stimulating environments, sharing their vision and passion about what they have done throughout their careers. Sharing the reasons for their success with others on a face to face basis, rather than through one off computer-based e-learning, would be much more meaningful and effective at ensuring these patterns are repeated, and will inspire others to visualise their own career progressions.

The evidence in this study, as discussed in the section headed Doctor-Patient Interaction in chapter 4, has shown how the interviewees had developed strategies to meet the needs of their diverse patient population and believed that they had been able to dismantle the power relationships that occurred with marginalised patients, in particular, white ones. Examples of good practice can be identified from further exploring in this area. The interviewees talked about the provision of healthcare that was sensitive to the linguistic and cultural needs of the Asian community, often in the absence of any particular direction from the NHS. There are, however, dangers in assuming that only Asian GPs provide high quality and culturally competent healthcare services. I argue this for two reasons. Firstly, the evidence in this study has revealed that the interviewees were often less sympathetic to the complexity of needs exhibited by Asian patients, in comparison to white working class patients, who they regarded as less problematic. This may be related to class difference and social hierarchies that exist in societies. Secondly, the evidence suggests that the majority of interviewees did not wish to be pigeonholed in any way and expressed a desire to offer their services to the wider society, rather than just a section of it. They very much believed in their professional ethos and viewed their role as universal. It is important to avoid the ghettoism that can arise from a concentration in certain specialties, as this would limit their opportunities to work in 'sought-after' specialties, which have so far been predominantly white and will continue to be so unless challenged (Esmail, 2001).

It is also important that policy makers recognise issues beyond the narrow use of domestic policies such as the community cohesion policy framework, with the roles it prescribes for migrants within its limited definition (one national identity, one national language and British values), and the NHS only considering medical migration in relation to securing staffing levels nationally. Policy makers should consider the implications of global migration around healthcare and the gains that can be accrued by developing countries from the migration of overseas-trained South Asian doctors. Evidence strongly suggests that these individuals are in a prime position as medical diasporas to take on more transnational roles, magnifying the resources in the countries of their origin, where some of them are already involved as social entrepreneurs. These roles need to be legitimised with a view to maximising the advantages that may be gained by means of human capital transfer and philanthropy when flows of expertise are potentially multiple and multi-directional, and whether it is temporary, virtual and/or in person. It means that individuals can have transnational identities; an aspect that should be respected rather than questioned. This will also have fewer implications for the sending developing South Asian countries, meaning the 'Brain drain' is thus replaced with 'Brain Gain'. Domestic policies need to be developed in concordance with the obligations of international healthcare polices, such as those of the World Health Organisation (WHO), which emphasises that health is a shared responsibility, involving equitable access to essential care and collective defence against transnational threats.[1]

A final point I would like to stress is that the doctors in the study had the perception that they had been accepted as a legitimate and valued part of British society. This, I believe, was to a large extent owing to the intersectionality of their professional, class and racial identities, which may not be afforded to others in circumstances where there is an absence of such

[1] World Health Organisation. http://www.who.int/about/en/

overlapping elements. It is also important to remember that the doctors in the study were elites, who were able to participate more fully in UK life than their non-elite counterparts, because the structure of their lives gave them exposure to a wide range of people and situations, such as interactions at work, with medical/educational professionals and patients and communities. This sometimes forced them to shift their reference frames as new skills were needed for them to be able to progress. They were instrumental adapters, who Levitt (1998, 931) describes as able to alter and add to their routines for pragmatic purposes, able to readjust their frames of reference to equip them to deal better with the challenges and constraints of migrant life. The extent to which the interpretative frames of migrants are altered is very much a function of their interaction with the wider society, which also depends upon their socio-economic characteristics and the opportunity structures available to them (Portes and Zhou, 1993). I believe that institutions and governments should not be allowed to escape from fulfilling their responsibilities. They must play a central role in ensuring equality of opportunities by eradicating entrenched disadvantages, rather than putting a disproportionate onus on the citizens themselves to achieve community cohesion. This study has consistently shown that while the elites in this study were in a privileged position as a result of their socio-economic background, and local structures that offered opportunities through which they were able to embed themselves, thus feeling more included and valued, thereby leading to their successful career trajectories. In spite of this, however, they also experienced structural inequality as a result of their ethnicity.

APPENDIX 1: DEFINITION OF RACIAL HARASSMENT USED IN INTERVIEWS

Box 8.1 sets out the definition of racial harassment developed for NHS employers, which included examples of racially harassing behaviours.

Box 8.1 DEFINITION OF RACIAL HARASSMENT

Racial harassment is unacceptable targeted behaviour motivated by racial intolerance affecting the dignity of women and men at work.

Racial harassment covers a wide range of unacceptable, and often unlaw, behaviour. There are the more obvious and over forms of harassment such as racist language and physical intimidation. However, racial harassment is frequently more covert. These more subtle forms of racial harassment, such as deprecating the way people dress or speak, are eqally distressing and can create an intimidating and unpleasant atmosphere at work.

Examples of racially harassing behaviours include:

- Patronising remarks
- Shunning or excluding people from normal workplace conversation or social events
- Being condescending or deprecating about the way people dress or speak
- Intrusive questioning about a person's racial or ethnic origin, culture or religion, or subjecting this to mockery
- Unjustified criticism of work performance
- Unfair allocation of work and responsibilities
- Racist 'jokes', banter and insults
- Display or articulation of racially offensive marerial, including racist graffiti
- Denial of access to training and/or overtime
- Black or minority ethnic staff being more likely to be disciplined than white staff
- Threatening and abusive language
- Physical abuse or intimidation.

Racial harassment may be deliberate and conscious, but it can also be unintentional, as when an individual is oblivious to another person's feelings and sensitivities.

Source: Collins (2001, 171) in Racism in Medicine.

REFERENCES

AHMED, R. & MUKHERJEE, S. 2012. *South Asian Resistances in Britain 1858-1947.*

AHMED, W. U., R, B. M. & KERNOHAN, E. M. 1991. General practitioners' perceptions of Asian and non-Asian patients. *Family Practice,* 52-56, 8.

ALDRICH, H. & ZIMMER, C. 1986. Entrepreneurship Through Social Networks. *In:* SEXTON, D. L. & SMILOR, R. W. (eds.) *The art and science of entrepreneurship*

ALDRICH, H. E. & WALDINGER, R. 1990. Ethnicity and entrepreneurship. *Annual review of sociology,* 111-135.

ALLEN, S. 1971. *New minorities, old conflicts: Asian and West Indian migrants in Britain,* Random House New York.

ALLPORT, G. W. 1979. *The nature of prejudice,* Basic books.

ANDALL, J. 2000. *Gender, migration and domestic service,* Ashgate Aldershot.

ANG, I. 2003. Together-in-difference: beyond diaspora, into hybridity. *Asian Studies Review,* 27, 141-154.

ANGELOU, M. 1997. *I know why the caged bird sings,* Random House LLC.

ANTONSICH, M. 2012. Exploring the Demands of Assimilation among White Ethnic Majorities in Western Europe. *Journal of Ethnic and Migration Studies,* 38, 59-76.

ANWAR, M. & ALI, A. 1987. *Overseas doctors: experience and expectations: a research study,* Commission for Racial Equality.

ATKINSON, R. & FLINT, J. 2001. Accessing hidden and hard-to-reach populations: Snowball research strategies. *Social research update,* 33, 1-4.

AXNER, M. The Community Tool Box, Healing from the Effects of Internalized Oppression. Chapter 27, Section 3. Available: http://ctb.ku.edu/en/tablecontents/sub_ section_main_1172.aspx.

BALLARD, C. 1979. Second Generations South Asians. *In:* SAIFULLAH KHAN, V. (ed.) *Minority Families in Britain: support and stress.* London: Macmillan.

BALLARD, R. 1994. *Desh pardesh: The South Asian experience in Britain. London: Hurst & Co, 5. On this, see also, John Wolffe (1994)'Fragmented universality: Islam and Muslims'.*

BASCH, L., SCHILLER, N. G. & BLANC, C. S. 1994. Nations Unbound: Transnational Projects. *Post-colonial Predicaments, and De-terrirorialized Nation-States, Langhorne, PA: Gordon and Breach,* 9.

BAXTER, C. 1988. *The black nurse: an endangered species: a case for equal opportunities in nursing,* Training in Health and Race.

BEAGAN, B. L. 2000. Neutralizing differences: producing neutral doctors for (almost) neutral patients. *Social Science & Medicine,* 51, 1253-1265.

BEAGAN, B. L. 2003. Teaching Social and Cultural Awareness to Medical Students:" It's All Very Nice to Talk about It in Theory, But Ultimately It Makes No Difference". *Academic Medicine,* 78, 605-614.

BEIDER, H. 2011. Community cohesion: the views of white working-class communities. *Joseph Rowntree Foundation. London, UK: Coventry University.*

BERGER, P. L. & LUCKMANN, T. 1971. *The Social Construction of Reality,* Harmondsworth Penguin University Books,.

BHABHA, H. 1994. The Location of Culture. *London in New York: Routledge.*

BHATT, R. M. 2013. Unravelling Post-Colonial Identity through Language. *In:* COUPLAND, N. (ed.) *The Handbook of Language and Globalization.* Wiley-Blackwell.

BHOPAL, R. S. 2008. *Ethnicity, Race, and Health in Multicultural Societies: Foundations for better epidemiology, public health, and health care: Foundations for better epidemiology, public health, and*

health care, OUP Oxford.
BHUGRA, D. & BECKER, M. A. 2005. Migration, cultural bereavement and cultural identity. *World Psychiatry,* 4, 18.
BILIMORIA, P. 1996. Ninian Smart Religion and nationalism the urgency of transnational spirituality and toleration. *Sophia,* 35, 131-137.
BLAU, P. M. & SCHWARTZ, J. E. 1984. Crossing social circles. Academic Press, Orlando.
BLINDER, S., FORD, R. & IVARSFLATEN, E. 2013. The Better Angels of Our Nature: How the Antiprejudice Norm Affects Policy and Party Preferences in Great Britain and Germany. *American Journal of Political Science.*
BOLOGNANI, M. 2007. The Myth of Return: Dismissal, Survival or Revival? A Bradford Example of Transnationalism as a Political Instrument. *Journal of Ethnic and Migration Studies,* 33, 59-76.
BONNETT, A. 2000. *White identities*, Prentice hall Harlow.
BORNAT, J., HENRY, L. & RAGHURAM, P. 2009. 'Don't mix race with the specialty': interviewing South Asian overseas-trained geriatricians'. *Oral History,* 37, 74-84.
BOWLING, A. 2009. *Research methods in health: investigating health and health services*, McGraw-Hill International.
BRAH, A. 1982. *Minority Experience*, Open University Press.
BRAH, A. 1985. The South Asians. *In:* HUSBAND, C. (ed.) *Ethnic minorities and community relations / Open University.* Miltone Keynes: The Open University.
BRAH, A. 1996. *Cartographoes of diaspora.* PhD.
BRAH, A. 2007. Non-binarized identities of similarity and difference. *Identity, Ethnic Diversity and Community Cohesion, London: Sage*, 136-145.
BRYMAN, A. 2009. *Social research methods*, OUP Oxford.
BURR, V. 2003. *Social constructionism*, Psychology Press.
BYGRAVE, W. D. & HOFER, C. W. 1991. Theorizing about entrepreneurship. *Entrepreneurship theory and Practice,* 16, 13-22.
CABALLERO, C., EDWARDS, R. & SMITH, D. 2008. Cultures of mixing: understanding partnerships across ethnicity. *Twenty-First Century Society,* 3, 49-63.
CANTLE, T. 2001. Community cohesion: a report of the independent review team.
CARGILL, D. 1969. Recruitment to general practice in Essex and Birmingham. *The Lancet,* 1 (7596) 669 - 670.
CASSELL, P. 1993. *The Giddens Reader.* , London, MacMillan Press.
CASTLES, S. & MILLER, M. J. 2003. *The age of migration: international population movements in the modern world*, London: Macmillan Press Ltd.
CHAKRABORTI, N. & GARLAND, J. 2004. *Rural racism,* Cullompton, Cullompton : Willan, 2004.
CHARLESWORTH, S. J. 2000. *A phenomenology of working-class experience*, Cambridge University Press.
CHEONG, P. H., EDWARDS, R., GOULBOURNE, H. & SOLOMOS, J. 2007. Immigration, social cohesion and social capital: A critical review. *Critical Social Policy,* 27, 24-49.
CHEW-GRAHAM, C. A., MAY, C. R. & PERRY, M. S. 2002. Qualitative research and the problem of judgement: lessons from interviewing fellow professionals. *Family Practice,* 19, 285-289.
CHEW, S. & RUTHERFORD, A. 1993. *Unbecoming daughters of the Empire*, Dangaroo Press.
CLARKE, T. 2001. Burnley Task Force report on the disturbances in June 2001. *Burnley Borough Council: Burnley.*
COKER, N. (ed.) 2001. *Racism in Medicine: An Agenda for Change*: King's Fund London.
COLE, E. R. & OMARI, S. R. 2003. Race, class and the dilemmas of upward mobility for African Americans. *Journal of Social Issues,* 59, 785-802.

COLLINS, M. 2001. Racial Harassment in the NHS. *In:* COKER, N. (ed.) *Racism in Medicine.* London: Kings Fund.

COX, O. C. 1948. *Caste,class and race,* New York, Doubleday.

CRESWELL, J. W. 2007. *Qualitative inquiry and research design: Choosing among five approaches,* SAGE Publications, Incorporated.

CUBA, L. & HUMMON, D. M. Constructing a sense of home: Place affiliation and migration across the life cycle. Sociological forum, 1993. Springer, 547-572.

CUBA, L. & HUMMON, D. M. 1993. A place to call home: Identification with dwelling, community, and region. *The sociological quarterly,* 34, 111-131.

CUTCHIN, M. P. 1997. Physician retention in rural communities: the perspective of experiential place integration. *Health & Place,* 3, 25-41.

DADABHOY, S. 2001. The next generation, the problematic children: a personal story. *Racism in medicine.* London: King's Fund.

DCLG 2008a. The government's response to the commission on integration and cohesion. *In:* COMMUNITIES, D. F. & GOVERNMENT, L. (eds.). Communities and Local Government Publications London.

DE HAAS, H. 2010. The Internal Dynamics of Migration Processes: A Theoretical Inquiry. *Journal of Ethnic and Migration Studies,* 36, 1587-1617.

DE LIMA, P. 2004. John O'Groats to Land's End: racial equality in rural Britain? *Rural Racism,* 36-60.

DEI, G. J. S. & JOHAL, G. S. 2005. *Critical issues in anti-racist research methodologies,* Peter Lang.

DENHAM, J. 2001. Building cohesive communities. *A Report of the Ministerial Group on Public Order and Community Cohesion (London: Home Office, 2001).*

DOUGLAS, D. 2000. *Assessing languages for specific purposes,* Cambridge University Press.

DOYAL, L., HUNT, G. & MELLOR, J. 1980. *Migrant Workers in the National Health Service: Report of a Preliminary Survey,* London, Polytechnic of North London, Department of Sociology.

DOYAL, L., HUNT, G. & MELLOR, J. 1981. Your life in their hands: migrant workers in the National Health Service. *Critical Social Policy,* 1, 54-71.

DYER, C. 2002. BMA has to pay£ 815000 in damages for indirect racial discrimination. *BMJ: British Medical Journal,* 324, 1541.

ELLIS, M., WRIGHT, R. & PARKS, V. 2007. Geography and the immigrant division of labor. *Economic Geography,* 83, 255-281.

ESMAIL, A. 2001. Racial Discrimination In Medical Schools. *In:* COKER, N. (ed.) *Racism in medicine: an agenda for change.* King's Fund London.

ESMAIL, A. 2007. Asian doctors in the NHS: service and betrayal. *The British Journal of General Practice.*

EVANS, H. 1988. *Thimayya of India,* Harcourt, Brace.

FARMER, J., LAUDER, W., RICHARDS, H. & SHARKEY, S. 2003. Dr. John has gone: assessing health professionals' contribution to remote rural community sustainability in the UK. *Social Science & Medicine,* 57, 673-686.

FEAGIN, J. & SIKES, M. P. 1994. Living with Racism: The Black Middle-Class Experience. Boston.

GIDDENS, A. 1984. *The Constitution of Society* Polity Press, Cambridge.

GILCHRIST, A., BOWLES, M. & WETHERELL, M. 2010. Identities and Social Action: Connecting Communities for a Change. *Economic & Social Research Council.*

GISH, O. 1971. Overseas-born doctor migration 1962–66. *Medical Education,* 5, 92-109.

GOLDSCHEIDER, C. 1986. *Jewish continuity and change: Emerging patterns in America,* Indiana University Press Bloomington.

HAGAN, J. & EBAUGH, H. R. 2003. Calling upon the sacred: migrants' use of religion in the migration process. *International Migration Review,* 37, 1145-1162.

HALL, R. E. 2003. *Skin color as a post-colonial issue among Asian-Americans,* Edwin Mellen Pr.

HALL, S. 1992. New Ethnicities. *In:* DONALD, J. & RATTANSI, A. (eds.) *Race, culture and difference.* Sage.

HANN, M., SIBBALD, B. & YOUNG, R. 2008. Workforce participation among international medical graduates in the National Health Service of England: a retrospective longitudinal study. *Human Resources for Health,* 6, 478-449.

HANSEN, E. L. 1995. Entrepreneurial networks and new organisation growth *Entrepreneurship Theory Pract.,* 19(4), 7–13.

HARVEY, W. S. 2011. Strategies for conducting elite interviews. *Qualitative Research,* 11, 431-441.

HEATH, A. & CHEUNG, S. Y. 2006. *Ethnic penalties in the labour market: Employers and discrimination,* CDS.

HEWSTONE, M., TAUSCH, N., HUGHES, J. & CAIRNS, E. 2007. Prejudice, intergroup contact and identity: Do neighbourhoods matter. *Identity, Ethnic Diversity and Community Cohesion,* 102-112.

HOLSTEIN, J. A. & GUBRIUM, J. F. 2010. Animating Interview Narratives. *In:* SILVERMAN, D. (ed.) *Qualitative Research.* Sage.

HUNTER, M. L. 2002. "If You're Light You're Alright" Light Skin Color as Social Capital for Women of Color. *Gender & Society,* 16, 175-193.

HUSBAND, C. 1982. Racial prejudice and the Concept of Social Identity,. *Ethnic Minorities and Community relations, part one.* Open University.

HUYNH, J. & YIU, J. Breaking blocked transnationalism: intergenerational change in homeland ties. Paper Presented at the Conference on Immigrant Transnational Organizations and Development, 2012.

IREDALE, R. 2001. The migration of professionals: theories and typologies. *International migration,* 39, 7-26.

IRVING, S. & SEIDMAN, I. 1991. *Interviewing as qualitative research : a guide for researchers in education and the social sciences,* New York ; London, New York ; London : Teachers College Press, 1991.

JACK, S. L. & ANDERSON, A. R. 2002. The effects of embeddedness on the entrepreneurial process. *Journal of business Venturing,* 17, 467-487.

JAYAWEERA, H. & CHOUDHARY, T. 2008. *Immigration, faith and cohesion: Evidence from local areas with significant Muslim populations,* Joseph Rowntree Foundation.

JENKINS, R. 1994. Rethinking ethnicity: Identity, categorization and power. *Ethnic and Racial Studies,* 17, 197-223.

JOHN, R. & REX, J. 1979. *Colonial immigrants in a British city : a class analysis,* London, London : Routledge and Kegan Paul, 1979.

JOHNSTON, R., FORREST, J. & POULSEN, M. 2002. Are there ethnic enclaves/ghettos in English cities? *Urban Studies,* 39, 591-618.

JONES, E. L. & SNOW, S. J. 2010. *Against the odds: black and minority ethnic clinicians and Manchester, 1948 to 2009,* Manchester NHS Primary Care Trust.

KALMIJN, M. 1998. Intermarriage and homogamy: Causes, patterns, trends. *Annual review of sociology,* 395-421.

KALRA, V. 2006. Policing diversity. *In:* KALRA, V., ALI, N., KALRA, V. & SAYYID, S. (eds.) *A postcolonial people: South Asians in Britain.*

KALRA, V. S. 2000. *From textile mills to taxi ranks: Experiences of migration, labour, and social change,* Ashgate Publishing.

KESKINEN, S. 2009. *Complying with colonialism: gender, race and ethnicity in the Nordic region,* Ashgate Publishing, Ltd.

KHAN, O. 2007. Policy, Identity and Community Cohesion: How Race Equality Fits. *In:* WETHERELL, M., LAFLECHE, M. & BERKELEY, R. (eds.) *Identity, Ethnic Diversity and Community Cohesion.* London: Sage Publications.

KHAN, O. 2007. Policy, Identity and Community Cohesion: How Race Equality Fits. *Identity, Ethnic Diversity and Community Cohesion.*

KOFMAN, E. 2004. Family-related migration: a critial review of European Studies. *Journal of Ethnic and Migration Studies,* 30, 243-262.

KRIEGER, N. 1990. Racial and gender discrimination: risk factors for high blood pressure? *Social science & medicine,* 30, 1273-1281.

KVALE, S. 2008. *Doing interviews*, Sage.

LADBURY, S. 1984. Choice, chance or no alternative? Turkish Cypriots in business in London. *In:* WARD, R. & JENKINS, R. (eds.) *Ethnic Communities in Business.* Cambridge University Press Cambridge.

LAHIRI, S. 2000. *Indians in Britain: Anglo-Indian encounters, race and identity, 1880-1930*, Routledge.

LAKHA, S. & STEVENSON, M. 2001. Indian identity in multicultural Melbourne. Some preliminary observations. *Journal of Intercultural Studies,* 22, 245-262.

LAWS, G. 1997. Globalization, immigration, and changing social relations in US cities. *The annals of the American academy of political and social science,* 551, 89-104.

LAWS, G. 1997a. Women's life courses, spatial mobility, and state policies. *In:* JONES, J. P., NAST, H. J. & ROBERTS, S. M. (eds.) *Thresholds in feminist geography: Difference, methodology, representation.*

LAZARSFELD, P. F. 1972. *Qualitative analysis; historical and critical essays*, Allyn and Bacon.

LEGARD, R., KEEGAN, G. & WARD, K. 2003. In Depth Interviewes. *In:* RITCHIE, J. & LEWIS, J. (eds.) *Qualitative research practice: A guide for social science students and researchers.* Sage.

LEVITT, P. 1998. Social remittances: migration driven local-level forms of cultural diffusion. *International migration review*, 926-948.

LEVY, R. 2012. *The Persian Language (RLE Iran A)*, Routledge.

LIGHT, I. & GOLD, S. J. 2000. *Ethnic Economies,* San Diego, CA, Academic Press.

LIGHT, I. & KARAGEORGIS, S. 1994. The Ethnic Economy. *In:* SMELSER, N. J. & SWEDBERG, R. (eds.) *The Handbook of Economic Sociology*. Princeton University Press.

LINBLAD, I. 1993. The Irresistable Anglo-Filiation of Ishrat *In:* CHEW, S. & RUTHERFORD, A. (eds.) *Unbecoming daughters of the Empire.* Dangaroo Press.

LOGAN, R. F. L., ROBERTS, J. A. & STOCKTON, P. 1979. General Practice - The immigrant doctor in N.E.T.R.H.A. *Medicos,* 4 (1), 3 - 5.

LOWNDES, V. & THORP, L. 2011. Interpreting'community cohesion': modes, means and mixes. *Policy & Politics,* 39, 513-532.

LUPTON, D. 2012. *Medicine as culture: illness, disease and the body*, SAGE Publications Limited.

LYKES, M. B. 1983. Discrimination and coping in the lives of Black women: Analyses of oral history data. *Journal of Social Issues,* 39, 79-100.

MACPHERSON, S. W. 1999. *The Stephen Lawrence Inquiry: report of an inquiry*, TSO.

MARS, G. & WARD, R. 1984. Ethnic business development in Britain: opportunities and resources GERALD MARS and ROBIN WARD. *Ethnic Communities in Business: Strategies for Economic Survival*, 1.

MARTINOVIĆ, B. 2013. The Inter-Ethnic Contacts of Immigrants and Natives in the Netherlands: A Two-Sided Perspective. *Journal of Ethnic and Migration Studies,* 39, 69-85.

MASSEY, G. C., SCOTT, M. V. & DORNBUSCH, S. M. 1975. Racism without racists: Institutional racism in urban schools. *The Black Scholar,* 7, 10-19.

MCAVOY, B. R. & DONALDSON, L. J. 1990. *Health care for Asians*, Oxford U.P.

MCKEIGUE, P., RICHARDS, J. & RICHARDS, P. 1990. Effects of discrimination by sex and race on the early careers of British medical graduates during 1981-7. *BMJ: British Medical Journal,* 301, 961.

MCPHERSON, M., SMITH-LOVIN, L. & COOK, J. M. 2001. Birds of a feather: Homophily in social networks. *Annual review of sociology*, 415-444.

MEJIA, A. 1978. Migration of physicians and nurses: a world wide picture. *International journal of epidemiology*, 7, 207-215.

MERRISON, A. 1975. *Report of the Committee of Inquiry into the Regulation of the Medical Profession*, HM Stationery Office.

MERTON, R. K. 1941. Intermarriage and the social structure: Fact and theory. *Psychiatry*, 4, 361-374.

MODOOD, T. 1992. British Asian Muslims and the Rushdie Affair. *In:* DONALD, J. & RATTANSI, A. (eds.) *Race, culture and difference.* London: Sage Publication.

MODOOD, T., BERTHOUD, R., LAKEY, J., NAZROO, J., SMITH, P., VIRDEE, S. & BEISHON, S. 1997. *Ethnic minorities in Britain: diversity and disadvantage*, Taylor & Francis.

MOSS, P. J. 2002. *Feminist geography in practice: Research and methods*, Blackwell Oxford.

NAVARRO, V. 1978. *Class struggle, the state and medicine : an historical and contemporary analysis of the medical sector in Great Britain*, Martin Robertson.

NAVARRO, V. 1978. *Class Struggle, the State and Medicine: An Historical and Contemporary Analysis of the Medical Sector in Great Britain,* London, Martin Robertson.

NEITERMAN, E. & BOURGEAULT, I. L. 2012. Conceptualizing Professional Diaspora: International Medical Graduates in Canada. *Journal of International Migration and Integration,* 13, 39-57.

NORTON, B. 1997. Language, Identity, and the Ownership of English. *TESOL Quarterly*, 31, 409-429.

NOWIKOWSKI, S. 1984. Snakes and ladders: Asian business in Britain. *Ethnic communities in business: Strategies for economic survival*, 149-65.

OGUNTOKUN, R. 1998. A lesson in the seductive power of sameness: Representing Black African refugee women. *Feminism & Psychology,* 8, 525-529.

OIKELOME, F. & HEALY, G. 2007. Second-class doctors? The impact of a professional career structure on the employment conditions of overseas-and UK-qualified doctors. *Human Resource Management Journal*, 17, 134-154.

OIKELOME, F. & HEALY, G. 2013. Gender, Migration and Place of Qualification of Doctors in the UK: Perceptions of Inequality, Morale and Career Aspiration. *Journal of Ethnic and Migration Studies,* 39, 557-577.

OPPENHEIM, A. N. 2000. *Questionnaire design, interviewing and attitude measurement*, Continuum International Publishing Group.

OUSELEY, H. 2001. *Community pride not prejudice: making diversity work in Bradford*, Bradford Vision Bradford.

PANG, T., LANSANG, M. A. & HAINES, A. 2002. Brain drain and health professionals: a global problem needs global solutions. *BMJ: British Medical Journal*, 324, 499.

PARAMESWARAN, R. E. & CARDOZA, K. 2009. Immortal Comics, Epidermal Politics. *Journal of Children and Media,* 3, 19-34.

PAREKH, B. 2007. Reasoned Identities: A committed Relationship. *In:* WETHERELL, M., LAFLÈCHE, M. & BERKELEY, R. (eds.) *Identity, ethnic diversity and community cohesion.* London: Sage Publications.

PAREKH, B. C. 2002. *Rethinking multiculturalism: Cultural diversity and political theory*, Harvard University Press.

PAULUS, T. M., WOODSIDE, M. & ZIEGLER, M. 2008. Extending the conversation: Qualitative research as dialogic collaborative process. *The Qualitative Report,* 13, 226-243.

PHILLIPS, C. 2007. Ethnicity, identity and community cohesion in prison. *In:* WETHERELL, M., LAFLECHE, M. & BERKELEY, R. (eds.) *Identity, ethnic diversity and community cohesion.* SAGE Publications Limited.

PORTES, A. & MANNING, R., D 1986. The immigrant enclave: theory and empirical examples. *In:* OLZAK, S., NAGEL, J. & (eds.) *In Comparative Ethnic Relations.* Orlando: FL: Academic Press.

PORTES, A. & ZHOU, M. 1992. Gaining the upper hand: Economic mobility among immigrant and domestic minorities. *Ethnic and racial studies,* 15, 491-522.

PORTES, A. & ZHOU, M. 1993. The new second generation: Segmented assimilation and its variants. *The annals of the American academy of political and social science,* 530, 74-96.

PUTNAM, R. D. 2000. *Bowling alone : the collapse and revival of american community,* New York, Simon and Schuster.

PYKE, K. & DANG, T. 2003. "FOB" and "Whitewashed": Identity and Internalized Racism Among Second Generation Asian Americans. *Qualitative Sociology*, 147-172.

RAGHURAM, P., HENRY, L. & BORNAT, J. 2010. Difference and Distinction?: Non-migrant and Migrant Networks'. *Sociology,*, 44, 623-641.

RAGHURAM, P. & KOFMAN, E. 2002. The state, skilled labour markets, and immigration: the case of doctors in England. *Environment and Planning A,* 34, 2071-2090.

RASHID, A. 1990. Asian Doctors and Nurses in the NHS. *In:* MCAVOY, B. R. & DONALDSON, L. J. (eds.) *Health care for Asians.* Oxford: Oxford : Oxford University Press, 1990.

RATCLIFFE, P. 2011. From Community to Social Cohesion: Interrogating a Ploicy Paradigm. *In:* RATCLIFFE, P. & NEWMAN, I. (eds.) *Promoting social cohesion: Implications for policy and evaluation.* The Policy Press.

RATCLIFFE, P., NEWMAN, I. & FULLER, C. 2008. Community Cohesion: a Literature and Data Review. Report commissioned by the Audit Commission. Warwick Business School.

REX, J. & TOMLINSON, S. 1979. *Colonial immigrants in a British city: a class analysis,* Routledge & Kegan Paul London.

RICH, A. C. 1986. *Blood, bread, and poetry: Selected prose, 1979-1985*, Norton New York.

RITCHIE, D. 2001. ldham independent review, one oldham one future.

RITCHIE, J. & LEWIS, J. 2003. *Qualitative research practice: A guide for social science students and researchers*, SAGE Publications Limited.

RITCHIE, J. L., J. ELAM,G 2003. Designing and selecting samples. *In:* RITCHIE, J. A. L., J (ed.) *Qualitative Research Practice:A guide for Social Science Students and Researchers.* London: Sage.

ROBINSON, D. 2005. The search for community cohesion: Key themes and dominant concepts of the public policy agenda. *Urban Studies,* 42, 1411-1427.

ROBINSON, D., IQBAL, B. & HARRISON, M. 2002. A Question of Investment: From Funding Bids to BME Housing Opportunities. *London: The Housing Corporation.*

ROBINSON, V. 1988. The new Indian middle class in Britain. *Ethnic and Racial Studies,* 11, 456-473.

ROBINSON, V. & CAREY, M. 2000. Peopling skilled international migration: Indian doctors in the UK. *International migration,* 38, 89-108.

ROGALY, B. & TAYLOR, B. 2007. Welcome to 'Monkey Island': Identity and community in three Norwich estates. *Identity, Ethnic Diversity and Community Cohesion. London: Sage,* 61-74.

RUBIN, H. J. & RUBIN, I. S. 2011. *Qualitative interviewing: The art of hearing data*, Sage.

SAMERS, M. 2010. *Migration,* Routledge.

SAXENIAN, A. 2001. Silicon Valley's New Immigrant Entrepreneurs. *In:* CORNELIUS, W. A., ESPENSHADE, T. J. & SALEHYAN, I. (eds.) *The international migration of the highly skilled: demand, supply, and development consequences in sending and receiving countries*

SAYEED, A. A. 2006. *In the Shadow of My Taqdir*, Memoir Club.

SAYYID, S. 2004. Slippery people: the immigrant imaginary and the grammar of colour. *In:* LAW I, P. D., TURNEY L (ed.) *Institutional Racism in Higher Education.* London: Trentham Books.

SCAIFE, B., GILL, P., HEYWOOD, P. & NEAL, R. 2000. Socio-economic characteristics of adult frequent attenders in general practice: secondary analysis of data. *Family Practice,* 17, 298-304.

SCHILLER, N. G., BASCH, L. & BLANC-SZANTON, C. 1992. Transnationalism: A new analytic framework for understanding migration. *Annals of the New York Academy of Sciences,* 645, 1-24.

SHAH, N. M. & MENON, I. 1999. Chain migration through the social network: experience of labour migrants in Kuwait. *International migration,* 37, 361-382.

SHAW, P. 2010. Diversity training: a DVD resource showcasing BME role models. *Community Practitioner,* 83, 30-33.

SHORTER-GOODEN, K. 2004. Multiple resistance strategies: How African American women cope with racism and sexism. *Journal of Black Psychology,* 30, 406-425.

SIMPSON, J. M. 2018. *Migrant architects of the NHS: South Asian doctors and the reinvention of British general practice (1940s-1980s) (Social Histories of Medicine)*, Manchester university press.

SMITH, D. J. 1980. *Overseas doctors in the National Health Service,* London, Policy Studies Institutes.

SONG, M. 2009. Is intermarriage a good indicator of integration? *Journal of Ethnic and Migration Studies,* 35, 331-348.

SONG, M. & PARKER, D. 1995. Commonality, difference and the dynamics of disclosure in in-depth interviewing. *Sociology,* 29, 241-256.

STILLWELL, J. C. H. & CONGDON, P. 1991. *Migrations models: macro and micro approaches,* Belhaven Press.

TABILI, L. 2012. Ghulam Rasul's Travel: Migration, Recolonisation and Resistance in Inter-War Britain. *In:* AHMED, R. A. M. S. E. (ed.) *South Asian Resistances in Britain,1858-1947.* London: Bloomsbury Publishing.

TAYLOR, D. H. & ESMAIL, A. 1999. Retrospective analysis of census data on general practitioners who qualified in South Asia: who will replace them as they retire? *BMJ,* 318, 306-310.

TAYLOR, D. J. & ESMAIL, A. 1999. Retrospective analysis of census data on general practitioners who qualified in South Asia: who will replace them as they retire? *BMJ,* 318, 306-310.

TAYLOR, I., EVANS, K. & FRASER, P. 1996. *A tale of two cities: global change, local feeling, and everyday life in the North of England: a study in Manchester and Sheffield,* Taylor & Francis US.

THOMPSON, J. L. 2002. The world of the social entrepreneur. *International Journal of Public Sector Management,* 15, 412-431.

TYLER, K. 2012. The English village, whiteness, coloniality and social class. *Ethnicities,* 12, 427-444.

UNWIN, L. 2001. Career progression and job satisfaction. *In:* COKER, N. (ed.) *Racism in medicine: An agenda for change.* London: King's Fund.

UNWIN, L. 2001. Career progression and job satisfaction. *Racism in medicine: An agenda for change.*

VALENTINE, G. 2001. *Social geographies: space and society*, Pearson Education.

VAUGHAN, R. & ROBINSON, V. 1986. *Transients, settlers, and refugees : Asians in Britain,* Oxford, Oxford : Clarendon, 1986.

VERTOVEC, S. 1997. Three meanings of" diaspora," exemplified among South Asian religions. *Diaspora: A Journal of Transnational Studies,* 6, 277-299.

VERTOVEC, S. 2000. *The Hindu diaspora : comparative patterns,* London; New York, Routledge.

VERTOVEC, S. 2002. *Transnational networks and skilled labour migration,* University of Oxford. Transnational Communities Programme.

VERTOVEC, S. & COHEN, R. 1999. Migration, diasporas and transnationalism. *Cheltenham, UK.*

WALDINGER, R., WARD, R., ALDRICH, H. & STANFIELD, J. (eds.) 1990a. *Ethnic entrepreneurs: Immigrant business in industrial societies*: Sage.

WARD, R. & JENKINS, R. 1984. *Ethnic communities in business: Strategies for economic survival*, Cambridge University Press.

WEEDON, C. 2004. *Identity and culture*, McGraw-Hill International.

WELCH, C., MARSCHAN-PIEKKARI, R., PENTTINEN, H. & TAHVANAINEN, M. 2002. Corporate elites as informants in qualitative international business research. *International Business Review,* 11, 611-628.

WELZEL, C., INGLEHART, R. & DEUTSCH, F. 2005. Social capital, voluntary associations and collective action: Which aspects of social capital have the greatest 'civic'payoff? *Journal of civil society,* 1, 121-146.

WENGRAF, T. 2001. *Qualitative research interviewing: Biographic narrative and semi-structured methods*, SAGE Publications Limited.

WERBNER, P. 1984. Business on trust: Pakistani entrepreneurship in the Manchester garment trade. *Ethnic communities in business*, 166-188.

WERBNER, P. 1990. *The migration process: Capital, gifts, and offerings among British Pakistanis*, Berg Oxford.

WETHERELL, M. 2007. Community Cohesion and Identity Dynamics: Dilemmas and Challenges. *In:* WETHERELL, M., LAFLECHE, M. & BERKELEY, R. (eds.) *Identity, Ethnic Diversity and Cohesion.* London: Sage Publications.

WETHERELL, M., LAFLECHE, M. & BERKELEY, R. 2007. *Identity, ethnic diversity and community cohesion*, SAGE Publications Limited.

WHITE, P. & WOODS, R. 1980. *The Geographical impact of migration*, Longman.

WHORF, B. L. 1941. The relation of habitual thought and behavior to language. *Language, culture, and personality: Essays in memory of Edward Sapir*, 75-93.

WILLIG, C. 1995. *Introducing qualitative research in psychology*, Open University Press.

WILTON, R. D. 1998. The constitution of difference: space and psyche in landscapes of exclusion. *Geoforum,* 29, 173-185.

WISE, J. 2010. Doctors are one of the "linchpins" in closing the UK health inequalities gap. *BMJ,* 340, c3060-c3060.

WORLEY, C. 2005. It's not about race. It's about the community': New Labour and 'community cohesion. *Critical social policy,* 25, 483-496.

WORLEY, C. 2005. Its not about race. 'Its about the community'. New labour and 'community cohesion'. *Critical Social Policy,* 25, 483-496.

YUVAL-DAVIS, N., ANTHIAS, F. & CAMPLING, J. 1989. *Woman, nation, state*, Macmillan.

ZHOU, M. 2004. Revisiting Ethnic Entrepreneurship: Convergencies, Controversies, and Conceptual Advancements1. *International Migration Review,* 38, 1040-1074.

ZHOU, M. 2008. Revisiting Ethnic Entrepreneurship. *In:* PORTES, A. & DEWIND, J. (eds.) *Rethinking migration: New theoretical and empirical perspectives.* Berghahn Books.

ZULFIQAR, Z. & HUSEIN, F. 2011. Elusive Dawn, Faiz Ahmed Faiz A people's poet.

Lightning Source UK Ltd.
Milton Keynes UK
UKHW010203070223
416581UK00004B/228